THIRD EDITION

ESTATE PLANNING MADE EASY

- The **Ten Most Common Mistakes** and How to Avoid Them
- The Real Impact **Recent Legislation** Will Have on Your Estate
- New Strategies to **Avoid Creditors, Predators, and the IRS**

DAVID T. PHILLIPS

BILL S. WOLFKIEL

Editorial Director: Jennifer Farthing
Acquisitions Editor: Karen Murphy
Development Editor: Joshua Martino
Production Editor: Mike Hankes
Cover Designer: Gail Chandler

Published by Kaplan Publishing, a division of Kaplan, Inc.

Printed in the United States of America

07 08 09 10 9 8 7 6 5 4 3 2 1

Kaplan Publishing books are available at special quantity discounts to use for sales promotions, employee premiums, or educational purposes. Please call our Special Sales Department to order or for more information at 800-621-9621, ext. 4444, e-mail kaplanpubsales@kaplan.com, or write to Kaplan Publishing, 30 South Wacker Drive, Suite 2500, Chicago, IL 60606-7481.

Dedication

We dedicate *Estate Planning Made Easy* to the thousands of Americans who have had the foresight, perseverance, patience, respect, and love for their families, heirs, and business partners to go through the estate planning process and take a proactive approach to fighting the uncertainty and often devastating problems that death inevitably creates.

More important, we dedicate this book to the countless thousands who have procrastinated on this critical phase of life planning because it seemed too difficult and cumbersome. For them, estate planning has now been made easy.

Furthermore, we dedicate this book to our clients throughout the country. Because of them we were able to report on the real-life case histories contained within these pages.

Acknowledgments

I would like to acknowledge the ongoing contributions of the staffs of Phillips Financial Services and Estate Planning Specialists. They have assisted us in many endeavors throughout the years with great responsiveness and creativity. Thanks especially to John Goodson and Richard Durfee, Craig Sullivan, Ken Barney, Karl Huish, W. Ryan Zenk, and Doug Freeman, attorneys at law, for their assistance with the technical issues.

Also thanks to Tony Sagami, Mark Gagliano, Gil Greer, Roger McCarty, Matthew Rettick, Vince Carfagno, Christy Harrison, and Brittany Cornelius for their support throughout the years. And thanks to Mark Skousen, Joann Skousen, Bill Donoghue, Tom Phillips, Adrian Day, Richard Band, Terry Savage, John Mauldin, Bob Carlson, Suze Orman, and Charles and Kim Githler for their past endorsement of this needed American dream.

A special thanks goes to my oldest son D. Todd Phillips, our Register Investment Advisor, for his guidance on the creative and content end.

A deep appreciation goes to my wife Jane for all her help with editing and patience.

And a most sincere thanks goes to the affiliate offices of Estate Planning Specialists throughout the country for their unyielding assistance and patience in helping to hone the estate planning process into an easy-to-understand and easy-to-execute reality.

—David T. Phillips

Contents

Preface

Remember the short story *Rip Van Winkle* by Washington Irving? Rip goes to sleep after a game of bowling and much drinking in the mountains with a band of dwarves. He awakens 20 years later as an old man. Back home, Rip finds that everything has changed: His wife is dead, his daughter is married, and the American Revolutionary War has taken place.

Since the passage of the Economic Growth Tax Relief and Reconciliation Act in mid 2001 (EGTRRA), wealthy Americans, for the most part, have been using Rip Van Winkle as their role model. It seems to many that because estate taxation rules have been in flux and the federal estate tax exclusion credit has now increased to $2 million per person, they are content to sleep it off and wait until they wake up in 2011 to do any estate planning. BIG MISTAKE!

First and foremost, estate planning is so much more than just taxes. It is the premeditated decision to determine who gets what, when they get it, and how they get it. It is a true act of love and respect for those we leave behind. If it is so important, why do 70% of today's affluent avoid estate planning altogether?

There are a litany of reasons why they avoid it, but top on the list is procrastination. Estate planning isn't an exciting task, but it is vital to the sanctity of the family. At a time when the greatest human emotions come forth—the time when we pass away—we should be the authors of family unity, not confusion, hate, and envy.

Another reason why only a small percentage plan their estates is that it appears confusing. Considering EGTRRA 2001 introduced more than 300 changes to transfer tax laws, and The Pension Protection Act of August 2006 was over 1,000 pages, it's no wonder we are afraid and put it off. *Estate Planning Made Easy* was written with that in mind. My overall goals with this book and my firm Estate Planning Specialists are to make the complex easy to understand and implement.

I realize that politicians would have us believe that estate planning is all about estate taxes, but it isn't. They've done a great job of selling us the idea of estate tax repeal; in fact, 70 percent of Americans polled call for repeal. But in reality, as the law is written today, with the estate tax exclusion credit at $2 million, only one to two percent of those dying in 2007 and 2008 will be affected. If the credit increases to $3.5 million in 2009 as scheduled, estate taxation will only apply to five out of every 1,000 Americans that die that year.

So what's all the fuss about? Why all the commotion? Why the diversion from the real issues? I agree, the abolition of the onerous DEATH TAX, as it is now called, makes for great political rhetoric and great dramatics, but it is only a small part of estate planning.

Virtually every article I've read and every speech I've heard references the current federal estate tax exclusion at $2 million per person and $4 million per couple. Not true! That's an $900,000 lie. The truth is, if you are married, the $4 million total exclusion only applies if you have prepared for it. If it becomes a post-death action, it is too late.

Recently, I've worked with clients with seven-figure IRAs and annuities. The real issue is income taxes for them as well as their heirs. There are ways, known to only a few, on how to "stretch" the tax liability over one's life expectancy. Furthermore, there are ways to control the funds long after we leave this existence. All of this requires prior planning.

Avoiding probate fees, avoiding spending down your assets to be eligible for Medicare, purchasing dollars tomorrow for pennies today, guaranteeing income for life, getting the equity out of your home while staying there, wealth creation, wealth replacement, medical power of attorney, personal guardianship, philanthropy—these are just a few of the reasons why proper estate planning is crucial and shouldn't be something to sleep on.

In *Rip Van Winkle*, Washington Irving told the story of an old man ill-prepared for his departure and a man who gets a second chance to make things right even after a long sleep. Now is the time to wake up, take the car out of cruise control, and take action. Your legacy depends on it.

Remember: Procrastination can be dangerous to your wealth!

Introduction

As a youth and a musician, I always appreciated the beautiful music of Karen Carpenter. Her voice was incomparable and her songs inspirational. At the same time Karen was topping the charts with "We've Only Just Begun," another musician was topping the charts in a totally different element. While the music scale was all they had in common, they both had extremely successful careers, making millions.

Interestingly enough, their propensity to make a fortune in the music industry wasn't their only commonality. The other was that they both failed miserable to plan their estate, and, as such, the IRS and creditors had a field day, confiscating their riches to the tune of 50%.

The other musical genius was none other than Mr. "Deadhead" himself. Jerry Garcia, the lead guitarist and lead singer of the Grateful Dead. As *USA Today* reported, "Even before Jerry's ashes had been scattered in the Ganges, his estate was being picked over like a yard sale. Current and past wives, jilted lovers, family members, his acupuncturist, car dealer, and a personal trainer all were jockeying for a piece of the multimillion dollar spoils. One claim against Garcia's estate was even filed by a guy who said he spent time 'babysitting' the rock star during a drug binge." Much to the dismay of his rightful heirs, Jerry felt he was immortal—so why plan?

Karen, on the other hand, was more realistic. She just didn't have any cash to settle her $6 million in estate settlement expenses. For some reason, she assumed that things would take care of themselves and the $2,721 she had in the bank would cover her debts. The result—because her assets were illiquid and she only had a few thousand in cash, her family had to sell virtually everything and watch her fortune shrink by 58%, simply because she failed to plan.

While these accounts highlight the horrors of improper estate planning for celebrities—and they get the press, what about the average American with a few assets? You know who I'm referring to: The homeowner with $300,000 in home equity, a $250,000 IRA, $300,000 in stocks and CDs, $200,000 in annuities, a $100,000 life insurance policy, and prized family heirlooms. By world standards, they are considered wealthy and affluent. Tragically, because of procrastination, most are no better off than Karen or Jerry. **In fact, 70% have no logical plan to distribute their wealth from one generation to the next.**

With all the press and political rhetoric the repeal of estate taxes has recently experienced, you'd think that estate taxation was the main problem facing most estates. Not true—with the passage of the Economic Growth and Tax Relief Reconciliation Act of 2001 (EGTRRA), the percentage of estate that will feel the impact of federal estate tax between 2007 and 2008 is estimated to be less than 2 percent of all estates.

Estate planning was never all about taxes. In reality, it has always been and will always be about predetermining: **Who gets what, when they get it, and the manner they will receive it.** Certainly, when necessary, it's important to insulate your estate from creditors, predators, and the IRS, but it is more important to plan for a logical distribution of your assets from one generation to the next.

Americans should be motivated to plan the financial legacy they will leave behind, influencing the timed, logical distribution of their wealth and assets. Most do not want their heirs to quit working and experience a lavish, unearned lifestyle. Without proper estate planning, however, that could be their choice.

During the next 20–30 years, $9 trillion will pass from one generation to the next. A logical estate plan, reviewed every other year, will make certain that your share of that fortune will be distributed to the people you love, in the way you want, when you want. Don't let the courts make that determination for you. Properly plan your estate today.

How to Use This Book

In an effort to address the needs of a wide variety of readers, we have divided this book into two parts.

Part One: The Elements of Effective Estate Planning

This part addresses the fundamental elements of estate planning. From property ownership and probate to various estate and gift tax regulations, it provides a basic framework for estate planning.

Part Two: Advanced Strategies for Estate Planning

This part takes an in-depth look at various estate planning strategies. For those readers familiar with the basic elements of estate planning, Part Two provides actual estate planning applications and sophisticated techniques to help format and execute an effective estate plan or modify an existing plan.

PART

I

The Elements of Effective Estate Planning

CHAPTER

1

Estate Planning

It's Your Money and More

Estate planning is often touted as money planning. Who gets what and when do they get it? The real issue, however, is people and the problems they face at your death. Spouses, children, grandchildren, dependents, business partners, and others will suffer not only emotionally but also economically if you fail to plan. Taking care of people problems is the main objective in estate planning. Estate planning is people planning.

Until each of us realizes the probability of our own mortality, estate planning lacks meaning and definition.

In our business, we meet wealthy people daily. We've always had a difficult time understanding why a large number of them refuse to address estate planning. Many have substantial (six-figure) estate tax liabilities at death. Recently we found the answer to this mystery. A client we had been working with for several weeks was having difficulty deciding on some basic estate planning issues. Although his spouse was concerned about problems that might occur at his death, he seemed to lack the motivation to address these issues. This individual finally informed us that he didn't expect to die, at least anytime in the near future. However, he is missing the point of estate planning: Until each of us realizes the probability of our own mortality, estate planning lacks meaning and definition.

We spend a lifetime raising families, creating income, taking care of people, and planning for the future, and in an instant, it can end. We lose our opportunity for a plan of continuation if we fail to plan before death. Estate planning is really living planning. It involves money—lots of it. Generally, planning takes time, thought, and guidance and can appear complicated and confusing, but it can be simplified.

We can bear witness through the years that almost all of us already have an agenda. Most people, with a little thought, know what they would like to accomplish. The difficulty is finding outlets for guidance to complete the process. Each of us deserves understanding and a comfort level that will facilitate the process and eliminate the mysteries.

If you were drafting a last will and testament, which of the following would you prefer?

■ Last Will and Testament #1

Being of sound mind and strong body, I hereby stipulate this to be my last will and testament. To the Internal Revenue Service, and my state of domicile, my lifelong partners, I hereby bequeath one-half or more of all my assets—both business and personal—which I have been able to accumulate throughout a lifetime of endeavor.

I further stipulate that this bequest be satisfied in cash and that only the most liquid and readily salable of my assets be utilized in fulfilling this bequest.

■ Last Will and Testament #2

With the knowledge and confidence that I have otherwise provided for the Internal Revenue Service and my state of domicile, I hereby bequeath my estate in its entirety to my personal beneficiaries in accordance with the provisions of my last will and testament.

Attaining Last Will and Testament #1 is automatic. You need do nothing to carry it out. Just sit back and relax, and our system of state and federal government will handle everything for you.

Attaining Last Will and Testament #2, however, will require some effort on your part. Primarily, it will demand the coordination of your financial and legal advisors to formulate and execute a plan for the proper distribution of your assets when you are gone. If your gross estate is worth $1,000,000 or more (which is not a whole lot these days), one integral part will be to provide the necessary funds to cover your tax bill when it comes due nine months after you are gone.

By making provisions today, you gain peace of mind knowing which part of your estate will pass to heirs and which part will go to the state and federal government.

The Economic Recovery Tax Act of 1981 (ERTA)

In 1981, President Ronald Reagan signed into law the **Economic Recovery Tax Act of 1981,** commonly called **ERTA.** ERTA afforded substantial relief to many Americans in such areas as income taxes, capital gains taxes, and gift taxes. The most significant relief was in the area of estate taxation, the assessment you pay to transfer your estate to your heirs.

Prior to ERTA, the tax rate on an estate valued over $60,000 started at 32 percent and quickly escalated to 75 percent. We distinctly remember hearing the sad story about the severe loss of Nat King Cole's estate during that time. When Mr. Cole passed away, his estate was valued at over $3.5 million. Unfortunately, after estate taxes and settlement costs, his daughter Natalie received less than $1 million.

The real tragedy of pre-ERTA estate taxes was felt by landowners, particularly farmers. Because farmers traditionally kept little cash on hand, the surviving spouse was often forced to liquidate a major portion of the farm to cover the enormous estate tax bill.

With the passage of ERTA, things changed for the better. That new law (1) introduced the **unlimited marital deduction** (the ability to pass applicable assets to a surviving spouse with no tax), (2) increased the estate and gift tax exemption amount to $600,000 per person, and (3) restructured the tax rates. Most important, it gave all of us the opportunity to plan our estates with less taxation and more options.

The Economic Growth and Tax Relief Reconciliation Act of 2001 (EGTRRA)

In June 2001, President George W. Bush signed into law one of the most controversial and confusing laws ever, the Economic Growth and Tax Relief Reconciliation Act. In 2000, estate tax repeal was one of Bush's campaign platforms, and even though the eventual law is riddled with unanswered questions and huge problems, Bush lived up to one of his campaign promises.

The biggest problem is the assumption by the American public that because estate taxes would be repealed someday in the future, there was no need for estate planning, and, in fact, many still have that false sense of accomplishment. However, after a closer look, even though the federal estate tax is supposed to phase out in 2010, because of a "sunset" provision, things will go back to how they were before EGTRRA and the tax will reappear with the unified tax credit limit dropping back to $1 million in 2011.

In addition, EGTRRA actually includes other provisions that increase the complexity of estate planning, such as the gradual repeal of the generation-skipping transfer (GST) tax; the reduction in the top gift tax rate but no repeal of the gift tax; increases in gift, GST, and estate tax exemptions; and the most critical yet most overlooked provision—**the repeal of the step-up in basis at death on appreciated assets**. Also, there is a growing increase in the number of states that are now implementing their own inheritance tax because of the huge loss of revenue they are experiencing with the increase in the unified tax exemption.

While many Americans are in a "wait-and-see" mode, estate planning is more important than ever—without proper planning, you could still lose to estate taxes and settlement costs a large share of what you've spent a lifetime creating.

Why You Should Avoid Do-It-Yourself Planning Strategies

If there is one specific caveat that we can offer the general public in its quest to properly plan estates, it is to *seek professional help.*

Over the past 25 years, we have handled estate planning for thousands of people. Estate sizes have ranged from less than $1 million to multimillion-dollar estates. If there is one specific caveat that we can offer the general public in its quest to properly plan estates, it is to *seek professional help.*

This book addresses such highly technical areas as the following:

- Federal estate tax
- Generation-skipping transfer tax
- Proper retirement planning distribution strategies
- Various revocable and irrevocable trusts
- Charitable gifting techniques
- The most appropriate use of the estate tax credit allowance
- Asset protection strategies
- How to pay potential estate settlement costs, including taxes at a huge discount

These issues are applicable to both small and large estates. However, they have to be designed and implemented correctly. These are not do-it-yourself planning strategies. Through the years, we have witnessed individuals with good intentions trying to accomplish estate planning without proper help and guidance. The results have been, and continue to be, devastating. Please make sure that you seek proper guidance before you attempt to create a plan. If you are unsure where to seek help, Chapter 4, "Assembling the Team," focuses on this dilemma.

CHAPTER

2

Objectives

What Do You Want?

Developing specific objectives and goals is the first step to creating an effective estate plan. If you are uncertain what your objectives are or should be, simply starting the estate planning process will usually provide a road map for you to follow. The initial issues to deal with are *to whom* will you pass *what,* and *when* and *how* will you pass your estate.

To Whom Will You Pass Your Estate?

The following are some of the people and organizations to consider when deciding for whom you want to make provisions:

- Spouse
- Children
- Stepchildren
- Parents
- Grandchildren
- Siblings
- Nieces or nephews
- Close friends
- Alma mater
- Religious organizations
- Other charities

Dividing your estate among these people or entities takes careful thought and consideration. For example, your death will have a considerable impact on your spouse, especially if minor children are involved.

What Assets Will You Pass?

Quite often, assets are positioned in ways that make passage to certain individuals extremely costly and sometimes disastrous. A business interest passed to children uninvolved in the business versus children involved in the business and competent to continue its operations can spell disaster for the continuity of the business. However, passing the business interest only to those children involved in the business may cause a lopsided distribution. If equality is an objective, this raises the question of estate equalization among the various beneficiaries.

When Should You Pass Your Assets?

Should certain assets be passed during your lifetime (now) or at death? By gifting assets now, you may avoid inclusion of those assets in your gross estate at death, thus lowering or eliminating estate taxation. However, if these assets are highly appreciated, based on current law, passing them at death may give the beneficiary a step-up in basis to date-of-death value, thereby eliminating or significantly reducing capital gains taxes when the assets are sold by the beneficiaries.

When you are trying to decide when to pass assets, consider the following specific objectives:

- Are you willing to give up the ownership, control, and benefits of these assets during your lifetime?
- Will you jeopardize your future income picture or that of your spouse if assets are disposed of now or before death?
- Can you ensure that your assets will pass to your spouse at your death?
- At the death of your spouse, will your assets pass to your children?
- Will disposition during your lifetime eliminate probable probate costs and delays? Will disposition now avoid or minimize estate taxes?
- Will there be enough liquid assets to pay taxes and the costs for settling the estate?

Federal estate taxation and probate costs are difficult to assess unless you employ competent help.

Each of these questions should be answered during the estate planning process. Federal estate taxation and probate costs are difficult to assess unless you employ competent help. This assessment starts with an in-depth look at asset inventory. Exact valuation of assets—and in particular business assets—can be extremely complicated to compute. Most people try to utilize book value or some other self-predetermined valuation formula. It is important to understand that the IRS's method of valuing your business or business interest may be extremely different from your formula.

This can spell disaster when business interests are valued low and improper planning results.

The IRS valuation method usually utilizes the following factors:

- Book value
- Capitalization of earnings
- Capacity to pay dividends
- Type of business
- Economic outlook expectation
- History of prior stock sales
- Goodwill
- Sale history of comparable businesses

Valuation of assets is just one element the estate planner should consider in the assessment of a current estate. The following list presents seven other elements involved in estate assessment:

1. How property is held and consequently how it will pass
2. Assets that will be subject to probate
3. Probate costs
4. Federal estate tax and state tax cost at death
5. Estate shrinkage at your death and the death of your spouse
6. Liquidity needs for the payment of taxes and other settlement expenses
7. Future problems as the estate grows or matures

The Written Estate Plan Summary

The previous seven elements are fundamental to assessing your current gross estate and identifying possible problems. In addition, once this information is gathered, your planner can then assemble, assess, communicate, and illustrate unknown problems and solutions, such as potential and existing tax liability. This is usually presented in a **formal written estate plan summary,** or **estate analysis.**

How Do You Accomplish Your Objectives?

The formal written estate plan summary becomes the basis of estate planning.

The **formal written estate plan summary** becomes the basis of estate planning. It identifies problems (such as tax liability, estimated probate fees, who gets what, and when they get it) and presents planning opportunities to solve these problems or makes adjustments to previous plans. To determine how to plan your estate, you need to be familiar with the problems and then begin to **format** a plan utilizing the various estate planning tools available.

The basis of constructing the estate plan summary is the accurate detailed information gathered by the estate planner. This is usually accomplished by completing a comprehensive asset inventory form, which lists all assets and property owned and included in the gross estate. This inventory should also include an accurate breakdown of ownership. Figure 2.1 is an example of a simplified form we designed for asset inventory and pertinent information. You'll also find this helpful form in Chapter 32 that you can remove for your use in listing your assets in preparation for an estate analysis.

Is Your Current Plan Effective?

If you have a formal estate plan in place or you have formulated one on your own, review or update it from time to time. The following guidelines will help you measure how effective your estate plan is since you first created and implemented it:

- Has your estate appreciated since your last planning was implemented?
- Have your goals or objectives changed?
- Have there been any deaths of beneficiaries or divorces?
- If you have created a living trust, have you funded it?
- Have you received an inheritance?
- Have you relocated since your last analysis?
- Have there been any children or grandchildren recently added to your family that should be considered?
- Do you have an insurance trust to remove your life insurance from your gross estate?
- Are you making use of your annual gift tax exclusion?
- Have you used your unified credit (set at $2,000,000 for 2007 through 2008)?
- If you have married, have you made provisions to utilize both your and your spouse's unified credit deduction?
- Are you taking advantage of the annual tax-free gift allowance (currently set at $12,000 per person, per year)?
- Are you gifting highly appreciating assets to affect an estate freeze?
- Are you familiar with the personal advantages of charitable giving?
- Is there adequate liquidity to pay estate taxation and settlement costs?

If you have not recently addressed any of these questions, we recommend a complete review.

FIGURE 2.1 Personal Estate Planning Profile

PERSONAL ESTATE PLANNING PROFILE—CONFIDENTIAL

IF YOU ARE SINGLE, WIDOWED OR DIVORCED, SIMPLY PROVIDE YOUR PERSONAL INFORMATION AND DISREGARD ALL REFERENCES TO A SPOUSE

FULL NAME			
DATE OF BIRTH / /	SMOKER? ❑YES ❑NO	CITIZENSHIP	OCCUPATION
WITHIN THE PAST FIVE YEARS HAVE YOU CONSULTED A PHYSICIAN, MEDICAL PRACTITIONER OR BEEN CONFINED TO A HOSPITAL, CLINIC OR MEDICAL FACILITY? ❑YES ❑NO IF YES, PLEASE GIVE DETAILS:			

SPOUSE'S FULL NAME			
DATE OF BIRTH / /	SMOKER? ❑YES ❑NO	CITIZENSHIP	OCCUPATION
WITHIN THE PAST FIVE YEARS HAVE YOU CONSULTED A PHYSICIAN, MEDICAL PRACTITIONER OR BEEN CONFINED TO A HOSPITAL, CLINIC OR MEDICAL FACILITY? ❑YES ❑NO IF YES, PLEASE GIVE DETAILS:			

HOME ADDRESS	CITY, STATE, ZIP	HOME PHONE ( )	BEST TIME TO CALL
MAILING ADDRESS	CITY, STATE, ZIP	WORK PHONE ( )	BEST TIME TO CALL

ASSETS & LIABILITIES Key: Use to indicate how title is held:
H=Husband's separate W-Wife's separate CP=Community property JT=Joint property TC=Tenancy in common TE=Tenancy by the entirety

DESCRIPTION OF ASSETS	FAIR MARKET VALUE	LIABILITY	NET VALUE	NOW TITLE IS HELD
RESIDENCE				
OTHER REAL ESTATE				
STOCKS & BONDS				
BUSINESS & INTERESTS				
CASH IN BANK (CDs, MONEY MARKETS, ETC.)				
NOTES RECEIVABLE				
PERSONAL EFFECTS (AUTOS, BOATS, ETC.)				
RETIREMENT PLAN (NOT RECEIVING INCOME)				
VALUE OF ALL ANNUITIES				
OTHER ASSETS				
OTHER DEBTS				
TOTAL VALUES				

LIFE INSURANCE (PLEASE LIST ADDITIONAL POLICIES ON SEPARATE PAPER)

COMPANY	INSURED	OWNWER	BENEFICIARY	POLICY DATE	FACE AMOUNT	CASH VALUE

CHARITABLE GIFT TOTAL VALUE OF ASSETS THAT YOU WILL BEQUEATH, BASED ON CURRENT DESIGNATION, TO CHARITIES AT YOUR DEATH: YOU? $ _______ SPOUSE? $ _______

INCOME JOINT ANNUAL GROSS EARNED INCOME $ ____________________ JOINT ANNUAL GROSS INCOME FROM INVESTMENTS $ ____________________

CHILDREN (LIST ALL LIVING CHILDREN: S=SELF SP=SPOUSE J=JOINT)

NAME	AGE	SEX ❑M ❑F	PARENT ❑S ❑SP ❑J	NAME	AGE	SEX ❑M ❑F	PARENT ❑S ❑SP ❑J
NAME	AGE	SEX ❑M ❑F	PARENT ❑S ❑SP ❑J	NAME	AGE	SEX ❑M ❑F	PARENT ❑S ❑SP ❑J

GRANDCHILDREN (IF YOU ARE PLANNING TO LEAVE AN INHERITANCE TO ANY OF YOUR GRANDCHILDREN, PLEASE INDICATE BELOW: S=SELF SP=SPOUSE J=JOINT)

NAME	AGE	SEX ❑M ❑F	GRANDPARENT ❑S ❑SP ❑J	NAME	AGE	SEX ❑M ❑F	GRANDPARENT ❑S ❑SP ❑J
NAME	AGE	SEX ❑M ❑F	GRANDPARENT ❑S ❑SP ❑J	NAME	AGE	SEX ❑M ❑F	GRANDPARENT ❑S ❑SP ❑J

PLEASE INDICATE THE ESTATE PLANNING TOOLS YOU CURRENTLY HAVE IN PLACE

❑ UPDATED WILL
❑ CREDIT SHELTER OR BYPASS TRUST
❑ REVOCABLE LIVING TRUST
❑ MEDICAL POWER OF ATTORNEY
❑ DURABLE POWER OF ATTORNEY
❑ FAMILY DYNASTY TRUST
❑ FAMILY LIMITED PARTNERSHIP
❑ FAMILY OR COMMUNITY FOUNDATION
❑ CHARITABLE TRUST
❑ IRREVOCABLE LIFE INSURANCE TRUST
❑ ESTATE LIQUIDITY THROUGH LIFE INSURANCE
❑ LIMITED LIABILITY COMPANY
❑ QUALIFIED PERSONAL RESIDENCE TRUST
❑ COMMON LAW TRUST
❑ GRANTOR RETAINED INCOME OR ANNUITY TRUST
❑ OFFSHORE ASSET PROTECTION
❑ OTHER (EXPLAIN) ____________________

The real value of the estate plan summary is to identify specific problems of which each one of us may be unaware in our own estates. Quite often clients will have established goals in mind, such as the who, what, when, and how of passing their estate. By producing a formal estate plan summary, problems can be identified and defined and then coordinated with the balance of the estate planning objectives. The types of problems that are ultimately identified by the summary process vary greatly. The most common are improper property ownership, identifying probate assets, assessing estate tax liability, and providing an accurate picture of any current estate planning in place.

CHAPTER

3

The Ten Most Common Estate Planning Mistakes and How to Avoid Them

Among the various political issues over the past eight years, there has been one common campaign issue: eliminate or reduce estate taxes. You would think that based on current law, federal estate taxation would impact anyone with a home, automobile, and a few bucks in the bank. In reality, if laws were to stay as they are today, less than 2 percent of all estates settled would be subject to federal estate taxation. So what's the reason for all the political rhetoric?

As far as we can determine, it makes for good press. In fact, if the truth were known, the small percentage of Americans that pay estate taxes do so because that's their choice. Estate taxes can be totally avoided with proper planning. But year after year, people die without a proper plan in place and governments and attorneys stand in line to confiscate the inheritance from your children, grandchildren, and great- grandchildren.

While people make a lot of mistakes when it comes to estate planning, most of which are mistakes of omission, there are ten common mistakes that should and can be avoided.

Mistake 1: Failure to Have a Plan or Having an Antiquated or Improper Plan

We often hear of families totally torn apart because a parent or grandparent fails to predetermine who gets what. "She wanted me to have it," claims one child. "No she didn't; she promised it to me," retorts another. Who is right? Only the deceased knows for certain. Too bad she didn't write it down. Too bad she didn't take a few minutes and let her true wishes be known.

At a time when we want the best feelings to exist in our family, when we want them to find comfort in each others' arms, heirs, out of selfishness, can foster the worst traits in the spectrum of human emotions. Anger, envy, jealousy, and even hate can be found when confusion is wrought—the result of failure to preplan the distribution of even the most modest estate. Sins of omission are still sins.

Antiquated plans pose similar problems. A will drawn up ten years ago may not appropriately reflect your current situation. A lot can happen in a ten-year span. I have seen more problems resulting from outdated wills than any other situation. New marriages, new domiciles, new tax laws, growth, more children and grandchildren, retirement income, new investments; the reasons to update your plan are endless. Anyone who has a will or a revocable living trust that hasn't been reviewed since the passage of EGTRRA in 2001 is asking for serious trouble. At a minimum, all estate planning documents should be reviewed every five years.

At a minimum, all estate planning documents should be reviewed every five years.

Improper plans also create problems, such as do-it-yourself kits that are never completely finished, nonfunded revocable living trusts, and multiple conflicting wills. All you accomplish with an improper plan is to create confusion, make life difficult for your heirs, and encourage disputes.

Solution

The way to rectify these types of problems is to follow the Nike's advice: "Just do it!" But do what? Where do you start? The first step with any foreign subject and new adventure is to gain an education. Inside the pages of this book you will find the answers. Arm yourself with knowledge and then be proactive. It will be a costly mistake to walk into an estate planning attorney's office and say, "OK, I'm ready. Plan my estate for me." If you do, you will end up with a plan that isn't really yours.

You have the power now to decide what kind of legacy you want to leave your heirs. Take control by implementing your wishes, not someone else's.

Mistake 2: Misunderstanding the 2001 Tax Act (EGTRRA) and the True Impact It Has on Your Estate

Many sighed in relief when President George W. Bush signed EGTRRA into law because they believed that estate taxes had been, or would soon be, abolished. By taking a closer look at the law, the gradual increase in the estate tax exclusion, and the onerous "sunset provision," one soon understands that proper estate planning is as crucial as ever. The need for proper estate planning will become a thing of the past only when all federal and state inheritance taxes are totally abolished, all capital gains taxes on inheritance are abolished, the costs of probate are abolished, and everyone absolutely knows how everything is to be distributed. Because none of these things have happened yet, Chapters 9 through 12 explore current and past estate settlement laws and how they could potentially affect your estate.

Solution

Have your estate professionally analyzed. A personalized estate analysis can give you a peek into the future by taking a snapshot of your assets today, calculate your net worth, and then estimate what your growth will be after subtracting any living gifts to charities. A well-thought-out estate analysis can be your road map to success and lead you in the right direction, suggesting what tools to implement in order to keep your wealth in the family while maintaining control.

Mistake 3: The Improper Use of Jointly Held Property

For some reason, many feel that if they transfer ownership of their holdings to a close relative, the transaction will side step probate. Perhaps they saw this strategy in some movie or heard it on a talk show. Don't be tempted! If your joint tenant or co-owner is sued or files bankruptcy, the creditors will attack your valued asset and you will lose it—even if it is your home. Furthermore, a spouse from a second marriage could totally disinherit children from a previous marriage. Again, proper prior planning avoids these mishaps, but it does require thought and action.

Solution

If your estate is valued in excess of $150,000, a professionally drafted revocable living trust avoids probate after assets have been transferred into the trust, and it gives you control after you depart this world. Your wishes will not only be carried forth, they cannot be contested.

A well-drafted will can accomplish much of the same; however, a will is always subject to probate and the associated costs. In addition, a will can be contested and becomes public knowledge. Chapters 5 through 8 address ways to correct this mistake in detail.

Mistake 4: Blindly Leaving Everything to Your Spouse

Since the tax act of 1981 and the introduction of the marital deduction, 80 percent of America's affluent have elected to pass their total estate to their surviving spouse. While that is generally our ultimate goal, it isn't necessarily good estate planning. In fact, for a joint estate currently valued in excess of $2 million or an estate with the potential to appreciate beyond that figure, passing everything to your spouse will be the most expensive and needless mistake you will ever make. To put it in dollars and cents, at the survivor's death, an estate valued at $3 million, will pay over $400,000 in federal estate taxes alone, not to mention state inheritance taxes. An estate worth $4 million will carry an estate tax of over $850,000, plus state taxes, all voluntary and unnecessary.

Solution

Currently everyone has the right to pass up to $2 million to the heirs free of the federal estate tax. It is vital that each spouse use this exclusion. That's $4 million per couple, and it is money that can pass from one generation to the next totally free of federal estate taxes. The most effective way to accomplish this tax-saving strategy is through the establishment of a credit shelter trust (CST) prior to the death of the first spouse.

Upon the death of the first spouse, assets valued in excess of the current estate tax exclusion (currently $2 million) are placed into the credit shelter trust, also known as a by-pass or b trust. The surviving spouse is not the trustee. That spouse can, however, access 5 percent of the trust's funds, all the interest, and whatever is needed for health, education, and support. Of course, they can live on their share of the estate however they please. Chapter 15 specifically covers this strategy in detail.

Mistake 5: Not Properly Using the IRS-Approved Annual Gift Allowances

The vast majority of affluent Americans don't comprehend the need to share their wealth with their loved ones while they are alive. Furthermore, they don't understand the power that leverage can create and the many estate tax benefits that can and will be realized if they apply this simple concept.

Each and every American can, by law, currently gift $12,000 annually to anyone they want. A married couple can each gift this allowance or $24,000 per beneficiary, per year. A couple with five children, five grandchildren, and two great grandchildren can gift up to $288,000 per year. It's a use it or lose it proposition, and some question the wisdom of gifting these funds to your family now, citing that they may depend on the gift and become counterproductive. However, there is no law requiring that the recipients must receive the gift in cash; nor do they need to have access to the gift immediately.

Solution

By placing the gift inside an irrevocable trust, such as a family dynasty trust, it can be stipulated that while the gift is given today it cannot be realized until certain parameters are achieved or the recipient reaches a given age. You should maintain as much control as you can over these gifts for as long as possible.

Another idea: Rather than giving the gift outright to your heirs today to do with it what they please, it's better to invest today's gift in something that significantly multiplies at a later date.

For example, for a couple age 65, a simple gift of $24,000 a year to just one child can create $1,676,000 of tax-free cash for delivery when the surviving spouse dies. This is done by establishing a joint and survivor life insurance policy inside an irrevocable life insurance trust and using the gift each year to pay the premium. The proceeds could be used to pay future estate taxes, create an estate, replace assets gifted to charities, or cover debt. This strategy can be further understood by reading Chapter 21.

Mistake 6: Failure to Properly Plan the Distribution of Your Pension/Retirement Accounts

The funds inside all qualified retirement accounts accumulate and compound tax deferred. When the money is distributed, the shelter comes off and taxes are due on April 15 for distributions received during the previous calendar year. The tax liability applies to not only the retiree, but to the beneficiary. Unless properly planned for, taxes can erode up to 70 percent of the value of the plan.

That's 70 percent gone forever! I can't imagine anyone desiring that outcome. Yet an alarming 80 percent of all pension/IRA monies are passed to named beneficiaries and not actually used as retirement income.

Solution

The first order of business should be to spend your pension/IRA monies. There is no reason to let these funds compound until age $70\frac{1}{2}$ when you are forced to take minimum distributions.

I love the bumper sticker on the massive RV that reads: I'm driving my children's inheritance. That's the way it should be. The inherent problem for some is that it can be very difficult to spend the money as fast as it is growing.

For example, a $2 million IRA growing at 10 percent will produce $200,000 in annual growth income (see Figure 3.1). Many retirees find it difficult to spend that kind of money and, as such, the estate keeps growing and the tax time bomb keeps ticking. So what's the real solution?

First, unless you have a prenuptial agreement, your spouse should always be the first in line as your primary beneficiary, so he or she can roll the funds into their own IRA at your death.

Second, by virtue of the August 2006 Pension Protection Act, distributions from a deceased taxpayer's pension/IRA can now be made in a lump sum over a five-year period, or over the life expectancy of the nonspousal

FIGURE 3.1 $2 Million Growth at 10%

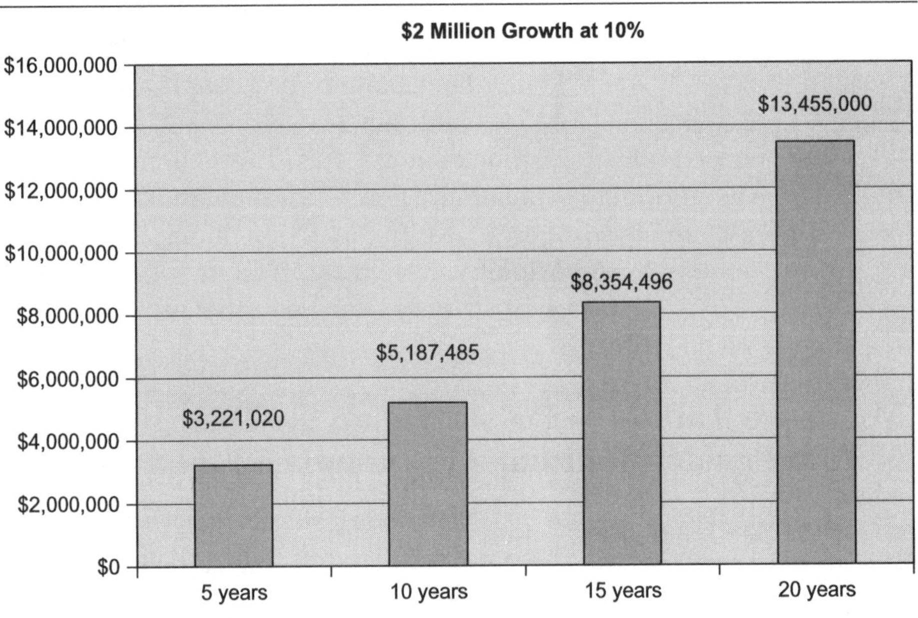

beneficiary. In other words, because the principal and earnings have never been taxed, when the funds are actually withdrawn, taxes are due. Now, the income tax liability can be spread out instead of being due the year following the death of the retiree. While this spells income tax relief for heirs, there is always the issue of the beneficiary taking a lump sum deposit for whatever reason. When this occurs, income taxes will be due.

> Never require your heirs to pay estate taxes with "qualified money."

Never require your heirs to pay estate taxes with "qualified money." They will not only have to pay the estate taxes, both federal and state, but they will have to pay income tax on the money used to pay the tax. Chapter 14, "The Retirement Time Bombs," focuses on this issue and the solutions that can help relieve the tax burden.

Mistake 7: Lacking Liquidity to Cover Estate Settlement Expenses

On the day you expire, there will be a financial assessment. If you have debt, if you owe taxes to the IRS or your state government, if you owe legal fees, or if you owe probate fees, your heirs will need cash. Because 70 percent of today's affluent people do not have a strategic plan, the net results are tragic because most lack the liquidity necessary to cover the bills. As a result, assets must be liquidated to generate cash.

Which assets will be sold first? Will they get top dollar? What if the market suffers declines? These are the types of questions we will force our heirs to answer if we don't have a strategic plan in place beforehand.

On the other hand, if we are fortunate enough to have sufficient liquidity, such as cash or highly marketable securities, our family could use those assets to pay the settlement costs. But is that really prudent? Isn't there a better way than paying 100 cents on each dollar?

Solution

Education is the first step in combating the IRS, state governments, and probate courts. There are viable tools and strategies one can implement to reduce these expenses, and they are found within the pages of this book.

Chapters 8, 15, 16, and 21 focus on proven legal techniques that can be used to allow you to retain 100 percent of what you have worked so hard throughout your life to create and pass on.

Mistake 8: Improperly Arranged and Owned Life Insurance

Recently, while reviewing a doctor's estate, I told him that his $2 million term life insurance policy would be included in his estate and would be taxed just as any other asset. He was upset. He claimed he had been told by his agent of many years the proceeds were not taxable. He even argued his point. I assured him that his agent was partially correct. The proceeds will be *income* tax free, but not *estate* tax free. That is, unless the policy is owned by someone other than himself. That's a critical mistake we see all too often.

The next mistake we encounter is failure to name a proper contingent beneficiary. Millions of dollars lay unclaimed simply because the insured named a secondary beneficiary that predeceased the insured. Furthermore, many people, for the lack of actually naming someone, list their estate as their primary and secondary beneficiary. By doing so, upon death, the proceeds are needlessly subjected to probate and the claims of the insured's creditors.

Millions of dollars lay unclaimed simply because the insured named a secondary beneficiary that predeceased the insured.

There is one other common problem we see with regularity when reviewing estates—existing policies are not performing to their initial expectations. In other words, they most likely will not survive based on the assumptions that were originally presented. This is a huge problem because the insured and his or her family are counting on the insurance policies to protect them. If the problem is not corrected, the policies will disintegrate.

Solution

First, let us give you the solution that we presented and implemented to a new client of ours in Baltimore. After careful review and analysis, we executed a tax-free exchange (Sec. 1035 IRC) of an old underperforming universal life policy for a new **guaranteed death benefit** policy. We placed the cash value of the previous policy inside an irrevocable life insurance trust, using a portion of the annual gifts and lifetime gift allowance. The net result was **more coverage for a lower premium**, and a policy fully insulated from creditors, predators, and, most important, the IRS.

Needless to say, a review of your life insurance and beneficiaries should occur every five years. This kind of vigilance will allow you to avoid these common mistakes and allow your policies to fulfill their stated purpose.

Mistake 9: Not Properly Preparing for the Exorbitant Cost of Long-Term Medical Care

According to the Health Insurance Association of America, "4 in 10 Americans age 65 and older will need long-term care—at a cost of $60,000 to $100,000 a year." At that rate, a lengthy illness could wipe out many estates, especially considering the fact that before one can be eligible for Medicare's financial assistance for long-term care, you must first "spend down" your assets.

Are you prepared to take the chance that your assets will cover long-term medical costs? Have you taken any steps to shield your investments from this cash drain? Could you financially survive a long-term illness or accident?

Solution

Learn these simple words: *long-term care insurance.* If your net worth is between $100,000 and $4,000,000 and you're relatively healthy, you're an ideal candidate for long-term care (LTC) insurance. The average age of LTC insurance applicants is 66. However, the sooner you apply, the easier it is to qualify and it is less expensive.

Recently a major insurance carrier introduced a long-term policy tied to a universal life insurance policy. In most cases, if you qualify, you get life insurance, cash value accumulation and LTC coverage for the same premium as a stand-alone LTC policy.

In addition to LTC insurance, you should also consider placing your assets inside irrevocable trusts or investments, such as Medicare safe annuities, that cannot be penetrated by creditors, predators, or the IRS.

Mistake 10: Not Leaving Your Life Story for Your Family to Enjoy Forever

As with all planning, the number one obstacle is procrastination. We are filled with great intentions, but when it comes to actually moving forward, we put it off until a more convenient time. Unfortunately, the things we put off today usually don't get done tomorrow.

Each of us has a personal life history. Each of us has a story to tell. For the most part, these histories are seldom recorded for posterity, and after a while they simply become faded memories. Your family loves and appreciates you. They love your stories of the Great Depression, World War II, the time you met your spouse, the day they were born, and your favorite family vacation. They want to remember forever your personality. Don't just stop at leaving a financial legacy; leave them your life's legacy.

Solution

With the technology and services of today there is little excuse for not preserving your life history for your loved ones. Write it down (there is software available to help), create a video (there are national companies like *www.leavingmylegacy.com* that can help), create a scrapbook of memories (there are more scrapbook stores than ever before), create a concise photo history (there are Web sites like *www.grandpatellme.com* that are designed to lend a hand in organizing your photos).

Preserve your legacy forever. You owe it to your family.

Conclusion: Procrastination Will Be Dangerous to Your Wealth

Why is it that 70 percent of America's millionaires fail to plan the logical distribution of their assets from their generation to the next?

There isn't just one answer. Fear, lack of education, cost, denial, etc. all contribute to **procrastination;** and that's the biggest mistake of all. No one cherishes the time they spend planning their estates, but that planning is vital. Estate settlement costs can be exorbitant. Estate taxes are the most unjust taxes we pay in this country. But when the IRS and state revenue departments give us an out, we need to jump on it. In no other situation does the phrase **"the waiting game is the loser's game"** apply more appropriately.

To repeat the Nike motto again: **JUST DO IT!**

CHAPTER

4

Assembling the Team

Finding a Quarterback

Constructing an estate plan takes professional help. Deciding who will help you accomplish your estate planning goals is probably the most crucial step in achieving your overall objectives. The enormous number of people who refer to themselves as **estate planners** complicates this decision. Today estate planners come in all sizes and shapes. The choices are wide open: insurance agents, financial planners, investment firms, bank trust departments, attorneys, and those who devote 100 percent of their time to the practice of estate planning.

How do you decide whose advice and guidance to seek? Perhaps the best way for you to make the selection is to have a set game plan from the start. But to have a game plan, you must first understand the game!

Almost everyone has watched an occasional football game on television. Have you ever watched a game in which an injury sidelines the starting quarterback? How well does the team perform? Most often, teams are decimated when the star player or the person who directs the team is out. In fact, quarterbacks who are lost for long periods from a severe injury cause losing seasons for most teams.

A person with the experience and resources to effectively direct and execute a plan can mean the difference between success and failure.

Winning the game of estate planning requires similar coordination and direction by a team leader. A person with the experience and resources to effectively direct and execute a plan can mean the difference between success and failure. This becomes quite clear when you begin to explore the various aspects involved in estate planning.

FIGURE 4.1 Three Basic Elements of an Effective Estate Plan

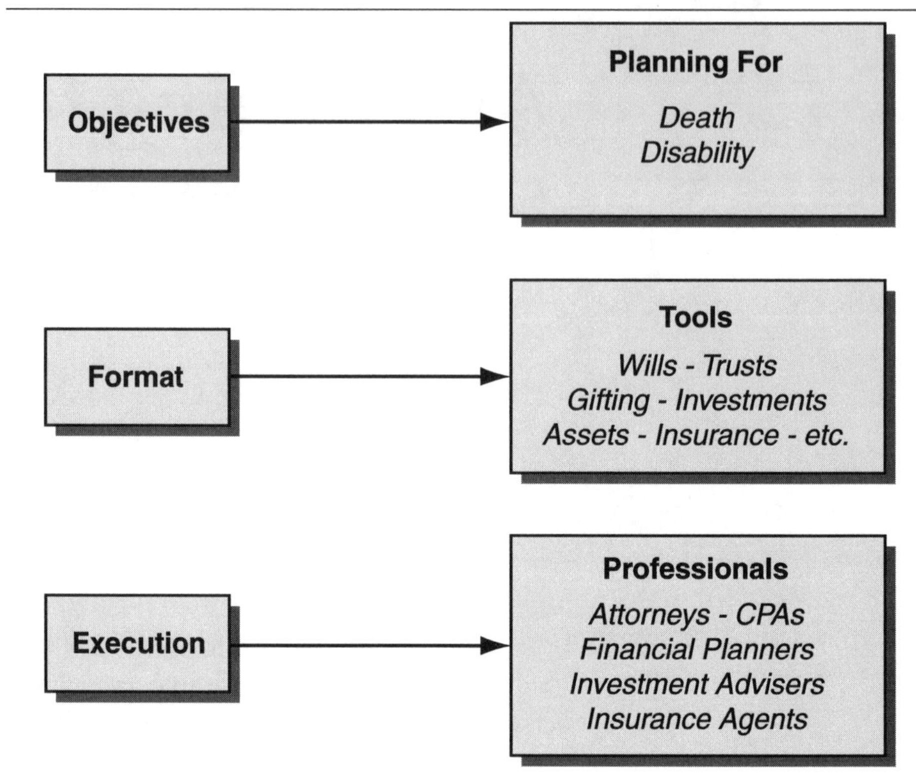

Attaining an Effective Plan

There are three elements basic to attaining an effective plan: (1) **objectives,** (2) **format,** and (3) **execution.** In Figure 4.1, these elements are categorized to illustrate each stage.

Objectives

Objectives in estate planning are not limited solely to death planning, testamentary planning, and disability planning, but include lifetime planning as well.

Format

Format planning consists of the various tools to facilitate objectives. In simple estate planning, there may be only one tool: a will. This tool facilitates the distribution of assets at death and usually indicates a minimal estate. However, the typical estate plan today contains many tools designed to achieve any number of planning objectives.

Execution

Execution, once a plan is formatted, it generally requires the use of an attorney to facilitate plan documents such as wills and trusts. The plan usually is coordinated with additional professionals such as estate planners, financial planners, investment advisors, and insurance agents. Valuing assets, retitling assets, measuring life insurance proceeds for inclusion in the gross estate, assessing tax liability, and many other elements are all integral parts of total estate planning.

Estate Planners and Quarterbacks

In the past five years, we have seen the advent of the **estate planner.** These individuals and their staff concentrate their efforts on and specialize only in estate planning. Their backgrounds are varied. Many hold business degrees, some are practicing attorneys, and others have extensive backgrounds in financial services and now specialize in estate planning. These individuals and firms have specialized in estate planning because of two factors: (1) the degree of sophistication in planning techniques required to be effective and (2) the need for systematic efforts across the United States to create entities that specialize in specific areas of estate planning. Examples of such specialized areas are business succession, estate freeze techniques, wealth transfer, charitable gifting, leverage techniques, and generation-skipping transfers.

Such hybrid planners are often referred to as **quarterbacks.** They usually facilitate objectives, format, and execution. These essential elements of planning are often integrated and achieved under one roof because the professionals are structured for and integrate all the various aspects of planning.

The quarterback method of planning does not exclude other established professionals the client may have. The quarterback simply coordinates the entire process with these other individuals and fills any voids where necessary. His or her most important function is to develop a written plan and familiarize all those involved in the process with the objectives, format, and execution of the plan.

Figure 4.2 illustrates how this method can be simplified. In the *client maze,* the client is faced with the multifaceted job of coordinating all the various aspects of the plan. In the *client simplification box,* the client allows the quarterback to facilitate all the various components of the plan. This approach usually eliminates the confusion most people feel when planning their estates.

FIGURE 4.2 The Quarterback Method Versus the Client Maze

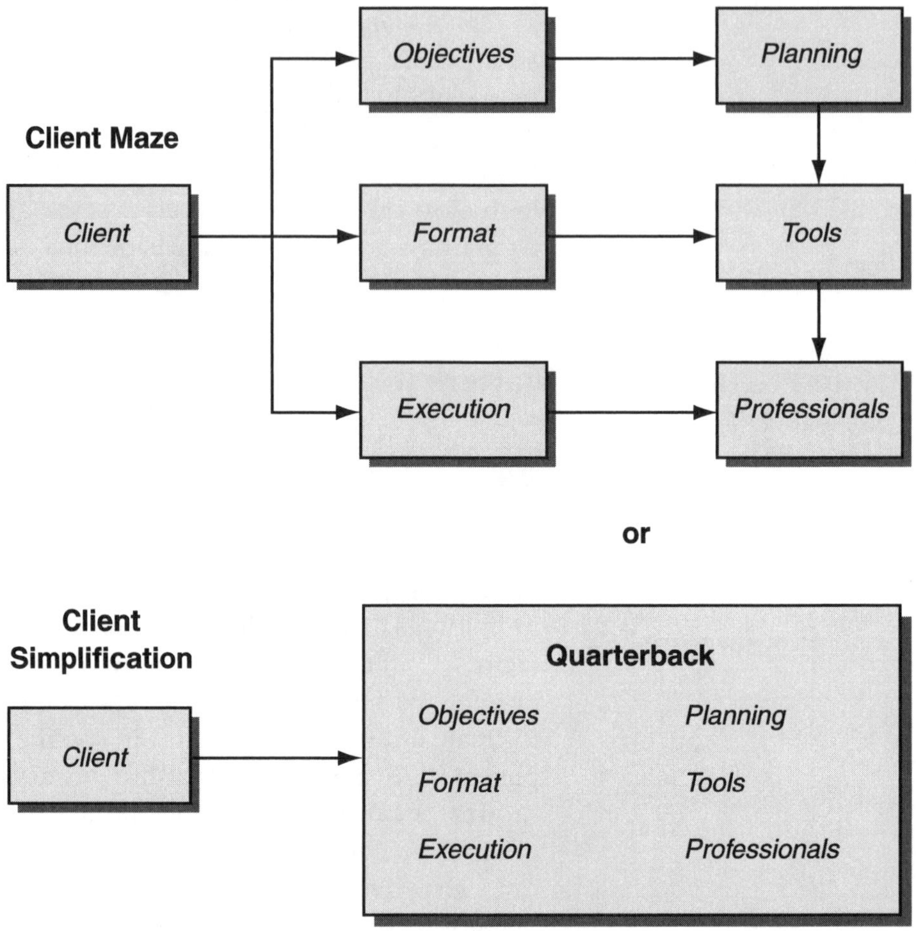

Finding the right planner should consist of finding a planner who can coordinate all the various aspects of your plan. This includes the coordination of objectives, format, and execution under one roof with all of your advisors. Coordinating the various tools that will be used and combining the various professionals will usually provide a clear, concise, and effective plan.

CHAPTER

5

Ownership and Title

The Built-In Estate Plan

If assets are not titled properly, your estate plan may prove to be ineffective.

In one of our recent client meetings, our client (let's call her Mary) divulged that she had arranged to give her house, which she currently shares with her husband, to her daughter upon death. Mary had recently remarried after being a widow for several years. The house was titled in joint tenancy with right of survivorship with her current husband. When we asked her how she intended to facilitate the transfer of this property, she said that she had made a provision in her will. Unfortunately, as we pointed out, based on how the house was titled with her new husband, it would pass directly to her husband upon her death by **operation of law.** Her daughter would not be entitled to inherit the house. Mary had no idea that her will had no effect on passing the house to her daughter.

This situation provides a good example of why accurate information gathering is vital. In this case, it revealed a potential problem with Mary's current estate plan based on her actual goals and objectives.

To explain how property passes, we must review how certain property is owned and the potential problems various forms of ownership present in passing property at death. But first, there are two basic forms of ownership: (1) property that is owned by one person **(outright ownership)** and (2) property that is held in conjunction with others **(joint ownership).**

Outright Ownership

Property that is owned completely by one person is the simplest form of ownership. This type of ownership is referred to as outright ownership or **fee simple** ownership. With this type of ownership, an individual is free to do everything ownership allows without the consent or constraints of other people. The owner has the freedom to sell, exchange, or manage the property any way he or she desires. The owner can collect any income that is applicable to the property, profit from any gain, and suffer from any loss while assuming all liability that goes along with property ownership. Examples of liability include maintenance, repair, taxes, and debts that may be secured by the property.

Joint Ownership

Unlike outright ownership, which deals with ownership by one individual, joint ownership has several different forms and can be more complex. The four types of joint ownership consist of the following:

1. Joint tenancy
2. Tenancy by the entirety
3. Tenancy in common
4. Community-owned property

Joint Tenancy with Right of Survivorship (JTWRS)

This type of ownership provides for any number of owners. All owners hold an equal undivided share of the property. If the property is disposed of, it must remain undivided. A tenant is free to sell his or her share of the joint tenancy. The new owner will own his or her interest with the other tenants and not as a separate share.

You cannot readily sell your interest as a separate share or as a separate part. Shares can be separated only under the direction of a court, more commonly referred to as remedy of *partition.*

■ Example

Mary Williams and Sam Perkins own stock as joint tenants. The value of the stock is $500,000. As joint tenants, each owns an equal share of the stock, or 50 percent. If Mary wants to sell her interest, she cannot divide or separate her interest from Sam's interest. A new owner will continue as a joint tenant with right of survivorship with Sam Perkins. If one of the two tenants dies, the survivor will succeed to full ownership.

Another interesting feature of joint tenancy deals with how the property passes at the death of the tenants. At the death of a tenant or co-owner, the surviving co-owners acquire the decedent's entire interest in the property by law. If you are a surviving tenant, the total property interest belongs to you. If you started with ten tenants (co-owners) and you survive all of them, you now own the entire property! In many cases, JTWRS provides automatic estate planning. In the case of property owned between spouses where each wishes to pass the entire property to the surviving spouse, transfer strategies need to be employed. The property will pass by law to the surviving spouse; a will or other estate planning document has no effect. However, other assets in the estate may be passed by a will or other methods structured into the estate plan.

Property passing by JTWRS has an additional built-in feature—this type of ownership generally avoids probate proceedings until the death of the surviving tenant or co-owner.

WARNING

Although JTWRS has some specific advantages in certain estate planning applications, it can also be a big mistake. If you want assets to pass to people other than joint tenants or co-owners, JTWRS can prevent you from accomplishing this.

In our practice, one of the largest problems we see is incorrect ownership, even in cases where clients have established elaborate estate plans.

In larger estates, tax planning may be a key issue. Using the allowable exemptions or each spouse's individual estate tax credit (currently $2,000,000 for 2007 through 2008) to maximize the amount allowed to pass without death tax can be foiled by JTWRS ownership. The cost of this mistake can create up to $850,000 in death taxes that is unnecessary and avoidable if proper ownership is accomplished.

In our practice, one of the largest problems we see is incorrect ownership, even in cases where clients have established elaborate estate plans. This problem might be one of the most costly as well as one of the easiest to remedy.

JTWRS property is specifically titled as right of survivorship and is usually spelled out in the title. If right of survivorship is not clearly stated, tenancy in common is generally assumed.

Tenancy by the Entirety

Tenancy by the entirety is a special type of joint ownership that exists only between spouses. This type of ownership provides for only two owners: husband and wife. Property is deemed to be owned equally by each spouse as long as both are alive. Under this type of ownership, property passes by right of survivorship to the surviving spouse.

A primary difference between JTWRS and tenancy by the entirety is that in tenancy by the entirety, neither spouse may dispose or convey an interest in the property without the consent of the other spouse.

Tenancy in Common

Tenancy in common contains no right of survivorship. Each owner may dispose of his or her interest without regard to the other co-owners. At the time of death, the owner's interest passes by will or the laws of intestacy (without a will) set forth by state statute. The co-owners have no automatic or survivorship rights to the decedent's share of the property.

Tenants in common may hold unequal shares. One tenant may hold a 30 percent interest, and a second tenant may hold the balance, or 70 percent, of the property. There is no limit on the number of tenants in common. Each owns a percentage or fraction of the undivided total property.

The instrument that conveys ownership of tenancy in common property usually spells out percentages in unequal tenancy. If the tenants equally own shares, the instrument should state "equally as tenants in common."

Community Property

Eight states have community property laws: Arizona, California, Idaho, Louisiana, Nevada, New Mexico, Texas, and Washington. In addition, Wisconsin has enacted legislation that closely resembles that of community property states, though it is not a true community property state. The other 42 states base property ownership on common law principals.

Understanding community property ownership, as well as other forms of ownership, is vital to effective estate planning. The value of a community property asset is different from that of an asset held fee simple or as tenants in common.

Community property deals with property specifically acquired during marriage. This type of ownership assumes that each spouse owns a one-half or equal interest regardless of the employment status of each spouse or specifically which spouse paid for the property. Under community property law, it is assumed that each spouse owns the property equally. Income generated from community property assets is deemed to be owned equally between each spouse. At the death of one spouse, community property is valued in the estate at 50 percent of the date-of-death value.

Contributions in acquiring the property is assumed to be equal by both spouses. At the death of one spouse, only half of the property may be

The most important legislation pertaining to estate planning took place in 1981, when Congress passed the Economic Recovery Tax Act (ERTA).

disposed of by the deceased spouse's will. This half passes to the surviving spouse only if specific provisions are made to do so.

Because community property deals only with property acquired during marriage, property acquired before marriage by either person remains separate property. Another exception is property that is acquired during marriage in the form of a gift. Property received by one spouse after marriage by gift or inheritance remains separate property unless it is actually transferred to the other spouse.

Community property retains its status as community property even if the individuals move to a non–community property state. It is extremely important to know how this property is treated, regardless of which state you reside in. The federal government recognizes the rights of each state, which is addressed in the Tenth Amendment to the U.S. Constitution.

Provisions Created by ERTA

In an effort to treat all states equally with regard to estate taxation, the federal government passed several laws starting in 1948. However, the most important legislation took place in 1981, when Congress passed the Economic Recovery Tax Act (ERTA). This act contained sweeping reforms in federal estate and gift tax law. Among other changes, ERTA provided that someone could leave all property (unlimited amounts) to a surviving spouse with no tax liability. This is referred to as the **unlimited marital deduction.** ERTA also allowed one spouse to make *unlimited lifetime gifts* to the other spouse free of gift tax. Later we will focus on these two changes and the significant advantages they provide in planning your estate.

WARNING

Under ERTA, the benefits provided individuals living in community property states were significantly improved or enhanced. If this circumstance applies to you, we strongly urge you to review your estate plan. Significant tax saving strategies are available that previously did not exist.

Figure 5.1 summarizes the most common forms of ownership and title.

FIGURE 5.1 The Most Common Forms of Ownership and Title

Ownership and Title Summary

Outright Ownership

1. Fee Simple	You own 100 percent outright. You are free to • gift the property, • sell the property, or • direct who will receive the property at death.

Joint Ownership

1. Joint Tenancy	You own all property with others. You are free to • gift your interest or • sell your interest. You cannot pass your interest at death.
2. Tenancy by Entirety	This type of ownership exists between husband and wife only. There are only two owners. Both are equal owners. The survivor gains full ownership.
3. Tenancy in Common	You own part of the property. There can be unequal owners. You are free to • sell your interest, • leave your interest at death, or • gift your interest.
4. Community property	You own 50 percent. This form exists between spouses only. You may pass your interest at death.

CHAPTER

6

Passing Property

Are Wills Enough?

Property passes in one of three ways at time of death:

1. By will
2. By contract or trust
3. By operation of law

The Will—A Misunderstood Tool

A **will** is a simple document that instructs how assets are to pass to heirs at time of death. Wills are functionless during the course of one's life and have no effect until a person dies. The will passes property that is excluded from passing by operation of law or by contract or trust.

A further examination of wills yields additional aspects that need to be addressed by many families with minor children. A will can make provisions for the following situations:

- *A personal representative.* Wills can determine who will act for you after your death (your *executor*). This person will have many duties to perform. The most important duties include the administration of your estate, distribution of assets to beneficiaries, payment of debts, filing income tax returns, filing estate tax returns (Form 706), payment of taxes and expenses, and the collection of life insurance proceeds and retirement benefits.
- *Guardianship.* One of the most important aspects of a will is the naming of a guardian or guardians for minor children. Most people assume that family members will automatically be allowed to function as guardians for their children. However, most states

have specific laws that apply to guardianship. Most problems can be avoided by naming specific guardians in your will. Additionally, the selection of these individuals can be changed when necessary.

- *A testamentary trust.* A testamentary trust creates provisions that continue after your death (e.g., continued needs or support for minor children or aging parents). The testamentary trust provision in a will creates a trust to hold liquid assets (cash or its equivalent) to provide continued income after your death to minor children or others who have long-term needs.

During a person's lifetime, the provisions of the will remain private. However, upon death, a will becomes public record when it is registered with the court. As such, the contents of a will are available to anyone who makes an inquiry. Those involved in business may be the most adversely affected; debts and asset holdings can become subject to public scrutiny.

Because wills do not hold title to property, many people face multiple probate systems at death. Consider the person who is domiciled in one state and owns real estate in one or more additional states. At death this person's estate is subject to probate in all states where he or she owns real estate. This can cause severe estate settlement complications and needless costs.

Because a will takes effect only at death, it offers no lifetime benefits.

Because a will takes effect only at death, it offers no lifetime benefits. So ask yourself this question: Have you made absolutely clear provisions for the management of your physical and financial well-being if you become disabled? We were all born unable to care for ourselves and we required complete care by our parents or guardians for many years until we could take care of ourselves. Adult disability requires complete care by others. The main difference however, is when adult disability occurs we usually have assets that require management.

Often clients disclose to us that their estate plans are complete. Many of these individuals have completed wills and assume all their property will pass under the terms of their wills. However, when we examine property in each state and further determine how it is owned or titled, many of our clients find that these wills cannot accomplish the objectives they set out to achieve.

We generally use wills in simple estates where assets are limited.

We generally use wills in simple estates where assets are limited. Estates that contain numerous assets, hold business interests, own property in other states, face multiple probate systems, have minor children to financially care for (single parent) or children from previous marriages, often require additional planning tools, such as trusts. Furthermore, estates that are in excess of $1,000,000 often benefit from tax planning that trusts can offer versus simple will planning. We will examine these issues in later chapters when we review taxation and trusts.

FIGURE 6.1 Summary of Advantages and Disadvantages of Wills

Advantages

1. They direct assets that pass by will to beneficiaries.
2. They name guardians for minor children.
3. They name personal representatives to settle estates.
4. They may create trusts at death to accomplish postdeath planning.

Disadvantages

1. They take effect only at death.
2. They provide no lifetime planning.
   - There are no provisions for your disability.
   - There are no provisions to name a guardian for you.
   - There is no system for the management of your assets during your lifetime.
3. They are subject to probate.
4. They become public at death.
5. They are ineffective interstate planning tools.
6. They can be especially ineffective when minors are involved, particularly after a divorce.

Wills often have little effect on how assets pass because assets may pass by operation of law or contract. In many applications, wills are not sufficient to provide proper planning. By following the estate planning process, use of tools—wills, trusts, and so on—can be determined. The effectiveness and timeliness of a will can be summed up in Figure 6.1. In essence, a will should be the only estate planning vehicle when the net estate is valued at less than $150,000.

CHAPTER

7

Passing Property Through Contracts, Trusts, and Operation of Law

The Beneficiary Designation

Examples of assets that pass by contract are life insurance policies, annuities, individual retirement accounts (IRAs), employee benefit programs, and other qualified retirement plans. These contracts often name individuals as beneficiaries. Upon death, the value (proceeds) of these contracts passes directly to those named individuals. A will does not affect the passing of these proceeds unless the will is the named beneficiary.

Examples of Contracts

Life Insurance Policies

Most of us own life insurance policies. If your estate consists solely of a large life insurance policy (a contract) with specifically designated beneficiaries, the entire estate at death passes under the terms of the insurance contract to the stated beneficiaries. Any will that exists has no effect on how or to whom the insurance proceeds will pass. However, if you name your estate as beneficiary, the entire proceeds of the insurance contract will pass to the individuals named in, or who pass under, the provisions of the will. If no will exists, the proceeds are distributed by statutory guidelines set forth by the state in which you reside.

Trust Agreements

Another example of a contract is a trust agreement. A **trust** is a contract between a **grantor,** or **settlor** (the person or persons who create the trust), and a **trustee** or **trustees** (persons or entities who hold legal title to property in the trust until the trust provides for distribution).

With a trust, the grantor predetermines beneficiaries.

With a trust, the grantor predetermines beneficiaries. These beneficiaries are usually entitled to trust assets in a manner set forth under the terms of the trust. Trusts can make distributions to beneficiaries during the lifetime of the grantor but usually distribute property at the death of the grantor. Common examples include income and principal, both of which can be distributed in a variety of ways as set forth under the terms of the trust agreement. Beneficiaries are not parties to the trust agreement but hold an equitable interest in the trust property, commonly referred to as the **corpus.**

Operation of Law

Earlier, we discussed types of ownership where the surviving co-owner or co-owners succeeded to full ownership at the death of other tenants. Property passes by operation of law in one of two ways.

Passing Property by Title

The first way property passes by operation of law deals with how property is titled. An example is property that is titled jointly with another person with a right of survivorship, commonly referred to as joint tenancy with right of survivorship (JTWRS). This type of ownership is often associated with property held between spouses. At the death of one owner, the surviving joint owner or owners succeed to total ownership of the property by law. A common example of an asset that passes by joint tenancy with right of survivorship is a residence titled jointly between spouses. At death, the residence passes to the surviving spouse under operation of law by right of survivorship. This also applies to property that is held under tenancies by the entirety.

Intestate Death

We have often wondered how much money (property, etc.) is distributed by each state to statute beneficiaries because people do not plan for the distribution of their own estates!

The second way that property passes by operation of law is defined when an individual dies without a will; in other words, he or she dies **intestate.** A good example of intestacy is the person who owns a residence outright—fee simple—who may be a widow or widower. If he or she dies intestate, the residence will pass by state law or statute that prescribes how property is to be distributed.

State laws generally provide for distribution of property to next of kin. Percentages and provisions for others, such as spouses, vary from state to state. We have often wondered how much money (property, etc.) is distributed by each state to statute beneficiaries because people do not plan for the distribution of their own estates!

Dower and Curtesy Provisions

Most states have enacted specific provisions that protect one spouse from being disinherited by the other spouse. These are referred to as **dower** and **curtesy** interests. Most often the surviving spouse is entitled to a certain percentage of the deceased spouse's estate, which is usually no less than one-third to one-half of the estate or probated assets. Thus, in the event that a spouse leaves all property to a third party under a will, such as children or other family members, state law allows the surviving spouse to elect against the will and collect a percentage of the property according to state law.

As previously stated, depending on the type of property, such as life insurance that passes by contract or joint tenancy property that passes by operation of law, quite often people die with property not covered by either contract or operation of law. We recommend familiarity with your state's provisions of property distribution if you decide not to plan your estate. Often their plan is far from your wishes, but will be implemented if you die intestate.

CHAPTER

8

Probate

The Unnecessary Last Resort

Assets that do not pass by contract or survivorship (law) are distributed based on the laws of intestacy and are administered under a system called **probate.** Furthermore, if you die with a will (**testate**), those assets that pass under the terms of your will are also probate assets and are subject to the probate system established in your state.

Figure 8.1 depicts typical examples of property passing under state intestacy laws, which vary from state to state.

Note that this figure is greatly simplified for illustration purposes only. An additional point to consider is the passing of property further down the family, or bloodline.

Property That Passes by Bloodline

There are two lines that direct most intestacy laws in the distribution of assets among heirs: (1) **per stirpes** and (2) **per capita.**

Per Stirpes Distribution

Per stirpes is representative of distribution by line of descent. If a person who had had two children dies and one of the children predeceased the decedent and left behind two children (grandchildren of the decedent), the decedent's surviving child receives one-half of the per stirpes distribution and the two grandchildren receive the other half. Thus, each grandchild receives a one-fourth interest in the decedent's intestate property.

FIGURE 8.1 Typical Examples of How Property Passes Under State Intestacy Laws

Widow or widower with one or more children	100% to children
Married, no children	75% to spouse, 25% to parents
Married with one child	50% to spouse, 50% to child
Married with two or more children	1/3 to spouse 2/3 to children
Unmarried, no children	100% to parents, brothers, and sisters equally

Note: Most state intestacy laws make additional provisions to pass property to heirs in the event that the above beneficiaries have predeceased the decedent.

Per Capita Distribution

Per capita distribution is representative of an equal distribution among a group of named individuals or beneficiaries. Family relationship or kinship has no bearing on this type of distribution. If a parent, son, granddaughter, and aunt are beneficiaries, they will all receive equal distributions of the decedent's property.

Other Lines of Distribution

What about distributions to adopted children, illegitimate children, posthumous children (children born after a parent's death), and half-brothers and half-sisters? How are they treated in intestate circumstances?

Adopted Children

Adopted children usually take a full child's share of property. In almost all states, an adopted child has the same right to share in the parents' estate as the full child.

Illegitimate Children

Illegitimate children share in property differently between mother and father. In most states, the illegitimate child is in the same position as a legitimate child in regard to his or her mother and bloodline relatives. Thus, an illegitimate child will take a grandchild's share of the estate of a maternal grandmother or grandfather. However, this is not true in the case of the father. An illegitimate child will share in the property of the deceased father equal to a normal child's share if the father eventually marries the mother, the father is determined to be the natural father by a court, or the father confirms the child as his own.

Posthumous Children

Posthumous children are those born after the death of a parent. They generally are treated as normal children and receive a full child's share.

Half-Brothers and Half-Sisters

Half-brothers and half-sisters have only one parent in common. Most states treat them as normal blood children. In other words, these children receive a whole share.

What Happens to Property When No Heirs Exist?

You may wonder what happens to property when there are no heirs. This is commonly referred to as *escheat.* In most states when there are no heirs, the decedent's property passes to the state, or the property "escheats" to the state.

When there is an unmarried person with no children, 100 percent of the property passes to parents, brothers, and sisters equally. However, what happens if there are no surviving parents, brothers, or sisters? In these cases, intestacy laws usually provide for assets to pass to nieces and nephews equally. If there are no nieces or nephews, the property can then pass to grandparents, aunts, and uncles. If none of these people survive, the state inherits the property.

If you fit into one of the categories just described, you should investigate the laws in your own state for an accurate picture of intestacy succession.

The Probate System: Its Functions and Disadvantages

The probate system incorporates courts in most counties of each state. The primary function of the probate court and the probate system is to pass property of deceased individuals to heirs. Probate functions both for those who die with a will and for those who die without a will.

As previously mentioned, probate has some definite disadvantages:

- Probate proceedings are public.
- Probate can be very costly.
- Probate can prolong settlement of an estate indefinitely.
- Heirs may be entirely cut off or may be prevented from inheriting property on a timely basis.

FIGURE 8.2 Functions of the Probate Process

- Appoint a probate agent (*administrator*) if there is no will.
- Interpret the will.
- Inventory and assess the value of all property.
- Locate and identify heirs.
- Identify and settle outstanding liabilities and creditors.
- Resolve conflicts between the estate and other parties.
- Complete and file various tax returns.
- Distribute all property.

If one of your objectives is to avoid probate, you have several ways to position your estate to accomplish this goal.

The probate system is fairly broad-based in settling estates. Not only does the probate system distribute assets to heirs, but also it is responsible for a number of other functions. (See Figure 8.2.)

Quite frankly, we don't understand why any of those with a moderate accumulation of assets ($150,000 and up) would choose to have their estate probated. In the case of small estates or estates in which all heirs or family members are deceased, individuals may lack motivation to arrange their estates to avoid the probate process. However, if one of your objectives is to avoid probate process, you have several ways to position your estate to accomplish this goal. Most of the following techniques involve proper ownership and titling:

- Title property joint tenancy with right of survivorship (JTWRS)
- Create and fund an **inter vivos,** or **living trust**
- Use correct designations of beneficiaries for life insurance and employee benefit programs
- If you live in a state that has adopted the Uniform Probate Code, you can use a designation on bank accounts known as **payable on death,** or **POD.**

Joint Ownership and Probate

In Chapter 5, we noted that property titled joint tenancy with right of survivorship (JTWRS) succeeds by operation of law to the surviving joint tenant. This type of property is not subject to probate or probate proceedings.

However, JTWRS property can create several problems. For example, consider property held in this manner between spouses. At the death of the first spouse, the property passes to the surviving spouse.

However, unless the surviving spouse retitles the property, it will become a probate asset at the survivor's death.

But what happens if the surviving spouse is unable to retitle the property? Serious problems can arise in situations of simultaneous death, advanced age of the survivor, or senility. Under these circumstances, retitling is improbable and property ownership between spouses under JTWRS provisions become ineffective.

JTWRS property delays probate at the death of the first spouse, but assets titled in this manner become probate assets on the death of the surviving spouse. If there are more than two tenants or in situations that involve tenants other than spouses, the surviving tenant succeeds to full ownership. Unless this person retitles the asset at the death of the first owner, it will become a probate asset. Furthermore, if you (the surviving spouse) retitle assets with your children, you then subject your assets to risk as a result of confiscation by your children's creditors, divorce proceedings brought by their spouses, and lawsuits that stem from their negligence.

Property That Passes by Contract

In Chapter 7, we examined property that passes by contract—for example, life insurance policies, annuities, and employee benefit programs (e.g., pension and profit-sharing plans containing beneficiary designations). It is important to remember that if named persons are designated beneficiaries of these contracts at death, the proceeds will pass directly to these named individuals and avoid probate. However, if the contract designates your "estate" as beneficiary, the contract proceeds will become probate assets at death subject to the provisions of your will. If you die intestate, these assets will pass according to state statutes.

One important aspect to consider when choosing beneficiaries with contracts is whether the beneficiaries are *minors.* If you elect minor children as beneficiaries, the proceeds from these contracts will become probate assets. Minors are subject to legal guardianship until they become of age. Legal age (usually 18) varies from state to state. If you have minor children, you must consider the use of trusts (see Chapters 16 through 20) for naming guardians and trustees to distribute assets to minors. Making your trust the beneficiary of a contract avoids probate and facilitates distribution of assets to minor children in a systematic way. Wills can provide for guardians of minor children and can also create trusts at death to distribute assets to your minor children. But remember that assets that pass through a will are probate assets and are fully subject to probate procedures and costs—a major factor when deciding whether to pass assets by will or by trust.

The Uniform Probate Code

Several states have adopted the Uniform Probate Code. If you reside in one of these states, you may profit from an additional technique to avoid probate that resembles passing assets by contract. Specifically, certificates of deposit, savings accounts, and checking accounts can provide a beneficiary designation that avoids probate. The beneficiary designation is termed *payable on death,* or *POD.*

When these accounts are set up, you will usually have the option of choosing a POD designation. If you are fortunate enough to reside in a state that has adopted this code and have elected to use this feature on your accounts, you must exercise caution where minor children are concerned. The same problems with making minors beneficiaries of life insurance and employee benefit plans hold true for POD designations on bank accounts. *Never use minors for these designations.* Instead, name a responsible adult or a trust that divides the property according to its terms.

The following 16 states have adopted the Uniform Probate Code:

Alaska	Minnesota
Arizona	Montana
Colorado	Nebraska
Florida	New Mexico
Hawaii	North Dakota
Idaho	South Carolina
Maine	Utah
Michigan	South Dakota

In addition, numerous states have adopted the UPC in an incomplete form. You should check with your state's probate system to see how the code applies in your state.

Using Trusts to Avoid Probate

The use of an **inter vivos,** or living, trust to avoid probate and reduce estate tax will be detailed in Chapter 16. It's important to keep in mind that trusts solve problems that no other forms of title or ownership can. As an example, consider the case of a husband and wife who own all of their assets jointly with right of survivorship. As previously illustrated, these are nonprobate assets. At the death of the first spouse, the surviving spouse will succeed to complete ownership—fee simple—by right of survivorship. When this happens, the assets become probate assets on the survivor's death.

If a husband and wife simply retitle all assets as tenants in common and each tenant titles his or her share under their respective trusts, the assets will escape probate regardless of who dies first. The survivor

Trusts solve problems that no other forms of title or ownership can.

is assured of nonprobate assets. If property is left outright to a spouse as tenant in common, this spouse can retitle the property to his or her trust to avoid probate at death.

Regardless of the size and scope of your assets, the living trust can be used to avoid probate for 100 percent of your property as well as solve numerous other issues that will be explained in later chapters. Although other techniques are applicable in estate planning, we feel that in most cases trusts should be an integral element of the basic format.

The Impact of Taxation

In previous discussions, we categorized estate planning into three phases: (1) objectives, (2) format, and (3) execution.

Most people have some idea of their objectives or what they would like their estate plan to accomplish before they consult an estate planning professional. A few know precisely what they want to accomplish. The main obstacles that we encounter are lack of motivation in addition to lack of knowledge—about both estate planning and whom to turn to for direction—all of which causes procrastination.

But one factor that motivates many to take action is taxation. When you finally realize that the federal and state governments will confiscate a significant portion of your estate through death taxes, you become determined to avoid this eventuality if at all possible.

Consider someone who currently has an estate of $2.5 million. If this person assumes that he or she can pass the entire estate to a child or grandchild, or anyone for that matter, this person obviously is not acquainted with "Uncle Sam's plan." The IRS's plan would collect about 10 percent, or approximately $230,000, before anyone receives anything. A $5 million estate would lose $1.4 million to federal taxation. Furthermore, the IRS would require its share in cash within **nine months** of the date of death. And then there is the matter state inheritance tax for each state where property is held. Tax ramifications are clearly the most planned-for aspect of estate planning.

Consider for a moment the following potential dilemmas that estate taxation creates when planning your estate:

- How will assets pass to an heir if they first have to be converted to cash to pay the estate tax liability, assuming there are not enough liquid (cash) assets to pay the tax directly?
- If your primary asset is a business, can the business continue to operate if it has to sell stock or assets to pay your death taxes?
- If your estate will be responsible for providing income to disabled children, will estate taxation impact this liability?

If a formal written estate analysis is developed from a clear and accurate picture of how assets are titled and an accurate valuation is placed on each asset, you'll be able to realize the impact this onerous confiscatory tax can have on your estate.

A professionally drafted plan should contain strategies to reduce death taxes, to the extent they can be reduced, and offset and pay death taxes. The tools that are commonly used to plan for death taxation will be a primary focus in Part Two.

CHAPTER

9

Estate Taxation

The Last Big Surprise

Most often, people are under the impression that because they have paid income tax throughout their lifetimes, taxes stop at death. In fact, and often to our dismay, we must inform clients about the cruelest tax of all—the **death tax,** or **federal estate tax.** In many circumstances the largest beneficiary isn't family members or other intended heirs; it is the federal government.

The federal estate tax has undergone many revisions since it was introduced in 1916. The maximum rate when the tax was first passed was approximately 10 percent—rather insignificant in comparison to today's rates!

The death tax is really a tax the U.S. government imposes on an individual's right to transfer assets or property to other people at the time of the individual's death. The tax is formally titled *federal estate tax* and is a transfer tax. We refer to this tax as the cruelest tax because it is capable of confiscating up to 45 percent of your estate. Some assets are subject to taxation beyond amounts of 70 percent. In Chapter 14, we will focus on individual retirement accounts and other qualified retirement plans wherein these assets are subject to estate taxes as well as income taxation.

Changes Initiated by ERTA of 1981

Before the Economic Recovery Tax Act of 1981 (ERTA) was passed and prior to 1976, only $60,000 of an estate was exempt from federal estate taxation. In 1976, the Tax Reform Act (TRA of 1976) revised the exempted amount to $175,625. This exclusion was referred to as the *exemption equivalent,* which was the tax-free amount that could be totally excluded from federal estate taxation. By 1981, because of the passage of ERTA the exemption had increased to an equivalent of $600,000 of assets per person.

While the increased exclusion was a significant change in estate taxation, the major change from ERTA was the introduction of the *unlimited marital deduction,* which made possible two key planning opportunities for married persons by providing the following:

1. The unlimited deduction means that the first spouse to die can leave as much property as possible to the surviving spouse without any tax liability. Thus, in properly planned spousal situations, the federal estate tax liability can be delayed until the death of the surviving spouse.
2. ERTA provides that spouses can gift during their lifetimes as much property to each other as they wish or make unlimited gifts to each other without any gift tax consequences.

The third change implemented by ERTA was the *restructuring of the estate tax rates* which began at 37 percent of assets valued in excess of the uniform tax credit and increased to 50 percent for estates of $2.5 million to $10 million. For estates over $10 million, the rate reflected the phaseout of the unified credit by imposing an additional tax of 5 percent. The law taxed estates and gifts of $10 million up to $18.34 million at 55 percent. Estates over $18.34 million were to be taxed at 50 percent.

In 1981, ERTA revised the exemption and made some additional sweeping changes:

- It amortized an increase of the exemption to a maximum of $600,000 by 1987.
- It introduced the unlimited marital deduction.
- It restructured tax rates.

TRA of 1997

The Taxpayer Relief Act of 1997 increased the unified credit or exemption equivalent starting in 1998. The unified credit was to be expanded through 2006 to exempt a maximum of $1,000,000 in assets for each individual as follows:

Year	Exemption	Year	Exemption
1998	$ 625,000	2003	$ 700,000
1999	650,000	2004	850,000
2000	675,000	2005	950,000
2001	675,000	2006	1,000,000
2002	700,000	2007	1,000,000

The Economic Growth and Tax Relief Reconciliation Act of 2001

The Economic Growth and Tax Relief Reconciliation Act of 2001 was a sweeping piece of tax legislation. It is commonly known by its abbreviation EGTRRA, often pronounced "egg-tra" or "egg-terra," but most often referred to as simply the "2001 Tax Act." The legislation made significant changes in several areas of the IRS tax code, including income tax rates, qualified retirement plan rules, and, most significantly, estate and gift taxation. Many provisions of EGTRRA were designed to be phased in over a period of up to nine years.

One of the most notable characteristics of EGTRRA is that its provisions are designed to *sunset,* or revert to the laws that were in effect before it was passed. EGTRRA will sunset, or terminate, on January 1, 2011 unless further legislation is enacted to make its changes permanent.

With regard to estate planning, the act gradually lowers the top estate tax rate to 45 percent by the year 2007, where it remains until 2010. The estate tax credit or exemption, which effectively exempts a large majority of small and medium-sized estates from federal estate taxes, gradually increases until 2010. The exempted amount for 2006 through the end of 2008 is $2 million per person. The exempted amount is set to increase to $3.5 million by 2009. In 2010, both the gift and estate taxes are to be eliminated completely. Because of the *sunset* provision, however, the estate and gift taxes are scheduled to be reinstated in 2011.

Over the past year, Congress has been half heartedly trying to pass permanent legislation. Some have been crying for total repeal, while most offer a compromise. The House actually passed complete estate tax repeal in June 2006 only to have the Senate postpone any permanent legislation until further studies can be done. The main question is, how much federal tax revenue will be lost with total repeal? While current estate taxes will only effect estates in excess of $2 million it is estimated that the federal tax loss caused from total repeal according to the Joint Committee on Taxation

FIGURE 9.1 EGTRRA 2001 Estate and Gift Tax Schedule

Calendar Year	Estate Tax Applicable Exclusion Amount	Highest Tax Rate	Gift Tax Applicable Exclusion Amount	Highest Tax Rate
2006	$2 million	46%	$1 million	46%
2007	$2 million	45%	$1 million	45%
2008	$2 million	45%	$1 million	45%
2009	$3.5 million	45%	$1 million	45%
2010	ZERO ESTATE TAX		$1 million	35%
2011	$1 million	55%	$1 million	55%

will be $78.8 billion by the year 2006, $100 billion from 2009–2012, and $740 billion from 2013–2022. With the pressure to raise revenue to pay for the huge deficit and the war on terrorism, there is little hope for permanent repeal, and in fact, we may see an actual decrease in the current $2 million exclusion rather than the scheduled increase.

Asset Distribution and Tax Planning

The devastating ramification of the death tax has segmented estate planning into two general areas:

1. Planning for asset distribution (*dispositive*), or who gets what
2. Tax planning

For people who have property cumulatively valued at over $2,000,000, integration of distribution and tax planning go hand in hand.

■ Example

Linden has an estate of $3 million. How can she plan for distribution when a tax of approximately $450,000 is due before any assets can be distributed to her heirs? Consider also that Linden has one primary asset—real estate. How does her estate pay the tax liability without being forced to sell the property? Selling the real estate may adversely affect her planning objectives and most likely will not be done in the best interest of her estate or heirs. The only entity that will benefit will be the federal government.

Tax planning is an integral part of estate planning and in most estates is the single largest factor to contend with before dispositive provisions can be structured.

Tax planning is an integral part of estate planning and in most estates is the single largest factor to contend with before dispositive provisions can be structured. Remember that federal estate tax is charged on the privilege to transfer property. However, the tax is applied and calculated on the asset value of the transfer. In other words, the tax is derived from the value of the property transferred. The tax is also all-encompassing and is levied from the total value of all property in your name at your death. The following are the only current exemptions (a few other interests affect only a small number of people, but they are beyond the scope of this publication):

- Social Security benefits based on your life now payable to your beneficiaries
- Life insurance proceeds on your life if you have no right of ownership
- Death-benefit-only plans created by employers, whose proceeds pass directly to designated beneficiaries and must meet certain IRS guidelines to qualify

- Money that passes directly to named beneficiaries from certain annuity purchases sponsored by employers and that also have to be structured to meet specific IRS guidelines
- Income annuities that end at the death of the annuitant

Life Insurance

Most people are under the impression that life insurance is not a taxable asset. While this is in part true, it is not the complete story.

One asset that remains a source of confusion is life insurance.

Most people are under the impression that life insurance is not a taxable asset. Many have been told by their insurance agents that life insurance proceeds pass tax-free to beneficiaries. While this is true in part, it is not the complete story.

Named beneficiaries do receive life insurance proceeds free of income tax. However, these proceeds are included in the gross estate of the deceased individual if the decedent has owned the insurance contracts, and thus are subject to estate taxes. The strategies that can be implemented to avoid the inclusion of life insurance in your estate will be discussed at length in chapters 18–22.

Understanding the correct tax liability and the amount of insurance owned by an individual can be a key factor in accomplishing an effective estate plan. Consider an individual with a $3 million estate. If $1 million of the estate property is a life insurance contract (or contracts), this individual's assumption that the insurance will pass estate tax free to a beneficiary becomes a very costly mistake. Let's examine why.

From our previous example, we know that the approximate total tax on the estate of an individual who currently transfers $2 million is zero. Adding an additional $1 million to the estate escalates the tax liability to approximately $450,000. How can this be? The following two things have occurred:

1. The size of the estate has increased and therefore so has the total tax liability.
2. The extra $1 million included in the estate because of the inclusion of the insurance has pushed the estate into the 41 percent estate tax rate.

Current Federal Estate Tax Laws

EGTRRA significantly changed the way that we now construct and format estate plans. If your plan was completed prior to the passage of EGTRRA on June 7, 2001, it may no longer be effective. We are constantly amazed by how many people have not been informed about, or have not updated their plans to take advantage of, the potential tax-saving elements

FIGURE 9.2 Federal Estate and Gift Tax Rates (1993 and Beyond)

If Your Tax Base Is Over	But Not Over	Your Tax Is	+	%	On Excess Over
$ 0	$ 10,000	$ 0		18%	$ 0
10,000	20,000	1,800		20	10,000
20,000	40,000	3,800		22	20,000
40,000	60,000	8,200		24	40,000
60,000	80,000	13,000		26	60,000
80,000	100,000	18,200		28	80,000
100,000	150,000	23,800		30	100,000
150,000	250,000	38,300		32	150,000
250,000	500,000	70,800		34	250,000
500,000	750,000	155,800		37	500,000
750,000	1,000,000	248,300		39	750,000
1,000,000	1,250,000	345,800		41	1,000,000
1,250,000	1,500,000	448,300		43	1,250,000
1,500,000	2,000,000	555,800		45	1,500,000
2,000,000	2,500,000	780,800		46	2,000,000
2,500,000	3,000,000	1,025,800		46	2,500,000
3,000,000	10,000,000	1,290,800		46	3,000,000
10,000,000	17,184,000	5,140,800		46	10,000,000
17,184,000	On Up	9,451,200		46	21,040,000

Note: All rates are before the application of the current (2006–2008) $2,000,000 estate tax exclusion.

EGTRRA provides. A review of the current federal estate tax law provides the following information:

> **W**e are constantly amazed by how many people have not been informed about, or have not updated their plans to take advantage of, the potential tax-saving elements EGTRRA provides.

- The federal estate tax is applicable to the fair market value of property.
- The federal estate tax is a tax on the right to transfer property.
- The federal estate tax must be paid in cash nine months from the date of death.
- The tax must be paid before property passes to beneficiaries.
- The tax starts at 18 percent after the application of the estate tax exclusions.
- The tax applies to estates that currently have a net value over $2,000,000.
- The tax code provides for an unlimited amount of property to transfer with no taxation to a surviving spouse in even a second or third marriage. (See information on QTIP trust planning in Chapter 17 and the credit shelter trust in Chapter 20.)

In addition, most of us are familiar with the standard deductions allowed on our income tax returns. The IRS also allows deductions that apply to federal estate taxation as follows:

- Debts (e.g., mortgages)
- Expenses incurred in the administration of the estate
- Funeral expenses
- Casualty losses
- Marital deductions
- Charitable deductions

These deductions will be discussed in detail in later chapters. The estate and gift tax rates are perhaps the greatest threat to many estates. The rates start at an effective rate of approximately 18 percent for each dollar over the estate tax exclusion amount. The rates are subject to change brought about by the need for increased revenues by our government. We can only speculate what future changes will be made as government tackles the deficit, the health care crisis, social security and the war on terrorism. Is it any wonder that planning for the tax bite in your estate has become a key planning issue?

What If Estate Taxes are Repealed? Should You Still Plan Your Estate?

For the past few years estate taxation has been a big question mark. Will the tax be totally repealed? Will the "sunset" provision be enacted? What will the estate tax exclusion be? What will the inheritance tax rate of your state of domicile be? These unanswered questions have given fuel to the estate planning procrastination fire. I often hear something like: "There's no hurry to get this done. I'll wait until Congress finally figures things out." Below I have listed 15 reasons why your estate should be planned even if estate taxes should, by some miraculous intervention, be totally abolished. In other words, there is much more to estate planning than taxes.

1. Planning for the disposition of your assets at your death—who gets what, how much and when?
2. Asset Protection Planning
3. Planning for disability and incompetence
4. Business succession planning
5. Planning for marital and other dissolutions
6. Charitable giving (income tax considerations would still be relevant)
7. Life insurance planning (other than to provide funds to pay taxes)

8. Planning for tax wise distribution of your qualified retirement accounts
9. Planning to avoid gift taxes (when you want to give more than the $1 million gift exclusion)
10. Planning for special needs children and grandchildren
11. Planning for spendthrift children
12. Planning for the distribution of real estate in more than one state
13. Planning for the distribution of property in other countries
14. Planning for nonresident aliens with assets in the U.S.
15. Planning for the possible reinstatement of the estate and gift tax

In previous chapters, we have discussed the importance of receiving a formal written estate analysis. It is the key, the road map, to proper effective estate planning. Now is not the time to put your affairs into cruise control thinking that legislation will take care of everything. The chances of a complete permanent repeal of estate taxes from both the federal and state government aren't likely, but even if total repeal occurs there is so much more to prepare for than just legally avoiding paying a tax to transfer your assets to subsequent generations. The bottom line: Have your estate professionally analyzed.

CHAPTER

10

States and Death Taxes

Getting Their Fair Share

Prior to the passage of The Economic Growth and Tax Relief and Reconciliation Act of 2001, the federal estate tax law allowed states a dollar-for-dollar credit against the federal estate tax for death taxes actually paid subject to a maximum amount under a table of percentages (based on the size of the estate). A majority of states were so-called "pick-up states" that based their state's estate (death) tax on the exact amount allowable as a credit under the federal estate tax. In other words, the state and federal governments engaged in sort of "revenue sharing" process under which the state would received the revenue on the portion of the federal estate tax up to the maximum credit amount. As a practical matter, the estate paid a total amount of tax equal to the entire federal estate tax liability but, because of the credit, the state received some of the tax.

Since EGTRRA and January 2005, the state death tax credit no longer exists. This has the obvious effect of increasing the amount of tax actually received by the federal government, but it leaves the states with a significant reduction in revenue. Given that most state governments are already operating under serious financial duress, those states which have a "pick-up" estate tax are "de-coupling" from the federal estate tax system. So far, 25 states have decoupled from the feds (see Figure 10.1), and have implemented their own estate tax structure. The type and amount of state death tax varies from state to state, thus making planning difficult. For example, if a person owns property in one state and lives in another state, then both states will be allowed to impose a tax on the value of the property and the size of the estate. So without proper planning, a client may be faced with both a federal estate tax and several state inheritance taxes.

FIGURE 10.1 Decoupled States As of December 2006

Connecticut	Maryland	Oregon
District of Columbia	Massachusetts	Pennsylvania
Illinois	Minnesota	Rhode Island
Indiana	North Carolina	Tennessee
Iowa	Nebraska	Vermont
Kansas	New Jersey	Virginia
Kentucky	New York	Washington
Louisiana	Ohio	Wisconsin
Maine	Oklahoma	

The states that currently have their own estate or inheritance taxes are: Indiana, Iowa, Kentucky, Maryland, Nebraska, New Jersey, Ohio, Oklahoma, Pennsylvania, and Tennessee. State estate taxes, like the federal version, are assessed on the estate as a whole. But states can have different rules about who pays. Inheritance taxes target bequests to the beneficiaries, rather than the estate itself. Typically, beneficiaries are divided up by their relationship to the deceased, with the biggest tax breaks going to those with the closest ties. In Iowa, for example, bequests to spouses, children, parents and other direct descendents (grandchildren, great-grandchildren) or ascendants (grandparents) are exempt from the state's inheritance tax. Property destined for brothers, sisters and siblings-in-law is assessed at rates ranging from 5 percent to 10 percent, while the rate for other inheritors runs from 10 percent to 15 percent.

It is important when estimating death taxes that you or your estate planner research the laws and tax rates of the state where you reside to determine your correct tax liability. The precise estate tax liability is a primary issue in every estate plan and should be fully understood when determining the strategies needed to properly plan your estate. A properly prepared estate analysis should take all these factors into consideration. You may also want to go online to the states where you own property and view their specific estate and inheritance laws.

It's anyone's guess what will happen between now and January 1, 2011, when estate tax repeal "sunsets" after just one year. Even if intervening legislation eliminates the sunset provision, does *permanent* really mean permanent? Taxes, especially federal estate taxes, have disappeared and then reappeared many times in our history. States that have de-coupled from the federal estate tax are likely to look favorably upon their individual estate tax regimes to revitalize the state Treasury and eliminate chronic deficits. Stay tuned.

WARNING

State death taxes are computed and apply in the state of domicile (state in which you primarily live). If you live in Colorado and have a winter home in Florida, you will be subject to Colorado's state death tax system. There have been cases where two states have applied their tax systems to the same estate, contending that the decedent was domiciled in both states. However, this is not the typical case.

CHAPTER

11

Estate and Gift Taxation

The Impact of EGTRRA 2001: The Annual Gift Tax Exclusion

The Impact of EGTRRA 2001: The Annual Gift Tax Exclusion

Because of the passage of The Economic Growth and Tax Reconciliation Act of 2001, each taxpayer is allowed to transfer at death up to $2 million to their heirs free of estate taxes. If, however, you want to gift your estate to your family while you are alive, the maximum allowed without incurring a gift tax is $1 million (see Figure 9.1 in Chapter 9). In previous years, the gift tax and estate tax were mirrors of each other. Since EGTRRA, all that has changed. While the lifetime estate exclusion is set to increase to a top of $3.5 million by 2009, gift taxes will stay at $1 million per person or $2 million per couple. In other words, estate planning just became more difficult because you are limited as to what you can gift through Family Limited Partnerships, Grantor Retained Income Trusts, and other high-end estate planning strategies.

The IRS still allows each individual the right to make an unlimited number of tax-free small gifts. The amount of these gifts is currently limited to $12,000 annually per recipient. The annual allowance is set to increase periodically based on an inflation index established by the IRS. If a person has one child or a dozen children, the gift can be applied to all.

For example, a person with two children may make a gift to each child of $12,000 per year. In addition to these small annual gifts to children, a person can make the same gift to as many unrelated people as desired.

■ Example

Steve, who has two children and an estate of $3 million, decides to gift each of his children $12,000 in 2007. Steve is able to do this without affecting his estate tax lifetime exclusion credit or his lifetime gift tax exclusion. Furthermore, neither he nor the children have to file a gift tax return, nor do they incur any gift tax.

One of the great family estate planning opportunities involves utilizing the annual gift tax exclusion between spouses to maximize the value of the gifts to children without adverse effects on the remaining estate tax exclusion credit.

The form of gifting we're discussing is referred to as the **annual gift tax exclusion.** For many years, the annual gift tax exclusion was limited to $3,000 per recipient. In 1982, the exclusion was increased to exclude gifts under $10,000. With EGTRRA it is now $12,000.

One of the great family estate planning opportunities involves utilizing the annual gift tax exclusion between spouses to maximize the value of the gifts to children without adverse effects on the remaining estate tax exclusion credit.

■ Example

Let's now assume Steve is married. He and his wife can combine gifts so that collectively they can gift each child $24,000, or a total of $48,000 each year. This total of $48,000 has no effect on either Steve's or his wife's $2,000,000 lifetime exemption.

If Steve and his wife had made gifts in excess of the combined $24,000 allowance to each child (say, $60,000), the additional $36,000 could be applied to the lifetime estate tax exclusion credit. If Steve is the over-contributor, he is also required to file a gift tax return (form 709) for the $18,000 over and above his annual exclusion amount. The amount over the gift tax exclusion can also be split between husband and wife. The couple may both elect to file gift tax returns for $18,000 each, thus leaving a balance of $1,982,000 for each lifetime estate tax exclusion credit.

The idea of using spouses to share in annual gifts to children is called **gift splitting.** In order for the gift to qualify for a split gift, the other spouse has to agree to share in the gift. When spouses share in a gift or split a gift, a gift tax return has to be filed in the year the gift is made.

With the advent of the unlimited number of these small annual gifts, a person can conceivably gift his or her estate into a position where no estate tax is applied at death.

If Steve and his spouse have an estate of $4,240,000, they could feasibly gift $48,000 each year to their two children, and in five years, assuming no net growth in the estate, they would have gifted $240,000 tax-free to the children. If death occurred to both parents after that time, and assuming the estate tax exclusion remains at $2 million, there wouldn't be any estate taxes due, if they have established provisions to utilize both estate tax exclusion credits, (refer to Chapters 15 and 20). The $240,000 that had been gifted would not be included in the estate for estate tax calculations, it would of course have not been available for income production throughout the years. We will explore this planning technique as well as others in later chapters.

It is important to note that the annual gift tax exclusion applies only to gift of a present interest. In other words, the gift must not have any strings attached. The recipient must be able to use and enjoy the gifted property immediately. There are certain exceptions, however, such as gifts to a College 529 plan where the gift can be used for future college expenses. This concept is covered in detail in Chapter 24.

Some are under the misconception that they can deduct the annual gift allowance from their income each year. If the gift is below the annual exclusion, then there isn't a gift tax, period. No income tax deduction is given unless the gift is given to a charity and in that case there isn't an annual limit.

Gifts from one spouse to another do not fall under the annual gift tax exclusion rules. That's because the gift tax laws exempt any and all gifts from one spouse to another. There is, however, an exception for spouses that are not U.S. citizens.

WARNING

Many of our clients believe the annual gift tax exclusion applies only to gifts made to their children. The annual gift tax exclusion applies to gifts of $12,000 or under and is unlimited in number as well as recipients. These gifts can be made to perfect strangers—as many as are deemed viable. Thus, you could give your entire estate away in one year by dividing the total estate value by 12,000 and then finding that exact number of people to gift to!

Gifts include not only gifts of cash but also other types of property or assets. It is always advisable to determine what property should be given and when. It is generally more advantageous for one to gift assets that are appreciating so the appreciation will accumulate outside of the estate and not compound the size of the estate, which could result in greater estate tax liability at death.

Summary

In summary, it is important for each person to understand the following:

- The annual gift tax exclusion is in addition to the $1,000,000 lifetime gift tax exemption.
- The annual gift tax exclusion is not limited to gifts made to children. Gifts made to any individual or individuals qualify.
- The annual gift tax exclusion is not limited in number. The gift can be made to one person or 100.
- These small gifts are currently limited to $12,000 each per gift per year.

These gifts may be split between spouses if both spouses agree to share in the gift. Thus, married persons may gift $24,000 to each recipient gift tax free. A gift tax return is required for gift splitting between spouses.

CHAPTER

12 Transfers at Death

A Stepped-Up Basis

The rules of cost basis often can determine when property should be given. The current laws regarding the basis of a gifted asset or an asset transferred at death are quite often misunderstood.

Cost basis in property can be a significant factor when trying to decide whether to gift assets during your lifetime or transfer them at death. Let's examine this in more detail.

Cost basis is the value of an asset when acquired. If John Minor purchased a house for $100,000 in 1965, his cost basis in the property is $100,000. However, in 2007 the fair market value of the house is $300,000. If Mr. Minor gifts the house to his son in 2007, his son takes on his father's cost basis in the property. If the son sells the property the following day for $300,000, he will incur both federal and state capital gains taxes on $200,000 (currently set at 15 percent for federal, to increase to 20 percent in 2011). The amount of gain is equal to the fair market value ($300,000) less the cost basis ($100,000) carried over from the donor (Mr. Minor).

In this example, Mr. Minor is referred to as the **donor,** or the person who makes the gift. His son is referred to as the **donee,** the person who receives the gift. When gifts are made during a donor's lifetime, the donee assumes the cost basis of the donor.

Under current law property transferred at death—**testamentary property**—receives a step-up in basis to the date-of-death value. The beneficiaries' basis reflects the date-of-death value of the transferred property. If the property is sold for an amount that reflects the date-of-death value, the beneficiaries incur no capital gains tax liability.

If Mr. Minor leaves the house to his son at death and the house is worth $300,000 the day he dies, his son's basis in the house is "stepped up" to reflect the $300,000. If the son sells the property the next day for $300,000, he will not incur a capital gains tax liability.

In this example, the amount of tax on the gain of $200,000 is by today's standard relatively small. However, consider the individual who started a business from scratch that became a booming enterprise! The start-up expenses generally are extremely low, and in some cases there may not be any cost basis. Furthermore, there may actually be a negative cost basis. The current value of stock and business holdings 20 to 30 years later is often in the millions of dollars. How do the owners transfer the value of the business to heirs or others without loss of value from capital gains and gift or estate tax ramifications? Should they gift stock and business assets during their lifetime or wait and transfer assets at death to give heirs a stepped-up basis?

The Tax Man Giveth and the Tax Man Taketh Away—The Truth About EGTRRA 2001

When President George W. Bush signed the Economic Growth and Tax Relief Reconciliation Act (EGTRRA) in 2001, it called for an eventual phase out of federal estate taxes, ending in 2010. But on the side of caution, Congress left the door open for the estate tax to reappear in 2011, referred to as the "sunset provision." Estate taxation would revert back to what it was in 2001. There was great applause for the apparent attempt at eliminating the onerous estate tax. There is, however, a little known clause seldom mentioned inside EGTRRA that if left unchecked would not only potentially increase the overall tax bill at death, it would create confusion and make accountants wealthy.

As the law was drafted, in 2010, when the federal estate tax is to be repealed, the generous stepped-up basis provision of the current law would be totally discontinued and estates being settled from descendants dying in 2010 would be subject to capital gains tax when an inherited asset is sold. This means that assets will be valued at what the deceased originally paid for them and any gain would be taxed to the heirs at the capital gains rates at that time. Of course, if the original basis information isn't readily available at the time of death, research will be necessary to estimate or compute the basis. This is where the accountants come in. The IRS will require legitimate original basis valuation, and someone with credentials will have to verify the figures.

Perhaps an example will help clarify this little-known secret.

Robert Wilson, a California widower, originally purchased investment property for $200,000, and it is now valued at $2,200,000. It is by far the largest single asset of his estate. If he dies in 2010 and his son Steve who is set to inherit the investment ever sells it, he will have to pay capital gains taxes on the difference between what it originally cost and what it sold for. Let's assume, Robert dies in 2010 and Steve sells the property that same year. Steve's capital gains tax assuming a federal and state rate of 25 percent and no reductions would be $500,000. If Robert had died in 2009, the capital gains tax would be zero and the estate tax would be zero. What a difference a day makes. Or in this case a year!

Confused? Let's just hope when the next round of estate tax reform appears it maintains the current stepped-up basis with a logical exclusion figure and moderate estate tax percentages. If not, the loss of this benefit could be more destructive than the estate taxes of the 1980s.

CHAPTER

13

The IRS "Assault" on Your Grandchildren

Extra Tax on Transfers That Skip Generations

If you transfer your assets to your grandchildren, the IRS has a longer period of time to wait before it can tax again.

In addition to the federal estate tax at your death, if your estate is large enough and you plan on passing some of your assets directly to your grandchildren, beware!

The IRS has refined its plan to "assault" those of you who wish to skip a generation (your children) and focus your tactical planning on your grandchildren. The same results can occur even if you plan to divide your estate between both generations—your children and your grandchildren.

This is in response to a delayed action of additional taxation to your children. Specifically, if you leave your wealth to your children, it will be taxed again at their death under the same guidelines as your estate at your death. However, if you transfer your assets to your grandchildren, the IRS has longer to wait before it can tax again. The period is measured by the length of time between the death of your children and the extended length of time until the death of your grandchildren.

The Generation-Skipping Transfer Tax (GSTT)

Because the GSTT is a tax on the right to transfer and is applied to direct transfers, it is referred to as the **generation-skipping transfer tax,** also known as the **generation-skipping tax.**

In 1976, the first version of the GSTT provided a method of taxation when a person had the power to control a trust. Applying this concept was the most complex aspect of the original law. The GSTT removed that dilemma, but it is still extremely complicated and should be approached with great care and expert advice.

Based on the Economic Growth Tax Relief and Reconciliation Act of 2001, the GSTT is scheduled for repeal in 2010 but is to be reinstated in its entirety in 2011. Until 2010, the exemption amount is set at $1 million to your grandchildren in total, not to each. The generation-skipping tax can be summed up as follows:

- The tax is based on the relationship of the person receiving property (the **transferee**) and the person who transfers the property or gifts the property (the **transferor**). The tax applies when assets transferred are transferred to, or for the benefit of, a person or persons at least two generations younger than the transferor, such as the transferor's grandchildren.
- These persons are referred to as **skip persons.** They are at least two generations younger than the transferor. A trust can also qualify as a skip person if the beneficiaries of the trust meet the definition of skip persons.
- Conversely, if a person is a member of the transferor's generation, prior generation, or one generation younger than the transferor, this person is referred to as a **nonskip person** (e.g., a transferor's child).
- GSTT is applicable on a transfer or gift to a skip person.
- The GSTT is an additional tax or stand-alone tax. It does not reduce or offset the gift tax or federal estate tax but is in addition to those taxes.
- After the current exemption is deducted, the GSTT is applied at the maximum unified (gift and estate tax) rate currently 46 percent.

With such a large exemption, many people are under the impression that the GSTT does not apply to their planning. This reasoning, however, may not be correct if you implement trusts to protect your children. Planning that provides for property to pass to a trust or trusts for your children at your death, with provisions for income and principal to be paid out to the child (who is a nonskip person), is exempt from application of the GSTT.

What If Your Child Dies First?

If you make provisions for property to go to your child's children (your grandchildren) and your child dies before reaching the date of the balance of the distribution of principal, GSTT may apply at that time.

If the trust does not give your child the power that makes the trust includable in his or her estate (such as the power to appoint property to himself or herself, to his or her estate, to creditors, or to the creditors of the estate), the death of your child can cause a taxable termination based on the termination of the interest of the child (who is a nonskip person) and the transfer of the benefit of the trust to a skip person.

If your child has a general power of appointment or a limited power to appoint property (such as to creditors of his or her estate), then the property will be included in the child's taxable estate and will not be subject to the GSTT. Generation-skipping laws usually apply to most family planning trusts in which provisions of gifts to the next generation below the children apply.

The negative aspect of the GSTT is that the property remaining in the trust at a child's death will be subject to tax at the 46 percent rate. Neither the transferor's nor the child's estate tax exclusion can be applied against the tax.

If property is distributed outright to your child or if your child has a general power of appointment over the property, the property will be subject to estate tax (beginning at the lowest rates) in that child's estate, and the child's estate tax exclusion credit will be applied to tax generated by that property. Because the property is subject to estate tax at the child's level, it will not be subject to the GSTT.

In many circumstances, the overall transfer tax may be higher when property is subject to the GSTT as opposed to being includable in a child's estate. If the property is taxed in a child's estate, then the child's personal estate tax exclusion could be used to shelter GST taxes.

Direct Gifts to Grandchildren

Taxing direct gifts to grandchildren requires review of all existing estate plans to determine whether there are any problems created by such gifts. Those who have completed estate planning would be wise to have their plans reviewed to determine whether adjustments need to be considered.

Direct gifts to grandchildren may not be large, but they can become a concern when added together with other property that is not exempt from the GSTT. This property may be kept in trust for your children's lives and thereafter pass to grandchildren. If this is the case, you should consider all the various applications of the GSTT.

Direct gifts to grandchildren may not be large, but they can become a concern when added together with other property that is not exempt from the GSTT.

- Direct transfers to a transferor's grandchild are, of course, subject to estate tax or gift tax.
- If the grandchild's parent is a child of the transferor or a child of the transferor's spouse, then the transfer *would be* taxable.
- If the parent of the grandchild is deceased at the time the transfer is made to the grandchild, then the transfer *would not be* taxable.

If the parent is deceased and we are not skipping the parent in terms of benefits, the rules permit direct gifts to grandchildren that are exempt from the GSTT. The end result is that the grandchild moves up a generation. Therefore, that grandchild is considered a child for applying the GSTT.

The trusts that will benefit the grandchild and then go on to benefit that grandchild's children are subject to the GSTT at the grandchild's death to the extent they are not protected by the current per grantor unified estate tax exemption.

Types of Generation-Skipping Transfers

The three GSTT applications are as follows:

1. **Direct skips.** These are outright transfers that also include transfers to trusts that benefit only skip persons.
2. **Taxable distributions.** These are distributions from a trust.
3. **Taxable terminations.** These are interests in trusts that terminate, such as income rights.

Calculating the GSTT

When you create a trust that is not exempt, or nonexempt, the GSTT exemption ($1,000,000) is a key part of calculating the tax that is levied on a taxable termination, taxable distribution, or direct skip.

The complexity of the calculation (ignoring all of the more difficult questions of applying the rules to get to the point of calculation) is beyond the scope of this publication. Estate planners universally agree that because of its complexity, reform or complete repeal of the GSTT is needed. It is a law too cumbersome to accurately administer.

Some deductions are allowed, including the amount of certain death taxes, debts, administrative expenses, and the like. However, no marital, charitable, or casualty loss deductions are allowed, nor is an application of the estate tax exclusion credit allowed.

CHAPTER

14

The Retirement Time Bombs

Losing Your Retirement Benefits Through Taxation and Poor Planning

The main goal in writing *Estate Planning Made Easy* was to educate Americans on how to legally avoid paying estate taxes and settlement costs. While our material naturally crosses over to income taxation, that is the subject of another volume. With regard to retirement planning, however, it is critical that we discuss both forms of taxation, because whatever isn't taxed as income either while living or at death will be inherited by someone.

The facts are clear. The proportion of the older population is growing dramatically. Between the years 2010 to 2030, the 65-plus population is expected to spike by 75 percent to more than 69 million. Furthermore, if you are married and make it to age 65, there is a 47% chance that one of you will live to see your 96th birthday. Americans need to immediately focus their attention on retirement income planning to ensure that we do not outlive our income. Obviously if you are over 60 and haven't saved a dime for retirement, your only recourse will be social security and family. If, however, you are fortunate to have accumulated wealth, there are ways to guarantee you never run out of money, no matter how long you live.

Throughout U.S. history, governments, both federal and state, have had their hands deep inside our retirement pockets. Fortunately that attitude is changing with the realization that social security and other federal and state financial aid programs will not be sufficient to support the tremendous number of baby boomers that are set to enter the retirement phase of life (7,918 boomers turn 60 each day—330 every hour). In addition, pension plans are in serious jeopardy with their numbers decreasing from 114,000 in 1985 to fewer than 30,000 in 2003. Furthermore, there is an increasing number of pension plans that are in default. For example, United Airlines defaulted on its pension plan, reducing the planned and promised retirement payout to its pilots and flight attendants by 75%. With this trend in mind, legislators are finally realizing that it is up to the individual to create their own retirement funds and by overly taxing them at any stage is counter-productive.

It is for this reason that the Pension Protection Act was passed and signed by President George W. Bush on August 17, 2006, with most provisions beginning January 1, 2007. While the new law did create some relief, there are many tax laws that remain. To understand what the new rules are we must first outline what remains in place and then briefly look at the benefits the Pension Protection Act gave us. We will look at these provisions first from the perspective of "qualified accounts," and second from the "non-qualified" view point. Currently, these accounts are allowed to accumulate free from income taxation; however, when the money is distributed either while alive or at death, **tax time bombs explode**. When and if those taxes are paid depend solely on when the funds are received and to whom they are given. Examples of qualified accounts are IRAs, 401(k)s, defined benefit pension plans, 403(b)s, and SEPs. Examples of non-qualified accounts are certificates of deposits, mutual funds, annuities and life insurance.

Like a bomb, these enormous tax liabilities catch most of us unaware and therefore helpless to defend against them.

The Retirement Plan Crisis

Tax time bombs describe these problems appropriately before and after the new legislation, because few people are aware of the severe tax liabilities applicable to their retirement plans until it is too late. To most of us, it is inconceivable that taxes can possibly confiscate the bulk of our retirement funds. Consequently, many of us will lose over 70 percent of the value of our plans to taxation:

- *Before-tax dollars* that have been carefully invested and earmarked for retirement years with the expectation of being taxed at a lower rate when distributed may be subject to a higher tax.
- *Remaining plan balances* left to heirs at death are subject to death tax. The combination of income tax and death tax yields the highest confiscatory tax structure in U.S. history.

In the early 1970s, heirs expected to receive at least 65 percent of plan balances. Today, without proper planning, heirs may realize as little as 30 percent.

The tax liabilities associated with retirement plans are extremely complex. The degree of taxation depends on a specific set of variables. Below is a list of the 12 most common variables:

1. Age of the plan participant and spouse (if married)
2. Plan balances at the time of retirement fund distributions
3. Plan balances at the time of death
4. Beneficiary designation named by the plan participant

5. Type of plan (e.g., IRA versus pension plan), 401k, tax deferred annuity, Roth IRA etc.
6. The size of the participant's gross estate inclusive of retirement plan balances
7. Current generation-skipping planning
8. Future growth of the plan
9. Future distributions of the plan
10. How the funds are "stretched" to the beneficiaries
11. Required minimum distributions
12. Inflation indexes

If you are concerned about or unsure of how to measure the potential tax explosion endangering your particular plan, you are not alone. Unfortunately, the majority of CPAs, attorneys, and financial service firms are not equipped to address this definitive and highly complex area of the tax code.

The Six Tax Time Bombs

If you are one of the millions of Americans who have contributed or are actively contributing a substantial amount of your income to a qualified retirement plan, congratulations!

- You have succeeded in avoiding income tax on contributions to the plan.
- You have succeeded in avoiding income tax on the growth of the plan.
- You have succeeded in accomplishing tax-free compounding on your qualified plan contributions.

If you are an employer, pension fund administrator, attorney, accountant, financial services professional, or individual who has established or helped others design, establish, and maintain these plans, you should be congratulated for your efforts. You are responsible for creating the means for your personal retirement funding as well as the means for many others!

However, these plans are subject to *extreme* confiscatory tax structures. In order to limit tax liabilities, participants will need to seek and attain extensive, professional, and well-structured planning.

For many individuals, a substantial portion of personal wealth consists of assets in qualified retirement plans. Qualified retirement plans are specifically defined as:

- Individual retirement accounts (IRAs), including retirement plans that are "rolled over" to IRA(s)
- Pension plans (including defined benefit and defined contribution plans)

- Profit-sharing plans
- 401(k) plans
- 403(a) and 403(b) plans
- Keogh plans or self-employment plans (HR-10)

Very few people are aware of the severe confiscatory tax structure of these assets or have any idea what to do about it.

Not many years ago, individuals could leave qualified plan balances intact until age 90. At death, they could pass plan proceeds to children and grandchildren with few tax ramifications. Deferral of income tax in qualified plans was easy and devoid of the enormous tax consequences that exist today.

Not many years ago, qualified plan assets were completely exempt from the federal estate tax (death tax).

Twenty years ago, only a few estates involved large qualified plan assets. Specific lifetime and death planning was an afterthought by most estate planning professionals.

Today, the tax structure of qualified plan assets has changed drastically. There are five reasons for this:

1. *The 1981 Tax Reform Act* repealed the estate tax exclusion on qualified plan proceeds and gradually phased in full estate taxation on plan balances.
2. Qualified plan balances have become the largest liquid asset in most estates within the United States.
3. The demise of the employer sponsored retirement plan
4. The Minimum Distribution Rules
5. The enactment of the Pension Protection Act of 2006

The six retirement planning tax bombs explode at two distinct time periods that apply to all plan participants:

1. Lifetime distributions from the plan
2. Death distributions from the estate to heirs or direct distributions

Applicable Lifetime Distributions: The First Three Tax Bombs

1. Income tax. Up to 35 percent federal income tax (plus state tax where applicable) is levied on distributions made during a lifetime.

2. The "too early" 10 percent tax. Distributions of taxable qualified assets before age 59½ are subject to an additional 10 percent excise tax intended to discourage spending tax-subsidized retirement savings before retirement.

3. The "too late, too little," or 50 percent penalty tax. A 50 percent penalty is imposed for failure to distribute a minimum amount of qualified assets (Required Minimum Distribution) each year beginning at the participants required beginning date, April 1, following the year in which the participant reaches age 70½.

Upon reaching the required beginning date payments, distributions from the plan must be made over the life expectancy of the participant and the participant's elected designated beneficiary.

Figure 14.1 illustrates the Uniform Lifetime Table the IRS uses to calculate the required minimum annual distribution amount. Here's an example on how to use the table: Assume that you are an 80-year-old male with an IRA valued at $100,000. The table indicates the distribution period to be 18.7 years. Your annual minimum distribution for 2007 will be $5,348 ($100,000 divided by 18.7).

FIGURE 14.1 Required Minimum Distribution Uniform Lifetime Table

To calculate the year's minimum distribution amount, take the age of the **beneficiary** and find the corresponding distribution period. Then divide the value of the IRA by the distribution period to find the required minimum distribution.

Age of Beneficiary	Distribution Period (in Years)	Age of Beneficiary	Distribution Period (in Years)
10	86.2	63	33.9
11	85.2	64	33.0
12	84.2	65	32.0
13	83.2	66	31.1
14	82.2	67	30.2
15	81.2	68	29.2
16	80.2	69	28.3
17	79.2	70	27.4
18	78.2	71	26.5
19	77.3	72	25.6
20	76.3	73	24.7
21	75.3	74	23.8
22	74.3	75	22.9
23	73.3	76	22.0
24	72.3	77	21.2
25	71.3	78	20.3
26	70.3	79	19.5
27	69.3	80	18.7
28	68.3	81	17.9
29	67.3	82	17.1
30	66.3	83	16.3
31	65.3	84	15.5
32	64.3	85	14.8
33	63.3	86	14.1
34	62.3	87	13.4

(continued)

FIGURE 14.1 *(Continued)*

Age of Beneficiary	Distribution Period (in Years)	Age of Beneficiary	Distribution Period (in Years)
35	61.4	88	12.7
36	60.4	89	12.0
37	59.4	90	11.4
38	58.4	91	10.8
39	57.4	92	10.2
40	56.4	93	9.6
41	55.4	94	9.1
42	54.4	95	8.6
43	53.4	96	8.1
44	52.4	97	7.6
45	51.5	98	7.1
46	50.5	99	6.7
47	49.5	100	6.3
48	48.5	101	5.9
49	47.5	102	5.5
50	46.5	103	5.2
51	45.5	104	4.9
52	44.6	105	4.5
53	43.6	106	4.2
54	42.6	107	3.9
55	41.6	108	3.7
56	40.7	109	3.4
57	39.7	110	3.1
58	38.7	111	2.9
59	37.8	112	2.6
60	36.8	113	2.4
61	35.8	114	2.1
62	34.9	115	1.9

Note: This table also can be used to determine the minimum distributions required from qualified company retirement plans, such as 401(k)s and profit-sharing plans. Roth IRAs are not affected by the new rules, because these accounts do not have required minimum distribution numbers. To calculate your personal required minimum distribution, go to *www.estateplanningmadEZ.com* or *www.guaranteedindexannuity.com*.

Applicable Distributions After Death: The Second Three Tax Bombs

4. Income in respect of a decedent (IRD). Plans are taxed for income in respect of a decedent (IRD) if distributed to the named beneficiaries after the death of the participant. Prior to January 1, 2007, and as a result of the Pension Protection Act (PPA 2006), only a spouse was permitted the privilege of rolling over the inherited retirement account into their own personal IRA. Anyone else that was fortunate enough to receive an inheritance from "qualified" retirement accounts was taxed in the subsequent year after receiving the funds. Now, because of PPA 2006, **all** individual beneficiaries that receive "qualified" funds have several excellent options:

1. All individual beneficiaries can elect to take full distribution of the inherited retirement account and pay income taxes at their tax bracket in the year following the inheritance.
2. They can elect to pass the inheritance to another generation.
3. The surviving spouse can elect to roll all or a portion of the inherited funds into their own personal IRA and, until age 70 ½ , when required minimum distributions are required, they can let the account continue to accumulate tax deferred without any income withdrawal requirements. The surviving spouse can also elect to receive their distribution over their life expectancy based on the IRS required Minimum distribution table (see Figure 14.1), paying income at a much slower pace over their lifetime.
4. All other individual beneficiaries now can roll all or a portion of the inherited funds into their own personal IRA. Unlike the surviving spouse, however, they are required to receive income from the inherited account in one of two ways:

   a. Receive the distributions over five consecutive years and pay income taxes after each year's inheritance.
   b. Spread the distribution over their life expectancy based on the IRS Required Minimum Distribution Table (see Figure 14.1), paying income taxes at a much slower pace over their lifetime. **Note: The inherited "qualified" money must be rolled into newly created IRA and cannot be deposited after a check has been received by the beneficiary.**

In other words, the beneficiary must make a conscientious decision to spread the income and therefore the income tax liability over their lifetime. It cannot be an afterthought. They can, however, change their mind later on to take a lump sum distribution of the account balance.

New Rules for Inherited 401k Accounts

With regard to inherited 401k accounts, the new rules are somewhat different. First, if allowed by the employer, the surviving spouse can continue the 401k as if it were their own. Frankly, we suggest that the surviving spouse roll the inherited 401k funds into their own IRA. No taxes will be due, unless the surviving spouse is age 70½ or above, and most important, he or she will be able to freely control the investment selections and not be tied only to the employer's 401k plan accounts.

Second, while most employers require that the inherited accounts by non-spouse heirs be emptied, or transferred on an accelerated schedule, heirs can opt to roll the funds into their own IRA and defer income taxes. To qualify, the non-spouse beneficiary must have the retirement account transferred directly from the employer's plan into an IRA. The beneficiary cannot receive a check and deposit that check into an IRA. In addition, new IRA must be created specifically to receive the rollover. Mingling with other IRAs is not allowed.

As with an inherited IRA, the rollover 401k must have the correct account title to qualify for tax deferral. The title must have the name of the deceased, the date of death, FBO (for the benefit of), and the name of the beneficiary. For example, the IRA's title should be similar to the following: "Sam Smith's IRA, deceased February 2, 2007, FBO Robert Smith as beneficiary."

Once the employer account is transferred correctly to the IRA, the deferral is not unlimited. The heir must begin receiving distributions immediately. But the required distributions can also be spread over the beneficiary's life expectancy as determined in the IRS minimum distribution table (see figure 14.1).

5. Estate tax—death tax. While the income tax rules have significantly lightened up, the estate tax laws remain the same with two exceptions. First, the estate tax exclusion has increased to $2 million for the years 2007 through 2008 and the top end estate tax bracket is now 46 percent. Second, the non-spousal beneficiaries now have the ability to "stretch" their IRA inheritance. Both of these reasons are extremely significant primarily because in many cases the single largest asset in the estate is the pension account (IRA, 401k, 403b, defined benefit plan). In fact, we have worked with clients that have had retirement accounts valued well above $10 million. A widow's or widower's estate with a $10 million IRA would subject their heirs to an enormous federal estate tax of $3,680,000. A married couple using both estate tax credits through their credit shelter trust provisions, still would generate an estate tax of $2,760,000 if they had a $10 million IRA. Don't forget your state's inheritance tax if applicable in your situation, and of course, all applicable federal and state income tax when distributions are made.

Note: The worst thing you can do is require that your heirs pay the estate taxes with your retirement accounts. Not only will they be paying the estate taxes, both federal and state, they will also be required to pay income taxes on the funds used to pay the estate taxes. This could result in an automatic loss of 70 percent of the overall value of your retirement account.

In addition to the establishment of a credit shelter trust there are a few additional strategies one can implement to avoid this huge estate tax liability:

1. Convert your retirement funds into an immediate or income annuity. This is a vehicle that is designed to generate guaranteed income for life, and if you are married, you can elect for your spouse to receive all or a portion of the same income for the balance of their life. At the death of the annuitant or the surviving spouse, the income ceases. Therefore there wouldn't be any remaining funds to be inherited by your heirs.

   For example: Marlon Walters is 70 years old, and his wife Carol is 67. Marlon has accumulated an IRA of $1 million. They are currently living off other income sources but will soon be required to receive the required minimum distributions. They elect to convert their $1 million IRA into a monthly income that will deliver a guaranteed monthly income of $6,000 per month or $72,000 annually to both of them for as long as they life. At the death of the survivor, the heirs would not be required to pay any taxes on the IRA because there isn't an inheritance. Many couples in this situation obtain a joint and survivor life insurance policy to replace the inheritance to their children and if it is set up correctly, no estate taxes will be due. Chapter 21 explains in detail how this type of wealth replacement insurance benefits the heirs without incurring any taxes.
2. Name a charity or family foundation, (refer to chapters 25, 26 and 27) as the IRA beneficiary. By so doing, there are no income and no estate taxes to be paid. If properly donated, you can maintain indirect multigenerational control of the philanthropic direction of the donation, plus you can re-inherit your IRA through wealth replacement life insurance.

   An example might help. Mary Wilson has an estate of $5 million. She has an IRA of $500,000, and she designates her Family Foundation as the beneficiary. She also establishes a life insurance policy for $500,000 inside an irrevocable life insurance trust (see Chapters 18, 19 and 21) with her granddaughter as the beneficiary of the trust. At death, the $500,000 IRA goes directly to the charity saving over $300,000 in income and estate taxes and her granddaughter receives the $500,000 proceeds from the insurance trust, totally tax free.

The Pension Protection Act of 2006 allows for taxpayers to avoid taxes when making a direct distribution from an IRA, either traditional or Roth, to a qualified charity for the year 2007. The amount of the distribution is limited to $100,000 per taxpayer. Under the old rules, the taxpayer was first required to take the distribution as income and then claim the charitable contribution deduction. This might sound like the same thing, but it isn't, because of the various limits on charitable contributions and tax computations driven by the adjusted gross income (AGI).

6. Generation-skipping transfer tax (GSTT). A 46 percent GSTT is levied if the distribution is made to a skip person. A skip person is usually defined as a person that is two generations below a decedent. For example, a father skips his own son in favor of a grandchild.

There is often a sense of comfort among plan participants as the value of plan assets continue to grow. Future growth is usually experienced through:

- Additional contributions
- Favorable investment performance
- Deferral of excessive distributions from the plan

Considering that 4,000 seniors are turning 70½ every day, and according to LIMRA, 85 percent don't have formal plans to transform their retirement savings into a steady stream of income, and now with the passage of the Pension Protection Act of 2006, it is vital that you not only have your estate analyzed, but also review the overall soundness of your retirement plan. Without proper planning you may be giving the major share of what you have worked a life time to accumulate for a comfortable retirement to government, both federal and state.

Understanding the Income and Estate Tax Implications of Annuities

According to LIMRA, more than $1.6 trillion is invested in annuity products. A great majority of this will pass to the next generation. Unless proper planning occurs from the onset, a great majority of this bonaza will be confiscated through taxation. Unfortunately, most annuity owners are unaware of the tax bill due on the annuity earnings they are planning to leave to their heirs. Furthermore, few understand what options their annuity offers their beneficiaries at death.

First in line as your beneficiary should be your spouse. Based on current law, he or she will be able to continue the annuity as is until their death. This process temporarily holds off the taxman. That is, until the survivor's death. At that time, or upon the death of the annuitant that names non-spousal beneficiaries, there isn't a step-up in cost basis, instead, any deferred income gain in the annuity will be taxable to the beneficiaries as ordinary income at the beneficiary's tax rate the year following the year they received the funds.

In 2001, the IRS issued private letter ruling PLR 200151038 regarding the distribution of annuities to beneficiaries (a private letter ruling applies generally to whom it is issued, currently only a handful of insurance companies have adopted PLR 200151038 for their policyholders). Before this ruling, and unless your annuity contract has specific language, owner driven non-qualified annuity contracts are required to distribute death proceeds to non-spousal beneficiaries under one of three basic methods:

1. Beneficiaries can receive the entire account value from the insurance company and pay income and applicable estate taxes in the year following receipt of the funds.

2. The entire annuity account value is required to be distributed within five years of the owner's death. This method forces beneficiaries to report all annuity earnings on their personal tax returns sometime during the first five years of receipt. This event could cause beneficiaries who don't want the income at this time to pay taxes in a higher bracket on all their other household income.
3. The beneficiaries can choose a traditional annuitization option (term certain and life, life only, etc.) within one year of the owner's death, which does not exceed the beneficiary's life expectancy. Under this method, most annuitzation options are not liquid if the heirs need additional funds other than the guaranteed monthly payments.

With the issuance of PLR 200151038, and only if your annuity company's product allows, beneficiaries can not only elect any of the first three methods to receive their inherited annuity, but they now have a forth choice. It's called the **stretch annuity**. Under this new and preferred method, beneficiaries can continue the tax-deferred growth in the annuity over their life expectancy. The only requirement is that they must take an annual required minimum distribution similar to the IRA distribution rules previously explained, using the same IRS table found in figure 14.1.

This is a critical movement in the right direction of estate and income taxation. Considering the options, it may be in the best interest of your nonspousal beneficiary to spread the income and tax liability over their lifetime. If, however, your annuity will not permit stretch provisions, depending on the size of your estate and the tax ramifications to your heirs, you may want to consider moving your annuity into an annuity that allows the "stretch." (Tax-free exchanges are made possible because of Section 1035 of the Internal Revenue Code.)

The stretch annuity gives annuity owners a simple way to pass their annuity to their heirs just like a stretch IRA. With the stretch annuity, children and grandchildren can continue growing the majority of their inheritance using tax-deferral over their life spans. The wealth creation possibilities become very exciting when you consider tax-deferral over two generations or more. Furthermore, the annuity owner gains peace of mind knowing that they have protected their annuity for use during their lives and the lives of their family to be used for needs such as, retirement, healthcare, or education.

Along with your estate analysis you should most definitely have your annuities analyzed to make certain they have the key components to allow the stretch option.

PART II

Advanced Strategies for Estate Planning

CHAPTER

15

Using Your Deductions

Use Them or Lose Them

The Unlimited Marital Deduction

As previously discussed in Chapter 9, the Economic Growth and Tax Relief Reconciliation Act (EGTRRA) of 2001 increased the individual unified credit or estate tax exclusion to $2 million for 2006, 2007, and 2008. The unified credit is set to increase even further in 2009 to $3.5 million, with estate taxes totally eliminated in 2010, and unless some quasi permanent legislation is passed prior to 2011, the credit will return to $1 million on January 1, 2011.

Under the Economic Recovery Tax Act (ERTA) of 1981, a surviving spouse, which may be the decedent's second or third (or more!) marriage, is entitled to receive all community property totally free of all estate taxes. This provision is known as the unlimited marital deduction. And is the reason why many planners suggest that the best estate planning strategy is to "never die single."

The Exemption or Estate Tax Exclusion

The unified credit amount in 1987 included an exemption amount of $600,000 for *each* individual. This deduction, as well as the unlimited marital deduction, allowed estate and gift taxes to be deferred and a total amount of $1.2 million to pass from a marital estate tax free *if planned properly.* Each spouse had a credit that could be applied against estate tax and also had an unlimited marital deduction. Both of these were a "use them or lose them" propositions.

When *all* property passed to the surviving spouse—whether by will, contract, or right of survivorship (or by intestacy, where a person dies without a will)—the benefit of the unified credit ($600,000 exemption) was lost to the estate of the first spouse to die because there was no tax to be paid at the first spouse's death as a result of exercising the unlimited marital deduction. Because there wasn't a tax to offset, the benefit of the $600,000 exemption was lost forever. This situation in actuality can be referred to as *too much marital deduction.*

With the passage of EGTRRA, the only thing that has changed is the amount of the credit or exemption. All property passes to the surviving spouse, and the entire amount is subject to tax when the surviving spouse dies. At that time, the surviving spouse can then use his or her exemption. The result is that only one credit is used, and one credit is lost. The net result of this mistake is the tax savings that the additional exemption is worth resulting in unnecessary taxes charged to the estate up to $900,000 for a joint estate of $4 million. Not only will your estate be reduced to $3.2 million, but your heirs also lose the potentiality of this inheritance forever.

Another effect of losing the benefit of one unified credit at the first spouse's death is the combination of inflation and growth that may increase the amount subject to tax at the second death. This can produce a disastrous result in terms of increased tax liability. The greater the projected annual growth combined with the longer projected life expectancy of the surviving spouse, the greater the potential loss if the exemption is not used at the death of the first spouse. If proper planning is used to ensure that both exemptions or credits are used, the potential savings are significant.

One huge common misconception in spousal estates is the notion that, regardless of proper planning, you are currently (2007 through 2008) entitled to pass $4 million estate tax free to your heirs.

One common misconception in spousal estates is the notion that, regardless of proper planning, you are currently (2007 through 2008) entitled to pass $4 million estate tax free to your heirs. This is a dangerous misunderstanding. Everyone is entitled to the exclusion. However, unless your estate is set up correctly with your spouse, one exclusion may be entirely lost. In fact, a recent survey of affluent Americans revealed that only 30 percent had previously employed the simple estate planning strategies needed to avoid this loss.

How to Avoid Wasting Both Exclusions

To avoid wasting the exclusion when the first spouse dies, the following two common planning options should be considered.

1. Make arrangements so that at the death of the first spouse $2 million in property is transferred to individuals other than the surviving spouse. To take advantage of the unified credit, or exclusion, at the death of the first spouse, $2 million in property can pass to someone else, such as the decedent's child or children. Providing the decedent passes exactly $2 million, an estate tax deduction for this amount can be taken with no tax liability.

The balance of assets can then pass to the surviving spouse under the unlimited marital deduction, also without tax liability. This will provide for the use of one exemption at the first death. At the death of the surviving spouse, the remaining exemption can be used for a total of $4 million passed with no applicable federal tax liability.

However, sometimes this method may be inappropriate and detrimental to the surviving spouse. Once the equivalent of $2 million in property passes to individuals other than the surviving spouse, it is no longer available for this spouse's continued lifetime needs. Caution should be used to ensure that the surviving spouse has adequate additional assets that can be used for income and other purposes for the remainder of his or her lifetime.

As an alternative to removing assets from the reach of a surviving spouse, a second common planning option can be implemented.

2. Pass $2 million in property to a trust that qualifies for the unified credit and preserves income and other benefits for the surviving spouse's lifetime. A proper plan can provide for an exact amount of the exclusion (currently $2 million), to pass to a trust that usually provides benefits for the surviving spouse. Property put into this trust is subject to estate tax. However, the tax is exactly equal to the lifetime estate exclusion; as a result, no taxes are due by the surviving spouse or heirs. This type of trust is referred to by several names, the most common being:

- the credit shelter trust,
- the bypass trust,
- the family trust, or
- the B trust.

Property in this type of trust is treated as on owned by the surviving spouse for estate tax purposes (if the trust is properly drafted). At the survivor's death, the entire trust passes totally tax free, including any growth or appreciation in the property.

In addition, the surviving spouse and family members can use the trust income. There are limitations on the use of the principal by the surviving spouse, however. The principal can be used for such things as **health, education, maintenance,** and **support,** which are often referred to as **HEMS.**

Such a trust is used to shelter the unified credit of the first spouse to die. Furthermore, the total balance of the trust principal (as well as growth) bypasses estate tax at the death of the surviving spouse, and the total value of the trust can be inherited by other family members.

The balance of the decedent's property in excess of the exclusion amount can be arranged to pass to the surviving spouse under the marital

FIGURE 15.1 Flow of Assets from a Marital Gross Estate

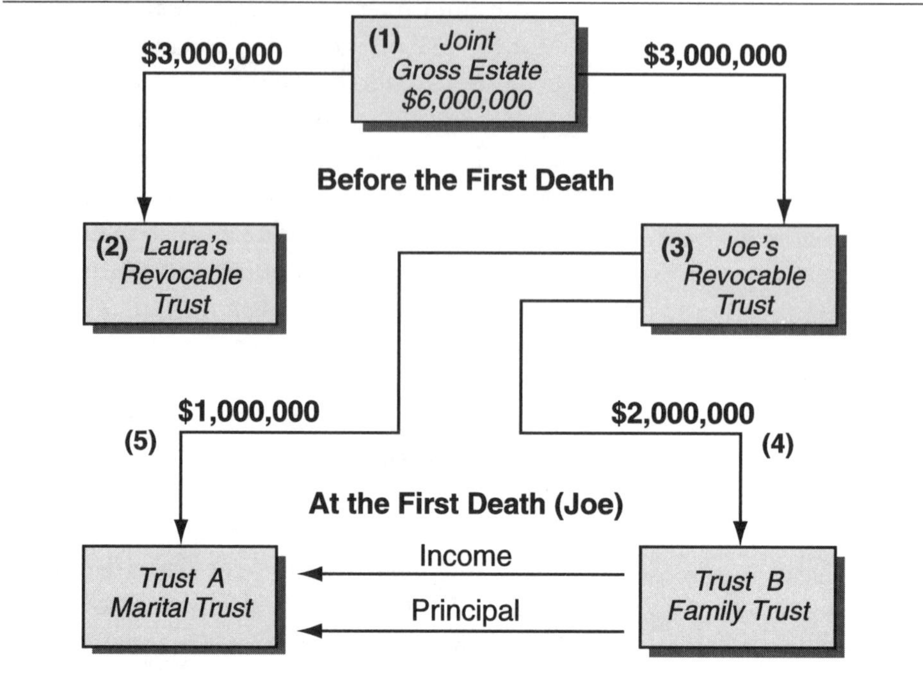

deduction, either outright or in a qualifying trust. The balance of property that passes qualifies for the unlimited marital deduction, so no tax is applied on this property. The net tax to be paid (after the benefit of the unified credit) at the first death is zero, regardless of the size of the estate! In Figure 15.1, we show the flow of assets from a marital gross estate to accomplish the use of both spouses' unified credits.

If your combined estate is currently greater than $2 million, this strategy will not avoid estate taxes. It simply defers them. Furthermore, all the marital deduction assets that remain at the surviving spouse's death will be taxed in his or her estate, together with any appreciation or increase in value of those assets. This type of trust arrangement is often referred to as the **optimal marital deduction** plan. You take a marital deduction only on the amount of assets necessary to reduce the net payable tax at the first spouse's death to zero.

Other Estate Tax Deductions

In addition to the two primary estate tax deductions, the unlimited marital deduction and the use of each individual's unified credit, there are several other estate tax deductions.

Gifts to Charities

Charitable gifting has become a premier estate planning tool.

Charitable gifting has become a premier estate planning tool. The enormous tax-sheltering effects of charitable giving have produced many estate planning strategies. The tax advantages are generally threefold:

1. Estate tax avoidance
2. Income tax deductibility for a predetermined remainder interest
3. Capital gains tax avoidance

Because gifts made to charities in trust have become a key planning tool, we will devote more time and explanation to this technique in Chapter 25.

Liabilities of the Decedent

Liabilities include mortgages, unpaid notes, open account balances, unpaid property taxes, or other types of assessed or determined taxes or claims that are enforced under state law.

Administration Expenses

Administration expenses include, but are not limited to, executor's fees, legal fees for court costs, trusts, and losses on property during the period of administration that were not claimed on any income tax return or the like.

Expenses for a Last Illness and Funeral Expenses

These expenses include the often-large medical bills resulting from a long-term illness.

Administration Losses

These are casualty losses directly related to estate assets that must be suffered during the actual estate administration.

Calculating the Estate Tax

The gross estate is reduced by the sum total of all the deductions. After all applicable deductions are subtracted, what remains is referred to as the *net taxable estate.* The estate tax rates are then applied to determine the estate tax payable. The unified credit or exclusion amount is then applied to offset the estate tax. The remaining tax is subject to payment with the estate tax return (Form 706).

Estate Taxation Credits

In addition to the various deductions and the unified credit, there are other credits that can be applied to offset estate taxation.

State Death Tax Credit

In Chapter 10, we illustrated the various ways in which states tax estates. Outside of the unified credit, the most important credit is the **state death tax credit,** which is a credit allowed for death taxes that are paid to the states.

Foreign Death Tax Credit

To avoid or minimize double taxation on assets owned by those who are subject to taxation in more than one country, the United States has treaties with many foreign countries that provide credit to be applied to the federal estate tax for taxes paid on property in other countries and is known as the **foreign death tax credit.** Because these treaties are numerous and extremely complex, we cannot discuss them in detail. It is important to keep this credit in mind, however, when consulting with your estate planner, particularly if you have foreign assets.

Credit for Tax on Prior Transfers

This credit is available when property has been inherited within a certain time frame (usually in the last ten years of life) and is consequently included in a decedent's estate. The amount of the credit usually is based on a percentage of the larger of the tax paid (either in the decedent's estate or in the estate of the person from whom it was inherited). The percentage decreases based on how long ago the property was inherited; recent inheritances receive larger credits. The credit is applicable to the estates of nonresident aliens as well as U.S. residents.

Nonresident Aliens

Estates of nonresident aliens are only allowed a meager credit of $60,000 with the maximum tax rate of 50 percent beginning with estates in excess of $2.5 million. If your spouse is a nonresident alien and you have a large estate, it may be prudent to have him or her naturalized to take advantage of the larger exclusions and the 100 percent marital deduction.

It also may be possible for a nonresident alien to avoid both gift tax and estate tax by holding title to U.S. assets in a foreign holding company. The Cayman Islands, Isle of Mann, and the Cook Islands are known for having many of these corporations. If these corporations are not treated as shams, the use of a foreign holding company to avoid transfer (estate and gift) taxes on U.S.-situated assets has been successful.

Estate tax has been found to apply to assets held by nonresident aliens in U.S. corporations, but gift tax usually does not apply.

WARNING

This is a very technical area of the law and one that continues to develop. Although the opportunity for tax sheltering is great, a specialist should be consulted whenever this type of planning is being considered.

The QDOT

Federal estate and gift taxes are imposed on taxable estates of all residents of the United States regardless of where property is located and whether the decedent was a U.S. citizen or a noncitizen. To prevent a noncitizen from removing assets from the United States, the unlimited marital deduction is not allowed. However, the noncitizen surviving spouse can use the unlimited marital deduction under the following two conditions:

1. The noncitizen spouse must become a citizen before filing the decedent's federal estate tax return.
2. The property must be passed to a **qualified domestic trust (QDOT).** No federal estate tax marital deduction will be allowed if the surviving spouse is a noncitizen unless the QDOT is used.

There are specific guidelines that need to be followed when transferring assets to a QDOT. These guidelines go beyond the scope of this book, but if applicable, it is important to discuss them with your estate planner and be aware that they need to be followed closely for the trust to qualify for the marital deduction if you are eligible for a QDOT.

In Chapter 16, we will continue discussing techniques that allow spousal estates to use both the unified credit and the unlimited marital deduction.

CHAPTER

16

The Magic of Revocable Trusts

A Shelter from the Storm

In Chapter 15, we reviewed the problems presented in spousal estates and the ramifications of not utilizing both spouses' unified credits or allowable exclusions (currently $2 million for 2007 through 2008). The solutions that were briefly mentioned were the bypass trust, B trust, family trust, or credit shelter trust. These trusts essentially are all the same.

And in Chapter 8, we outlined the need (especially in estates that contain numerous probate assets) to avoid probate, if possible.

We previously discussed the need to plan for the management of your assets in the event of your disability (temporary or permanent) and for the orderly distribution of assets at death.

Trusts can accomplish these tasks and more. In this chapter, we will focus on how trusts can be structured to:

- Plan for your possible temporary or permanent disability
- Avoid probate
- Facilitate the use of both estate tax exclusions and in particular the exclusion of the first spouse to die
- Plan for your current spouse or a spouse from a previous marriage
- Omit your current spouse, who may be your second or subsequent marriage partner, and focus on your own children
- Make special lifetime provisions, such as lifetime income, for people who are disabled or dependent on you for support

Types of Trusts

Trusts that are created after an individual dies by a provision in that individual's will are called **testamentary trusts.** Trusts that are created during an individual's lifetime and hold title to property are referred to as

> **W**ills that create testamentary trusts (family, marital, or other) can be effective estate planning tools. However, wills are ineffective for probate avoidance and disability planning.

inter vivos trusts. Inter vivos trusts are also commonly called **living trusts, revocable living trusts, loving trusts,** and probably some additional titles that we have yet to discover. Regardless of the various titles assigned to the inter vivos trusts, these trusts are identical.

Inter vivos is Latin for *living*. We will refer to this trust as a revocable living trust. An additional type of trust, the irrevocable trust, will be discussed in Chapter 18.

The primary difference between the testamentary trust and the living trust is the time at which these trusts are created. As previously stated, the living trust is drafted and executed during an individual's lifetime. That individual is referred to as the *grantor* or *creator.* The testamentary trust, on the other hand, is created at the death of an individual through a provision in that individual's will. Testamentary trusts do not hold title to property until the creator or grantor dies. Both testamentary and revocable living trusts can create additional trusts at the death of the grantor that will be covered in detail later in this chapter.

Wills as Estate Planning Tools

Wills that create testamentary trusts (family, marital, or other) can be effective estate planning tools. However, wills are ineffective for probate avoidance and disability planning, and we do not recommend their use in the majority of estate planning applications as they *contain no living benefits.*

Figure 16.1 illustrates the primary differences between planning with a will and planning with a revocable living trust.

Disadvantages of Wills

Some disadvantages of wills are as follows:

- Your will does not hold title to property and thus contains no systematic provisions for asset distribution to you in the event of your disability. There is no trustee, conservator, or guardian. There is no one to step in and manage your assets for you during your lifetime.
- Assets may be titled so that they pass outside the provisions of your will, such as assets held in joint tenancy with right of survivorship (JTWRS) or assets that pass by contract.
- Assets that pass by will are subject to the expense and inconvenience of probate proceedings.
- Wills can provide for the creation of trusts at the death of the maker. However, quite often these trusts may not be funded properly because assets may pass outside the provisions of the will.

FIGURE 16.1 Primary Differences Between Wills and Revocable Living Trusts

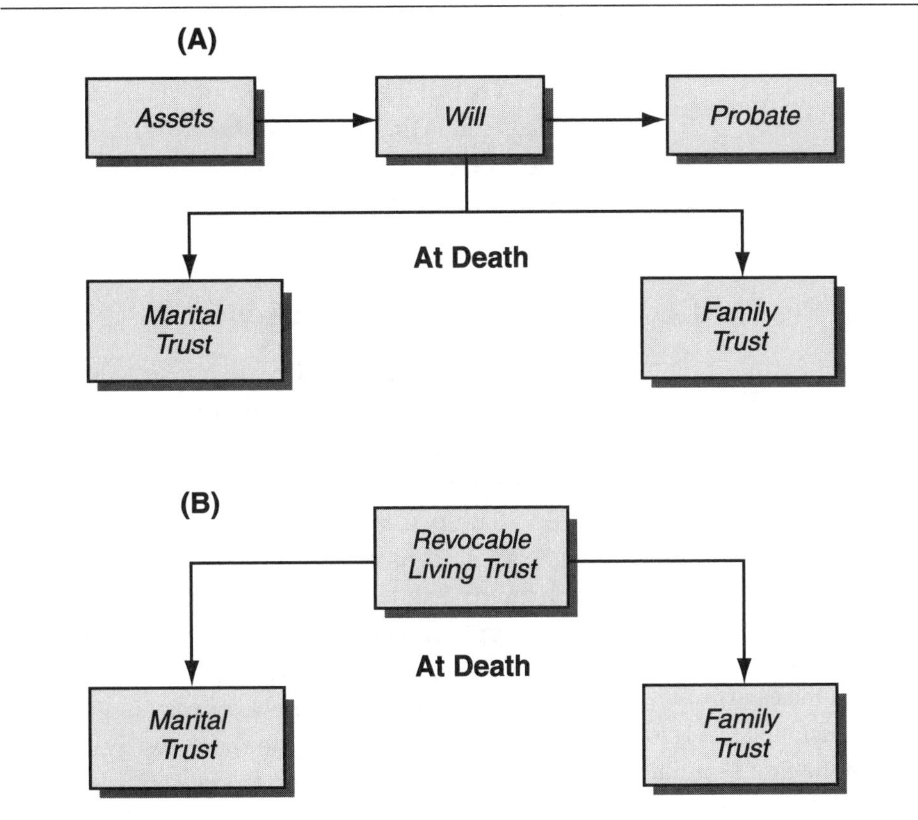

Advantages of Revocable Living Trusts

The advantages of revocable living trusts are as follows:

- Revocable living trusts hold title to assets before death.
- Revocable living trusts provide a center for management when they are funded (i.e., hold title to your property). You can name a trustee, guardian, or conservator to act in your behalf during your lifetime.
- Assets held or titled to your trust are not subject to probate.
- Revocable living trusts can split into additional trusts (marital and family), and the grantor can make certain that these additional trusts are funded under the terms of the living trust.

Avoiding Probate

Assets that are placed in a testamentary trust at death *do not* escape probate, such as assets that are titled and owned by an individual at the time of death.

The living trust is created during the life of the grantor and can hold title to assets. When assets are titled to the trust, the trust is referred to as "being funded." Assets titled to a living trust escape probate. At death, the grantor does not own these assets; his or her trust is the actual owner even though the grantor retained total control of the trust during his or her lifetime. *If an individual* ***does not*** *own an asset at death, the asset will not be subject to probate.*

One of the most common estate planning mistakes we have seen over the years is the neglect of funding, transferring, and titling property to living trusts after the trusts are created. Not funding a living trust makes the instrument an absolutely ineffective estate planning tool.

Using the Unified Credits of Both Spouses

As we described earlier, a key element in estate planning for spouses is to maximize the use of the unified credits of both spouses. This can avoid a potential unnecessary federal estate tax of up to $900,000 in the event that only the surviving spouse's credit is used.

The primary element involved in maximizing the use of the unified credit is to have the first $2 million (based on current tax law for 2007 through 2008) of the estate of the first spouse to die pass to a trust. Because this type of trust has several names, we will refer to it as the **family trust, credit shelter trust, trust B,** or **B trust** in this chapter. Simply stated, it is the trust that holds the exemption—that is, shelters the estate tax exclusion credit of the spouse that dies first.

The primary element involved in maximizing the use of the estate tax exclusion credit is to have the first $2 million (based on current tax law for 2006 through 2008) of the estate of the first spouse to die pass into a trust.

At the death of the first spouse, arrangements can be made for exclusion amount (currently $2 million in assets to pass to a family trust (trust B). These assets, including any increase in their value over time, are sheltered (not estate taxed) at the death of the survivor no matter when death occurs! This is true even though the survivor can receive all the income generated by the family trust as well as have access to the principal for defined needs.

The attorney drafting the revocable living trust must specifically add language that creates the B, or family, trust. The exact amount of property going into this trust should not exceed the unified credit unless the intent of the overall plan is to create a tax liability at the first death.

In addition, it is absolutely imperative (if the estate is large enough) that each spouse title at least the exclusion limit in assets to his or her respective trusts to ensure that at the first death there is at least the exclusion amount (currently $2 million) to fund the family trust.

The family trust is usually held for the surviving spouse for the remainder of his or her lifetime. The balance of assets passes to the **marital trust, trust A,** or **A trust.**

Figure 16.2 outlines the use of the revocable living trust and the A and B trusts based on the following example:

FIGURE 16.2 Sample Plan for the Revocable Living Trust

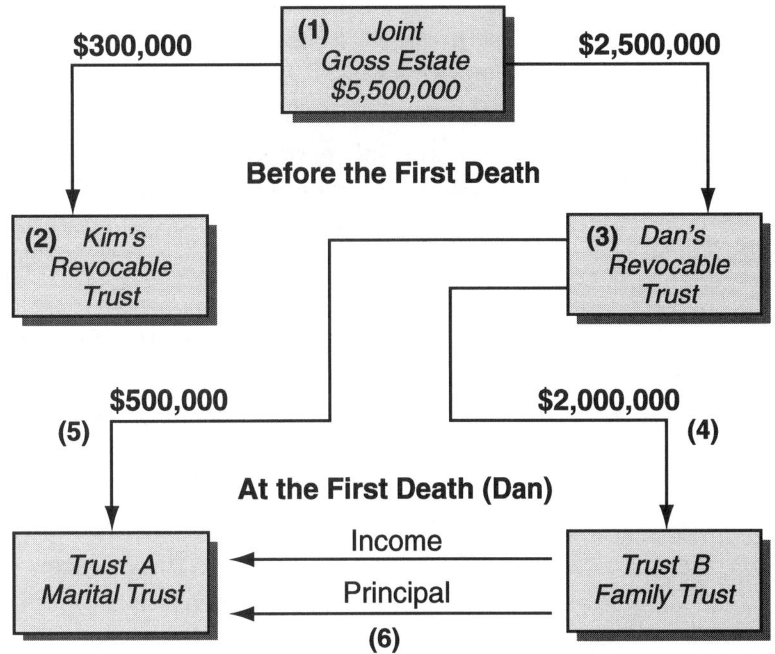

1. They retitle their jointly held assets so that Dan owns $2,000,000 outright and Kim owns $3,000,000 outright.
2. Their attorney drafts a revocable living trust for each of them. Dan titles his assets to his trust, and Kim titles her assets to her trust. Both trusts are now funded.
3. Assuming that Dan dies first, his revocable living trust will split into two separate trusts—A and B. Trust B will be funded with the unified credit amount of $2,000,000.
4. & 5. The balance of Dan's estate $500,000 will pass to trust A, the marital trust. The $500,000 that is placed in trust A qualifies for the marital exclusion.
6. Kim is the trustee of trusts A and B and has access to the income and principal from both trusts during her lifetime.

Note: Other variations of ownership could achieve the same results; however, for our illustration we assume each owns assets separately.

■ Example

Dan and Kim Young have a combined estate of $5.5 million. They know if it is arranged correctly, they can pass up to $4 million without federal estate tax simply by using each of their estate tax exclusions of $2 million each.

They reside in the state of Colorado, a non–community property state. After talking to their estate planner, they decide to implement the plan outlined in Figure 16.2.

This simple and easy trust arrangement saved the estate tax on one estate tax exclusion, or $900,000 in federal estate taxes.

The Estate Freeze Strategy

In addition to sheltering the exclusion amount (currently $2 million), a further tax planning tool is created with the family trust. Provided that the surviving spouse has sufficient assets outside of the family trust and has no need to invade the interest or principal of the family trust (trust B) for annual income, this trust may be used as an **estate freeze** strategy. Assets placed in the trust currently escape estate taxation to the extent of $2 million at the death of the first spouse. In addition, at the death of the survivor, the trust escapes estate taxation regardless of the total amount of growth.

In the previous example, if we assume the family trust (trust B) holds $2 million of securities and is able to average 7 percent growth each year, and Kim (the surviving spouse) does not withdraw the income or principal, the trust will increase to $3,934,303 at the end of ten years. At Kim's death (the death of the survivor), not only could she use her personal estate tax exclusion credit of $2 million, but the total value of trust B ($3,934,303) can pass to the children with no estate tax. The $2 million in the family trust in essence was *frozen* and allowed to grow outside either estate and pass tax free to heirs.

At Kim's death, both the A and B trusts terminate and the proceeds pass equally to their two children. Kim's revocable living trust also terminates, and the proceeds of that trust also pass equally to their two children (as illustrated in Figure 16.3).

FIGURE 16.3 Sample Trusts at the Death of the Survivor (Kim)

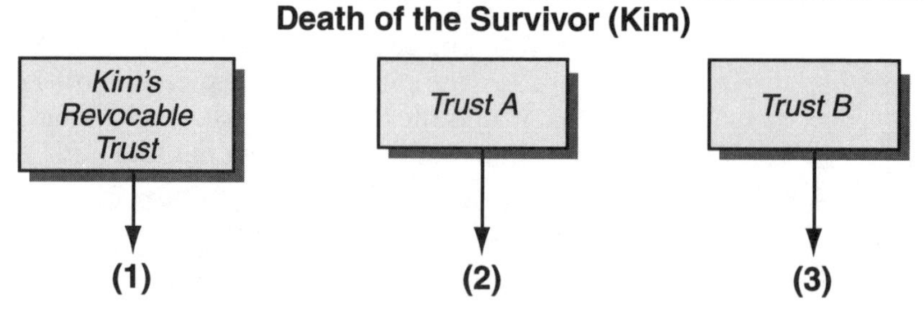

1. Kim's revocable living trust terminates and is divided equally between her children.
2. The marital trust (trust A) also terminates, and the proceeds are distributed equally to her children. There is no estate tax on the balance of Kim's revocable trust or trust A unless the sum of these trusts exceeds $2 million (Kim's unified credit). If the sum of these trusts exceeds Kim's $2 million exclusion, her estate will be taxed accordingly. The balance then passes to her two children.
3. Trust B passes tax-free to heirs regardless of the balance of assets contained in this trust.

In this example, it is likely that Kim would need the income from the family trust. The balance of assets in the marital trust and her revocable trust may not be sufficient to support her in the lifestyle to which she is accustomed. However, in larger estates, the freeze strategy is highly advantageous and readily deployed.

Dealing with Income from the Family Trust

The right to all the income from the family trust may be the easiest formula for dealing with the income, but it may not always be the smartest. This approach will force payments of income to the survivor even in the event they are not needed.

Any income paid to the surviving spouse is taxable as income.

Any income paid to the surviving spouse is taxable as income. Additional income from the trust, together with the survivor's separate property, the marital trust, and income that the survivor continues to receive from employment after the death of the first spouse may cause additional tax. Income that is not disposed of and allowed to accumulate or compound will be subject to estate tax as a part of the survivor's taxable estate.

Allowing the trustee to accumulate income in the family trust will create an additional taxable entity. Income that accumulates is taxable to the trust and can be divided between the family trust and the surviving spouse. In many cases, less income tax will result by not giving all of the income to the surviving spouse.

The Need for a Co-trustee

The type of planning we've been discussing often requires a co-trustee to distribute income to the surviving spouse. The use of a co-trustee reduces the possibility that income from the trust will be taxed to the survivor even if it is left in the trust.

A danger exists if the trustee has the power to either pay out or accumulate income. If the surviving spouse has this power as sole trustee, the IRS has taken the position that all of the accumulated income will be taxed to the survivor. Therefore, trusts generally provide for a co-trustee to make decisions regarding allocation of income in the family trust.

Tax savings can also be achieved by requiring that all income be accumulated in the trust. Through the trustee's powers, arrangements can be made for the trustee to lend accumulated income to herself or himself. Such arrangements create a separate income tax entity and the availability of funds to the survivor, with the added benefit of building up a liability (a loan to the survivor) to reduce the survivor's estate for estate tax purposes.

Planning for Your Spouse, Children, Lifetime Income, Other Family Members, and Divorce

In many cases, estate planning focuses on providing support to minor children for income, education, or an array of other objectives and is a key element in proper planning. If all income from the family trust is required to go to the survivor (as previously mentioned), it will be taxed in addition to other income. The survivor is then forced to use after-tax dollars to pay for such expenses as college or other support for the children.

The Sprinkling Provision

As an alternative, a provision can be structured in your trust so that the trustee can "sprinkle," or distribute at his or her discretion, income among the trust beneficiaries. These beneficiaries can be a group comprised of children, the surviving spouse, parents, an ex-spouse, and other people that can benefit from the income. **Sprinkling** may allow a trustee to distribute income to people who may be taxed at a lower rate than the surviving spouse. A sprinkling provision can also be an income tax benefit by providing income to children under the age of 14.

Ultimately, a sprinkling provision can be combined with an accumulation provision, allowing a trustee to pay the income to trust beneficiaries or to let the income accumulate.

Withdrawal of Trust Principal

Another provision of the family trust allows the surviving spouse to make withdrawals of trust principal within certain guidelines.

An income beneficiary usually has a right or power to withdraw principal from a trust. If the beneficiary fails to withdraw the principal, a gift of the amount not withdrawn is in effect made to the *remainder persons*—the people who receive property after the life beneficiary.

An existing rule allows a beneficiary the right to withdraw the greater of $5,000 or 5 percent of the principal from a trust without causing the entire trust property to be included in the beneficiary's estate for federal taxation.

An existing rule allows a beneficiary the right to withdraw the greater of $5,000 or 5 percent of the principal from a trust without causing the entire trust property to be included in the beneficiary's estate for federal taxation. In addition, the same rule does not trigger gift tax. The $5,000 or 5 percent rule is referred to as the **five and five power** and can give the survivor peace of mind from knowing that withdrawals from the principal can be made.

The five and five power is evident in small trusts, where the survivor may be forced to take principal at various intervals. The amount withdrawn under the five and five power in the year of death will be included in the survivor's estate for estate tax purposes. Withdrawals of principal may be included in the decedent's taxable estate, whereas the principal left in the family trust avoids estate tax at the death of the survivor. It may be advantageous for the survivor to borrow needed funds from the family trust. A loan will offset any assets withdrawn from the trust. Loans usually result in a net reduction of the survivor's taxable estate in the amount of the unpaid balance.

The family trust is usually held for the surviving spouse and children. If the estate is large enough, the surviving spouse may not have a future need to invade the trust for income or principal. The grantor may arrange for the family trust to benefit others.

Children from a Prior Marriage

The family trust can be structured to benefit children from a prior marriage. The trust can be formulated to distribute income for a period of time or to a certain age. Ultimately, the trust can distribute the balance of assets outright to the children and is a widely used family trust provision. In addition, this provision will not disrupt or void the use of the estate tax exclusion credit, as illustrated in Figure 16.4.

As we see in Figure 16.4, the family trust can be divided into a number of different trusts with portions of the property going to or for the benefit of parents, children, grandchildren, and children from a prior marriage or marriages. The family trust can also be drafted to protect disabled persons, for example, who are dependent on income.

Quite often a grantor may want to give property to individuals that exceeds the amount of the estate tax exclusion. In such cases, an estate tax is imposed at the death of the first spouse regardless of other planning. Planning should be done to ensure liquidity for payment of this tax.

The Marital Deduction Trust (Trust A)

We have discussed the massive legislation reform created under the Economic Recovery Tax Act of 1981 (ERTA), which had a significant effect on all estate planning. Because of that legislation, property amounts either given during one's lifetime or left at death to a spouse in a qualifying manner are subject to a marital deduction that results in no transfer tax (estate tax) being applied to the property. Regardless of whether the spouse owns assets valued at $500,000 or $10 billion, you can arrange for zero tax at the death of the first spouse. It doesn't matter which spouse holds title or who owns the property as long as the property qualifies for the marital deduction and is left to the surviving spouse in a proper manner—outright or in a trust that qualifies for the marital deduction.

The marital deduction is now 100 percent of a decedent's property. All property that qualifies for the marital deduction at the death of the first spouse will be subject to tax at the death of the surviving spouse. This

FIGURE 16.4 Example of How a Family Trust Can Benefit Other Family Members

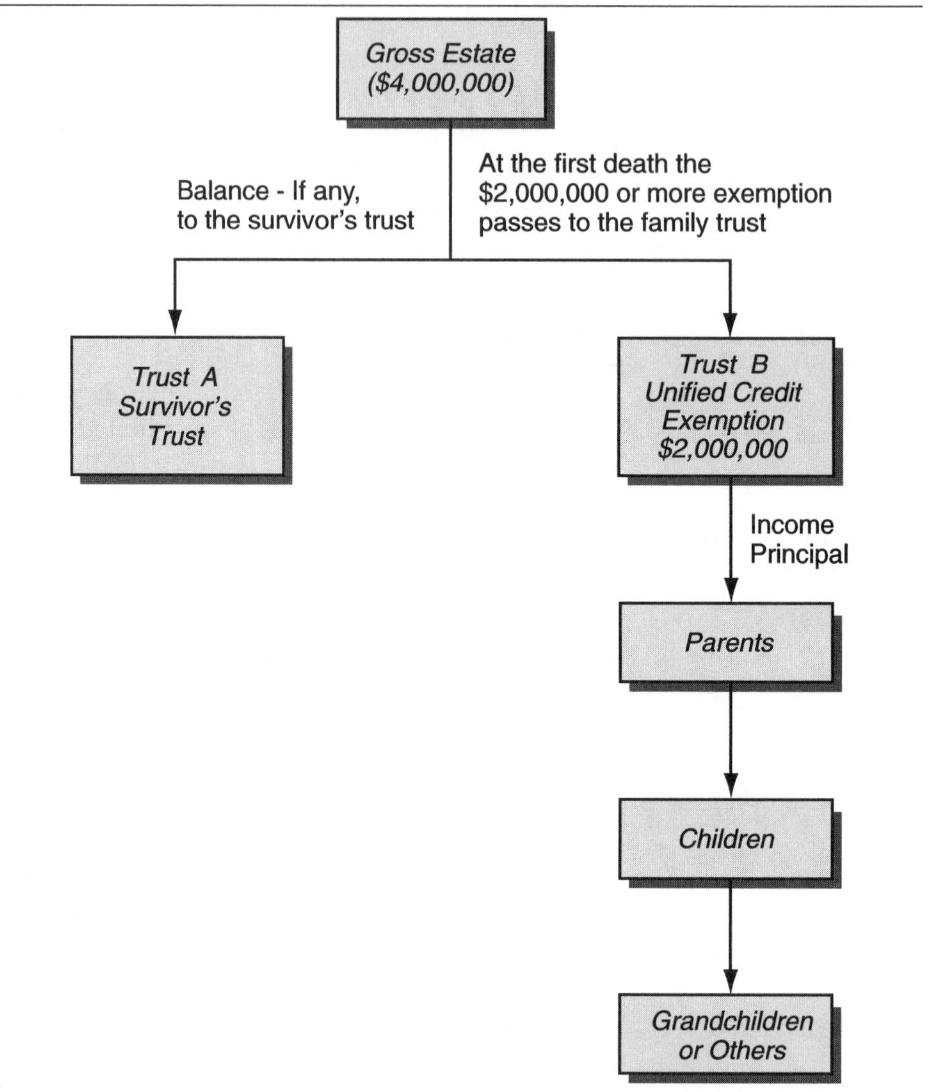

applies only if the survivor owns or has the right to benefit from the property. For estate tax purposes, the result is the same whether the property went to the surviving spouse outright in a qualifying marital deduction trust or always belonged to the survivor. The marital deduction property available for secondary or subsequent beneficiaries of the estate will be offset by the estate taxes payable at the death of the survivor.

Higher estate taxes may be encountered at the death of the survivor if the assets are allowed to grow or appreciate in value.

Assets or property transferred to the surviving spouse without any constraints or "strings" attached are subject to the marital deduction. With few exceptions, most property qualifies. Property that does not qualify includes some annuities—property in which an interest expires, terminates, or is given for a term of years, such as an immediate or income annuity with a period certain.

Today a major issue is the right of the surviving spouse to give property to people who may be irresponsible or who are outside the immediate family circle, such as a new spouse.

In many circumstances, transfers made outright may not meet with the donor's objectives. The surviving spouse has the property and the unrestricted right to its use and may abuse his or her power and control of the property. Today, a major issue is the right of the surviving spouse to give property to people who may be irresponsible or who are outside the immediate family circle, such as a new spouse.

A primary concern for each spouse is deciding to whom he or she would like the property to go at the death of the survivor. And there are no better vehicles than trusts to answer the questions of *who, what,* and *when.* Trusts are often used to protect the surviving spouse by ensuring that property left for the benefit of the survivor is wisely invested and administered and/or that it is kept intact for the ultimate benefit of the children.

Before ERTA 1981, property placed in trust for a surviving spouse would not qualify for the marital deduction unless the survivor was given the right of free reign over the property, a power that could be delayed until the death of the survivor. The result was that the surviving spouse had the power and control to give the property to anyone, including a new spouse, quite often to the detriment of the donor's children. The largest abuse was usually noted when the children were from a previous marriage.

Because of ERTA 1981, proper estate planning can eliminate this problem. New laws now allow the marital deduction even though property goes to individuals other than those the survivor would have favored. A spouse can be ensured of a marital deduction by leaving property in trust to a surviving spouse and know that at the second spouse's death, the (net of tax) property will pass to the individuals the first spouse previously designated.

Even people who have net estates under $2 million and are currently exempt from estate taxation may wish to set up a trust for living benefits and also for the protection it affords others, including children.

Selecting Trustees

No matter what type of trust you ultimately select for your estate planning, the selection of a trustee or trustees is clearly one of the most important steps involved.

When dealing with administration for minor children or for parents and others who may not have the maturity or financial wherewithal to manage and administer funds, a third-party trustee may be the only alternative.

We encourage clients to choose trustees wisely. Family members are the most widely used candidate. However, in many estate plans, circumstances may not allow you to consider family members. We have found a great reluctance among clients to use outside trustees such as banks.

There is always the possibility that an individual originally chosen to act as trustee will not be able to continue in this role. Trustees can become incompetent, disabled, or even predecease the grantor. Comprehensive planning usually provides for a corporate trustee to take over in the event of the death of any individual trustees.

You can make provisions for the trustee or trustees to elect successor trustees if circumstances dictate. Trusts should contain a provision that details how a trustee should be selected if no appointment is made. The selection usually is accomplished through petitioning the local probate court and generally requires legal representation that may be expensive and time-consuming.

The most common arrangement that exists today between spouses is to have each spouse be the trustee of his or her own revocable living trust during his or her lifetime.

You may be content using a brother, sister, or even a parent for managing your assets. These options should be thoroughly reviewed with your estate planner or attorney. Even if an individual does not have experience in managing money, assets, property, bookkeeping, tax filings, and recordkeeping, help is available.

Visiting with the trust officers at one or more banks or trust companies to explore the possibility of using a corporate trustee is an option worth consideration.

In family situations, quite often one spouse manages the business affairs of the household and even the financial assets during marriage. Consequently, it may be quite normal and fitting to have that spouse step in and serve as trustee if the other spouse dies first.

The most common arrangement that exists today between spouses is to have each spouse be the trustee of his or her own revocable living trust during his or her lifetime. At the death or disability of the first spouse, the other serves as trustee. We also recommend that individuals consider the use of co-trustees to serve with them in later years.

It is an excellent idea to make provisions to protect and assist in asset management in the event of mental or physical disability. If a surviving spouse has limited experience with asset management or rejects the idea of being put in the position of having to learn to manage assets, a co-trustee arrangement may eliminate the need for an outside trustee. Often family members can adequately serve as co-trustees.

A co-trustee can provide an array of services to the surviving spousal trustee. Such services can include investment, accounting, tax computation, and the day-to-day management necessary for trusts that hold substantial assets and property.

Your trust should also include a provision for the removal of a commercial trustee or co-trustee if needed. The surviving spouse should have the power to seek additional trustees or change trustees in the future. In trusts that provide income to beneficiaries and where beneficiaries have continuing income rights, the beneficiaries should have the right to change trustees. The ability to elect corporate trustees with adequate financial strength should always remain an option.

CHAPTER

17

QTIP and Reverse QTIP Planning

Gaining Control

Property placed in a QTIP trust flows to people chosen by the grantor (i.e., the decedent).

Often trusts will give all rights to income to the survivor for that person's lifetime. At the death of the surviving spouse, the balance of property then passes to a third person. The surviving spouse holds a **terminable interest** in the property because the right to income terminates at the death of the surviving spouse.

Terminable interests usually do not qualify for the marital deduction. There are exceptions to this rule, however. One requirement for qualification under the exception is to make provisions in the trust that prevent the surviving spouse from appointing trust property to herself or himself or to her or his estate.

One such trust that holds property to qualify for the marital deduction is referred to as a **qualified terminable interest property** trust or QTIP trust.

Advantages of the QTIP Trust

The QTIP trust differs greatly from other types of marital deduction trusts. While provisions under the typical marital trust (trust A) usually allow the surviving spouse to control where the property will go and how it will be used, property placed in a QTIP trust flows to people chosen by the grantor (i.e., the decedent). Property in this trust is subject to estate tax at the survivor's death in the same fashion as trusts that give the survivor the power to appoint where property will go.

Control

The function or advantage of a QTIP trust is *control.* The grantor, or creator, of this trust controls the distribution of property (under the terms of the trust) after death.

In the traditional marital trust (trust A), continued control by the decedent is lost if the trust gives the survivor the right to appoint property distribution or if the property is given outright to the survivor. In the QTIP trust, the decedent controls property distribution under the terms set forth by the trust.

The QTIP trust assures decedents that their property will ultimately go to those they select. This trust is widely used to plan for continued income for a surviving spouse. At the death of the surviving spouse, the property can be directed to pass to the decedent's children and not to the survivor's potential new spouse. This planning tool has become a primary strategy in planning for people in second marriages. It is a preventive measure for avoiding the inheritance of property by anyone other than family members and usually results in a win-win situation for both husband and wife.

Broad Use of the Marital Deduction

QTIP trust arrangements can allow for broad use of the marital deduction. When there are children from a prior marriage involved or children, parents, brothers, or sisters who need to be considered in the estate plan, the QTIP trust is a clear winner!

When there are children from a prior marriage involved or children, parents, brothers, or sisters who need to be considered in the estate plan, the QTIP trust is a clear winner!

■ Example

Bill Jones, 63, is a widower who retired two years ago. Bill just married Beth, age 45. Bill has two children from his previous marriage, and Beth has one daughter from a previous marriage. Bill's estate is valued at about $5 million; Beth has a small estate of about $500,000. Because of their age difference, Bill wants to ensure that Beth has adequate income for her lifetime if he predeceases her. Bill also wants to ensure that his assets eventually pass to his children. Bill has not used any of his estate tax exclusion credit and has a revocable living trust in place. Thus, Bill creates the plan outlined in Figure 17.1.

Bill has his revocable living trust updated to create the following three trusts at his death:

1. *At Bill's death, his living trust creates a family trust (trust B) to hold his unified credit, or the $2 million current exclusion. Under the terms of the family trust, his spouse has no access to income or principal. All assets in trust B flow to his children in any number of ways that Bill desires. Bill can also amend this trust right up until the time of his death.*
2. *Bill also makes provisions in his living trust to create trust A (a marital trust). Bill decides to allocate $600,000 to this trust at his death, which will allow his surviving spouse the right to all principal and income in*

FIGURE 17.1 QTIP Family Medical Trusts

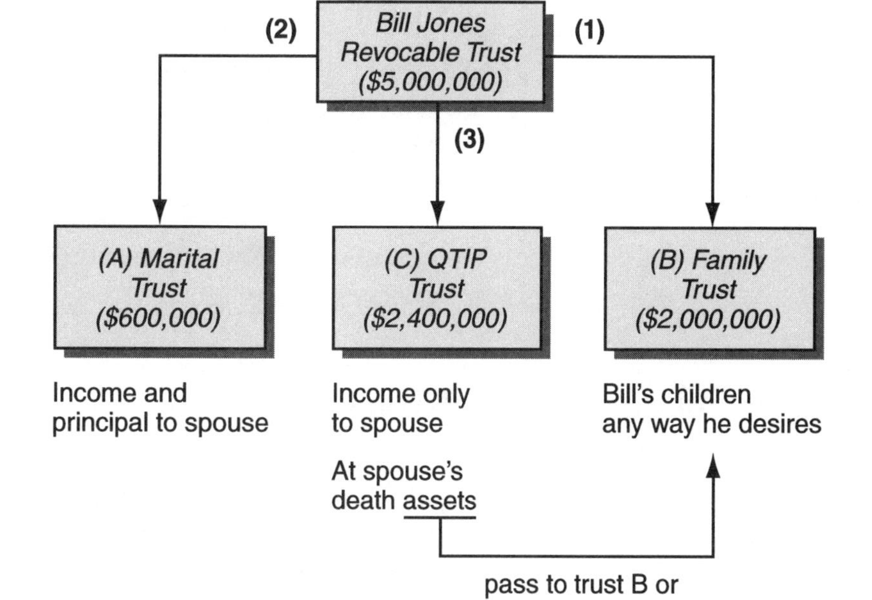

any manner she chooses. She plans to leave this trust for her daughter but may direct its proceeds to anyone.

3. *Bill plans to pass the balance of his estate to the QTIP trust, which is also created at his death by his revocable living trust. Beth will be limited to income only for her lifetime. At Beth's death the QTIP trust will pass to the family trust. The family trust will distribute all trust assets to Bill's children only.*

Because Bill elected to fund the B trust (family trust) with no more than his $2 million exclusion, no estate tax will be due at his death. The balance of his assets will be divided between the marital trust and the QTIP trust, both of which qualify for the marital deduction. Bill has planned his estate so there will be no tax at his death, assuming that he dies before Beth. He is assured that his beneficiaries will eventually inherit estate assets at the death of his spouse.

Bill could have elected any number of combinations in this multiple trust arrangement. He could have elected to fund the family trust with $3 million. However, the balance over his current $2 million exemption ($1 million) would be subject to approximately $350,000 in estate tax at his death.

The QTIP trust has income requirements: *All* income must be made available to surviving spouses for their use. This provision must be made in order for property in the trust to qualify for the marital deduction and avoid being taxed in the estate of the spouse that dies first. This income right must be vested in the *surviving spouse only.*

> **WARNING**
>
> If the trust contains any provision for income to be used by, or diverted to, anyone other than the surviving spouse, the entire marital deduction will be disallowed for property in the QTIP trust. Similarly, the surviving spouse must not be required to provide any income for the benefit of any other person, or else the marital deduction will be disallowed.

The Power of Appointment Trust

In addition to the QTIP trust, there is a similar trust that also qualifies for the marital deduction—the **power of appointment** trust. Power of appointment is a right to direct the trustee to distribute property as determined by the holder of the power. QTIP trusts, as well as power of appointment trusts, facilitate the ultimate distribution of assets in an estate plan.

Power of appointment trusts have the following two aspects that make them eligible for the marital deduction:

1. The right to all of the income
2. A power to "appoint" the property to anyone

In addition, the power to appoint includes the following:

- Uses must be for the spouse's own benefit.
- The right to direct the trustee to distribute property as determined by the holder of the power must be present.
- Income payable to the spouse must be received free of constraints.
- No provisions can exist that require the spouse to use income to benefit anyone else.
- The spouse should not be required to do anything that jeopardizes his or her complete and absolute right to all income from the property.

Cases where a seemingly harmless power was vested in the trustee of a trust to deprive the survivor of an income right have disqualified these trusts for the marital deduction.

Many attorneys construct limitations on the power of appointment by providing for an effective date of the power to take place after the surviving spouse's death. This does not alleviate the problem of property passing to the survivor's new husband, wife, or other family members. Diversion from the surviving spouse of principal that would otherwise provide income to the surviving spouse will trigger the loss of the marital deduction.

It is imperative that powers not be given to anyone (including the spouse) to shift property in the QTIP trust to someone other than the spouse. Use of a QTIP trust will not give the survivor a planning opportunity for reducing estate taxes. Other trusts provide additional planning opportunities to reduce estate taxation by the ability to gift or divert trust assets to others, which may be a drawback of the QTIP trust.

Distributions made to the survivor under the terms of the QTIP trust can be gifted to children or others if the survivor does not need the income. The survivor is free to decide what to do with these funds or assets.

There must be no requirements for survivors to use the funds in any way. Fund usage must be left strictly to their discretion.

QTIP trusts contain a number of drafting issues that can spell disaster in the form of disqualifying the trust for the marital deduction. Small things, such as providing income that is accumulated but unpaid to pass to the next beneficiaries at the surviving spouse's death, may put the marital deduction in jeopardy. Caution should be used and competent legal advice sought when considering the use of this trust.

QTIP planning has a flexibility that other marital deduction arrangements do not.

QTIP planning has a flexibility that other marital deduction arrangements do not. For example, the QTIP provides postmortem planning based on situations existing at that time, such as the ability to pay some of the tax at the first death (which is an exceptional advantage). An estate that has good growth potential from investing or inflated value assets may minimize future estate taxation if some tax is paid early.

Assets that pass to a surviving spouse under the marital deduction generally are treated as being owned by the spouse for the purpose of generation-skipping taxation. If the spouse is the person transferring the property, he or she is referred to as the *transferor* of the property when it passes to the next generation.

The GSTT and the Reverse QTIP

In Chapter 13, we touched on the generation-skipping transfer tax (GSTT) and how it can affect planning techniques. The GSTT has a $1 million exemption. In creating a marital QTIP, or family trust, care should be taken so that the exemption is fully utilized. When property in excess of the current $2 million estate tax exclusion credit passes under the unlimited marital deduction, the result can cause the utilization of the decedent's $1 million generation-skipping exemption.

The use of the QTIP trust can conserve the decedent's full generation-skipping exemption by providing that the decedent be the transferor of the property in the QTIP trust, referred to as a **reverse QTIP,** as illustrated in Figure 17.2.

When generation skipping is an objective in conjunction with the marital deduction, the QTIP trust is a clear winner. Some plans will use

FIGURE 17.2 Reverse QTIP Trust

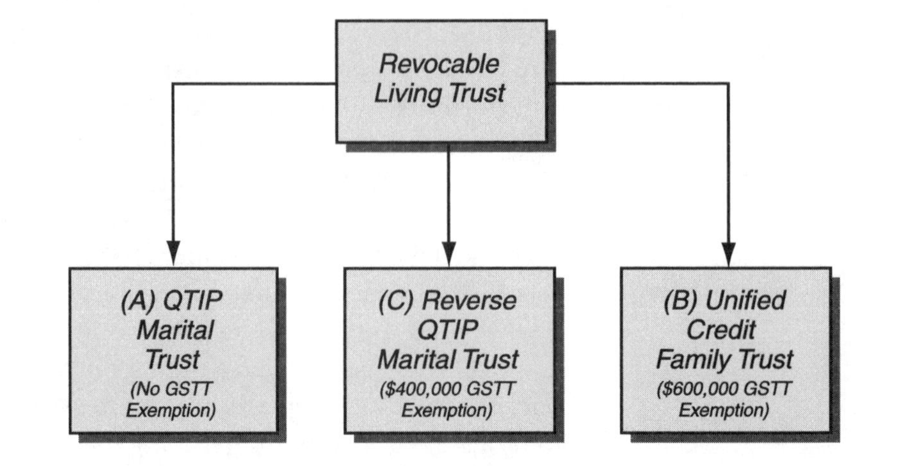

two QTIP trusts: One will allow the decedent to be transferor, and the other will focus on the spouse as transferor!

Summary

QTIP trusts have three outstanding planning opportunities as follows:

1. Provision of several options for dealing with estate tax at the first death
2. Full use of the marital deduction without loss of control of the ultimate disposition of the assets
3. The ability to preserve the full generation-skipping exemption ($1 million) of the first spouse to die

The unlimited marital deduction and the use of a QTIP trust are tantamount in planning for estates of spouses and children, especially if there are children from a prior marriage.

CHAPTER

18

Irrevocable Trusts

The Keys to Disinheriting the IRS

Irrevocable trusts are trusts created for the permanent transfer of property.

In the previous chapter, we discussed the use of the revocable living trust, which people create during their lifetime to hold title to property until death. The revocable trust may be terminated or amended at any time before the death of the grantor (person that creates the trust). At the death of the grantor, the revocable trust becomes irrevocable.

The creator of an irrevocable trust gives up all rights to make any future changes.

Irrevocable means simply *no changes.* The creator of an irrevocable trust gives up all rights to make any future changes. These trusts usually are set up for the purpose of completing gifts to trust beneficiaries. Gifts to irrevocable trusts are completed gifts with no strings attached. Under the IRS definition, to qualify as a gift, a gift must be irrevocable.

If you transfer assets into an irrevocable trust, you give up a degree of control of the assets. You cannot revoke or amend the trust; but you can have some control by incorporating the following elements into the trust:

- *Who* benefits from the trust
- *When* they benefit from the trust
- *What* the benefit will be (income, principal, etc.)

The various types of irrevocable trusts are illustrated in Figure 18.1. The three primary uses for irrevocable trusts in estate planning are:

1. expanding,
2. replacing, and
3. conversion, or shifting.

FIGURE 18.1 Types of Irrevocable Trusts

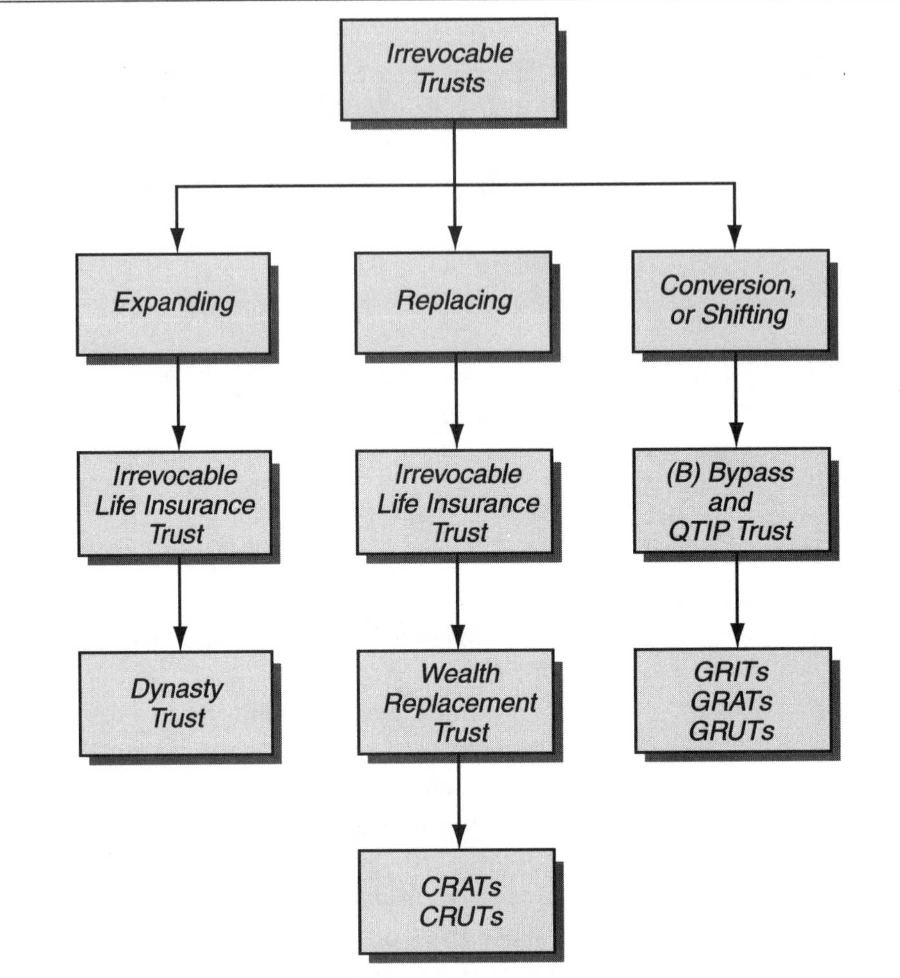

Expanding

Irrevocable, or expanding, trusts are used to create large amounts of cash that remain outside the grantor's estate and therefore are not included in the grantor's estate for federal estate tax computation. The three basic irrevocable trusts used to expand an estate are the **irrevocable life insurance trust (ILIT), spousal support trust (SST),** which is a variation of the ILIT, and the **dynasty trust.**

Each of these trusts use life insurance to expand the estate. The basic use of the ILIT and spousal support trust is to hold enough life insurance to expand the estate to cover any potential future estate settlement expenses, such as estate taxes, and to create a guaranteed inheritance. The creator typically makes small gifts to children or others that qualify for the annual gift tax exclusion. These gifts are usually waived by donees (persons who receive the gifts) and are used by the trustee of the trust to

FIGURE 18.2 The Primary Use and Structure of the Irrevocable Life Insurance Trust and the Dynasty Trust

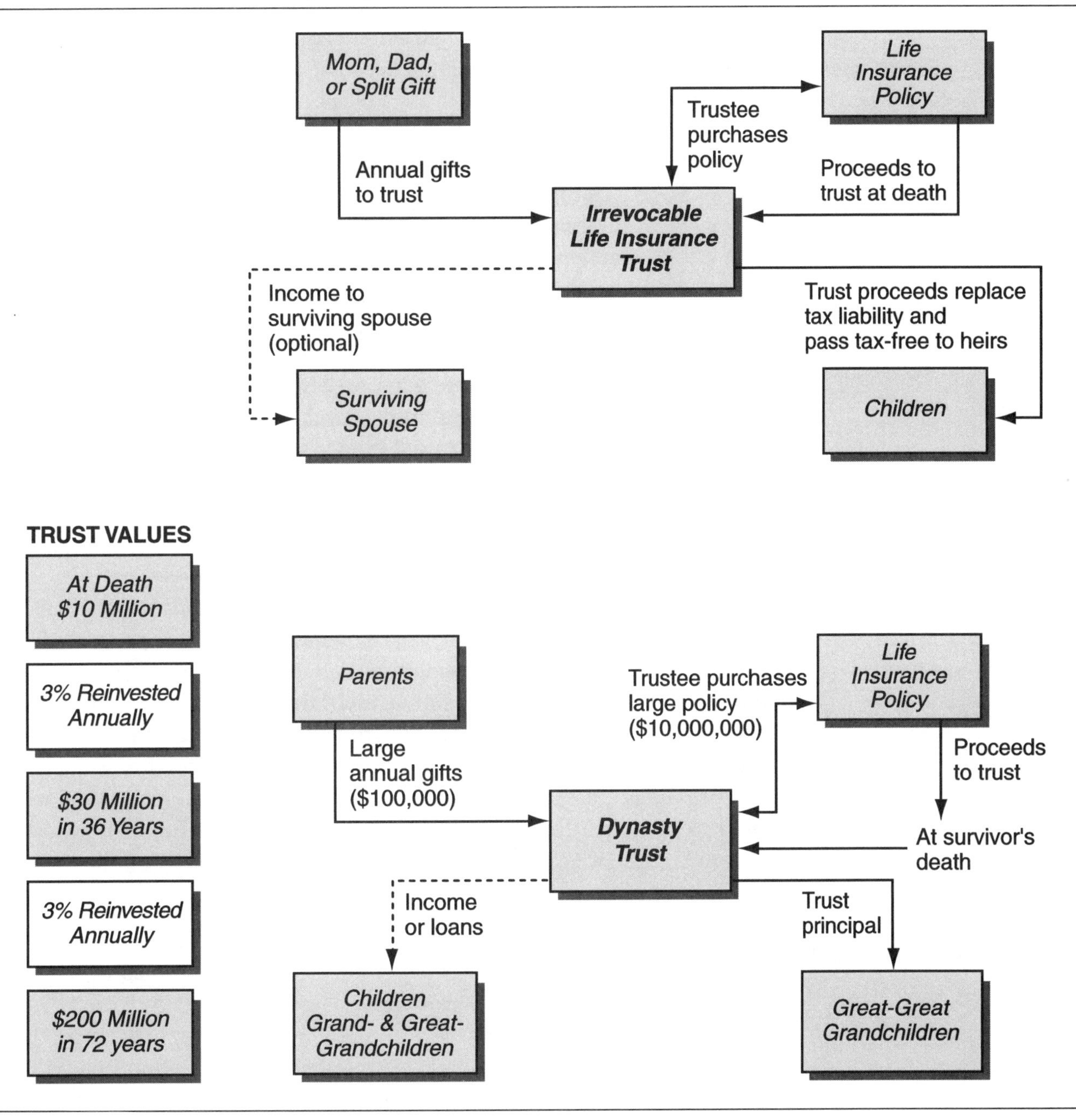

purchase life insurance. Because the trust is the owner of the insurance, it avoids inclusion in the estate of the grantor. The ILIT can also be used to expand a smaller estate (nontaxable estate) and allow the expanded portion (the life insurance amount) to remain outside the gross estate and not be subject to estate taxation. We will explore the ILIT, the SST, and the family dynasty trust in Chapters 19 through 22.

Replacing

Irrevocable, or replacing, trusts are used to replace the value of assets reduced by taxation and settlement costs, and to replace the value of assets gifted to a charity or charities. The irrevocable trusts used to replace assets are:

- Irrevocable life insurance trust (ILIT)
- Spousal support trust
- Wealth replacement trust (WRT)
- Charitable remainder annuity trust (CRAT)
- Charitable remainder unitrusts (CRUT)

The ILIT, although used to expand an estate, is more commonly referred to as a *replacement* vehicle because it often replaces that part of an estate lost to federal estate taxation.

The **wealth replacement trust** is used to directly replace assets given to charity during one's lifetime or at death; it usually is associated with gifts made to charities in trust.

Several kinds of **charitable trusts** will be covered in Chapter 25. The most common charitable trusts are *charitable remainder annuity trusts (CRATs)* and *charitable remainder unitrusts (CRUTs); in addition, there are charitable gift annuities (CGAs).* When donors make gifts to a charity in a CRAT, CRUT, or CGA, they retain a remainder interest in income from the trust for a certain period or for life. At the death of the grantors, the charity retains and owns the gifted asset. Consequently, heirs (such as family members) are deprived of the ability to inherit the gifted assets. Often donors will elect to replace assets donated to charity with life insurance that will be paid to heirs or other beneficiaries to replace the value of the donated assets. Figure 18.3 illustrates the basic use of the basic charitable trusts.

Conversion, or Shifting, Vehicles

In Chapters 16 and 17, we discussed the use of the family trust (trust B) and the QTIP trust (qualifying terminable interest property trust). These trusts are created at the time of death either by a provision in a will or a provision set forth in a revocable living trust. Although it is important to remember that provisions are made to create these trusts during your lifetime, these trusts are actually created at death and are irrevocable.

The family trust, or trust B, which is also referred to as a bypass trust or credit shelter trust, is used in spousal estates to qualify for the federal estate tax exclusion of the first spouse to die. Therefore, the exclusion of the first spouse to die is shifted to the family, or B trust and escapes or "bypasses" estate taxation.

FIGURE 18.3 Basic Use of the Charitable Remainder Trust (CRT)

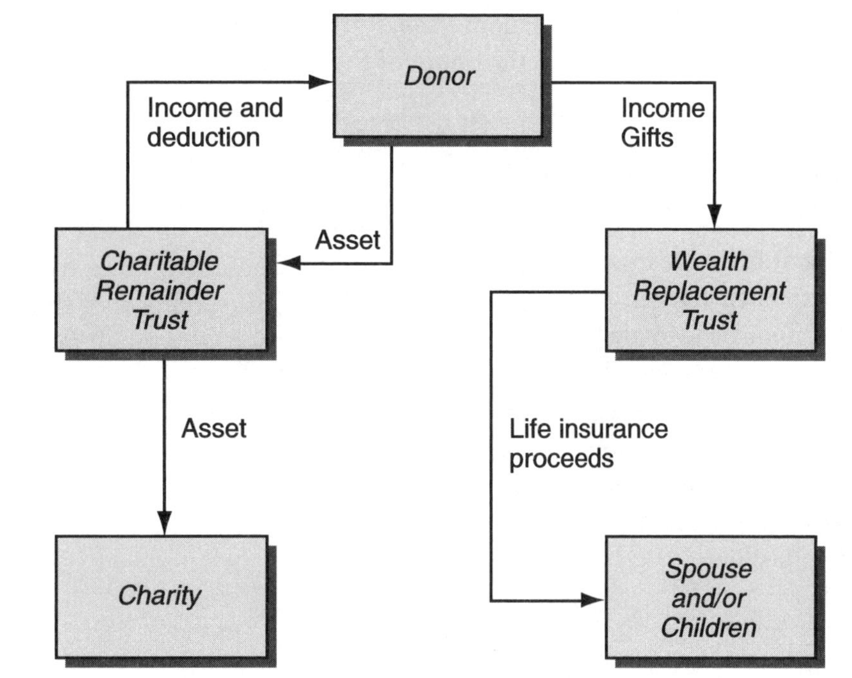

Although it is important to remember that provisions are made to create these trusts during your lifetime, these trusts are actually created at death and are irrevocable.

QTIP trusts are used to shift assets away from the surviving spouse. They usually convert assets into income to be paid to the surviving spouse for the remainder of his or her lifetime. They terminate at the death of the surviving spouse and shift the principal assets of the trust to others whom the grantor has chosen as beneficiaries.

Grantor-retained income trusts (GRITs), grantor-retained annuity trusts (GRATs), and *grantor-retained unitrusts (GRUTs)* are irrevocable trusts that convert assets to income that is paid to the grantor for a period of time. The asset is then shifted out of the estate with an estate tax discount. A common use of these trusts is the qualified personal residence trust (QPRT) explained in Chapter 28.

Selecting Trustees for Irrevocable Trusts

In Chapter 16, we discussed the importance of selecting trustees and the various options available in making this selection. When working with irrevocable trusts, the selection of trustees is critical. In some irrevocable trusts, it is imperative that the person creating the trust not act as trustee. Additionally, the use of a spouse as trustee may also have adverse consequences. One of the potential problems caused by using the person who creates the trust or that person's spouse as trustee is the possibility of having the value of the trust assets at death included in the creator's gross estate. This usually produces adverse tax liability and can negate the original motive for planning and the use of the irrevocable trust. One of the main uses of irrevocable trusts is to shelter trust assets from estate tax at the death of the creator.

Summary

The ILIT can be used to expand a smaller estate (nontaxable estate) and allow the expanded portion (the life insurance amount) to remain outside the gross estate and not be subject to estate taxation.

Irrevocable trusts are used to expand, replace, and convert, or shift, assets in an estate. Generally, these trusts contain assets that have limited ownership rights by the creation of the trusts. Ultimately, these trusts are estate tax exempt and free from all taxation in some cases.

CHAPTER

19

The Family Dynasty Trust

Breaking the Tax Chain

The FDT protects the life insurance so that it is available to take care of the family and to provide second-to-die (joint and last survivor) insurance for paying estate taxes similar to the irrevocable life insurance trust.

A **family dynasty trust (FDT)** is an irrevocable trust with special provisions designed to enhance the benefits to the family. The FDT is a receptacle for family assets and life insurance. It provides families a structure that will safeguard income and emergency funds for its members for up to six generations if grandparents are alive.

The FDT is an ideal receptacle for all life insurance on the lives of the husband and wife that set up the trust (grantors). The FDT protects the life insurance so that it is available to take care of the family and to provide second-to-die (joint and last survivor) insurance for paying estate taxes similar to the irrevocable life insurance trust.

In addition to the life insurance, other assets may be placed in the FDT, including the following:

- Stocks, bonds, and other securities
- Limited partnership and limited liability company ownership percentages
- Family corporation stock
- Household goods and personal effects of grantors
- Real estate rentals that are not in the **family limited partnership**
- Furniture, equipment, and other personal property rentals
- Second homes
- Secured receivable loans

The FDT can provide emergency funds not only for the grantors but also for the children, grandchildren, great-grandchildren, great-great-grandchildren, and, in some instances, the grandparents if they are still alive. Most of the time, these emergency funds are transferred out in the form of loans. These loans are secured by the property of the borrowers, resulting in a "creditor block" on the borrowers' assets that protects them from having their property taken away by outside predator creditors.

The FDT may also be used to provide retirement funds for the husband and wife who created the trust, the grandparents, the children, or grandchildren. Funds may be disbursed as loans so that the distribution will not subject the recipient of the cash to income taxes.

Additional Benefits of a Family Dynasty Trust

Protection from predator creditors. In conventional circumstances, a predator creditor could wipe out most of your and your family's hard-earned assets and decades of dedication. The assets in the FDT are not subject to predator creditors and therefore protect the integrity of the family dynasty.

Security from divorce claims. No matter how hard you try, the potential exists for the property that you inherited from your parents or that you give your children to end up in a divorce court where an in-law makes a claim on your family property. If you keep your assets in the FDT, the assets will remain the separate property of the family member and will not be subject to a divorce claim.

No exposure to gigantic medical bills. In today's world, escalating medical bills can wipe out a family's estate. The assets of the FDT, however, are not subject to those medical bills. The ill family member is allowed to qualify for federal and state aid like everyone else. The funds in the FDT are available as extra funds to make the family member more comfortable during a disastrous medical calamity.

Avoidance of probate expenses. No assets of the FDT, regardless of the generation, are subject to probate either on the death or the incompetence of the family member.

Protection from the "dead branch" of the family tree. Possibly one or more children of the family will not have children of their own. Rather than have the inheritance go to that child or children and end up in the hands of an in-law, it is recirculated within the FDT to the other branches of the family tree down to the great-grandchildren and great-great-grandchildren of those family members who have children to carry on the family name, traditions, and bloodlines.

Reduction of estate taxes. When a loan is made from the FDT to a family member, the loan becomes a debt of the family member's estate and thereby reduces the potential estate taxes of that family member.

To the extent that various family members pay interest on this kind of loan, the interest payments further reduce the future estate taxes of the various family members.

Reduction of need to use commercial financial institutions. The FDT essentially becomes a family "bank" either with investments or with the proceeds from the life insurance that was placed in the trust. The family bank is available to lend money to the family businesses, secured with collateral, and to give the family the benefit of (1) providing the funds the family needs, like a bank; and (2) structured interest rates affordable to the borrowing family member.

Avoidance of unscrupulous landlords. To the extent that property has been placed in the FDT, the trust acts as a landlord, leasing property to various family members and their businesses. As a landlord, the FDT protects the leased property from the creditors of the various family members and is always available to provide living quarters and business opportunities for family members.

Reduction of family unemployment. The FDT may own the controlling interests in the businesses of the family. In such situations, the family businesses are protected from the creditors of all the family members. At the same time, the FDT provides employment and business continuity as a controlling owner of the family businesses.

Guaranteeing the Perpetual Stability of Your FDT

If the actions of a trustee warrant the removal of the trustee, the trust permits a so-called protector to remove the trustee without court proceedings. If the tax laws change or if the assets are imperiled, the protector may shift the jurisdiction or change provisions of the trust subject to careful checks and balances. Normally, the attorney drawing up the trust is the protector because that person knows the most about the overall estate plan and the purpose of the trust. The family CPA, however, may be set up as a co-protector when the CPA is very close to the family. In addition, a religious person whom the family trusts may be set up as a co-protector with the attorney to provide adequate checks and balances. In any event, before the single protector or the co-protectors act, they must obtain the approval of one or several family members designated in the trust so that there is little chance for abuse by the protector. Essentially, the trust is set up like the U.S. government with various checks and balances so that none of the trustees, beneficiaries, or protectors may go astray without being restricted by other officials involved in the trust. The mere fact that

Essentially, the trust is set up like the U.S. government with various checks and balances so that none of the trustees, beneficiaries, or protectors may go astray without being restricted by other officials involved in the trust.

checks and balances exist will in all probability prevent aberrant conduct by anyone concerned with the trust.

If the family wants privacy, it may designate family members solely as trustees. The family need not involve outsiders in the trust or designate outsiders as trustees. Because the trust does not become involved in the probate process, it remains very confidential with few people ever knowing the terms of the trust.

Shifting Assets Out of Your Estate with the FDT

You can use all or a portion of your federal estate tax exclusion when transferring assets into your FDT. The transfer can then generate the income necessary to purchase any life insurance you might need to pay estate taxes and other settlement costs. This leverage concept, using pennies to create dollars, is explained in detail in Chapter 21.

To the extent that income is generated within the trust to pay life insurance premiums or for other purposes, the income taxes on those funds are charged to the grantors—that is, the parents. Normally, one would consider this income tax transference as being a bad event. Actually, it's good because it is, in effect, a phantom estate tax reducer. When the grantors pay the income taxes of the FDT, the payments reduce the size of their estate. For example, if their estate is within a 45 percent estate tax bracket, the government essentially pays 45 percent of the income tax payment in the form of reduced estate taxes!

The family dynasty trust follows and uses the normal exemptions, deductions, and other tax laws that were set up as social legislation by Congress to bring about various public benefits. In this instance, the FDT ensures that the family unit will be financially strong for many generations.

If we agree that our nation is a collection of families, the more strong and secure families there are, the stronger the entire nation will be. Those families that do not use the six-generational family dynasty trust will be subject to substantial losses and be weakened in later generations.

Imagine how strong, solid, and lasting our country and cultures would be if every family had a funded family dynasty trust drafted with uplifting character qualities that could assure multigenerational prosperity.

Figure 19.1 shows how the dynasty trust can be used.

FIGURE 19.1 The Use of the Dynasty Trust

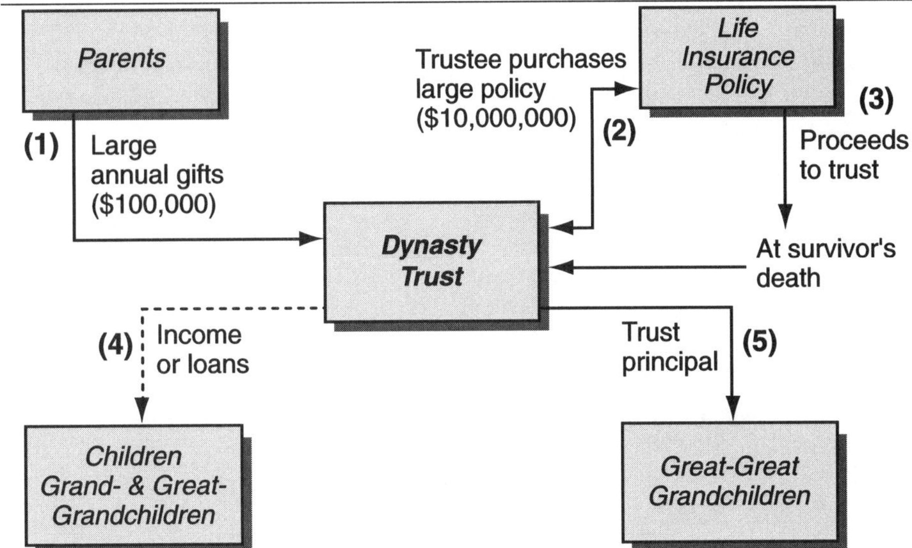

With the dynasty trust, the following occurs:

1. Parents make large gifts to the dynasty trust, usually over and above the extent of their annual gift tax exclusion, depending on the number of children, grandchildren, and great-grandchildren they currently have.
2. Under the terms of the trust, the trustee is allowed to purchase large amounts of life insurance. The insurance policies are not limited to, but most often are, second-to-die (joint and last survivor) life insurance contracts.
3. At the death of the parent or surviving parent, insurance proceeds are paid to the trust.
4. A portion of the trust income can be paid out to children, grandchildren, and great-grandchildren. An additional portion of this income is reinvested each year, and the value of the trust multiplies over the course of the lives of the children, grandchildren, and great-grandchildren. The fund may have started at $10 million but with proper investing could, over the course of 30 to 40 years grow to $40 million to $60 million.
5. The principal portion of the trust is then paid out to great-great-grandchildren.

CHAPTER

20

The Credit Shelter Trust

Creating True Leverage

The CST Dilemma

One of the main problems with the credit shelter trust (CST) is to decide which assets at the death of the first spouse are placed inside the "A trust". In the past, it was customary for the trustee to transfer assets that had a high potential for appreciation. The logic behind this strategy was that all new growth would never be subject to the estate taxation of either party's assets. In theory, that plan of attack was valid; however, in practice it was difficult to transact. The actual transfer of the precise allowable dollar figure of assets into the "A trust" has always been, and always will be, a huge challenge.

Creating Leverage

A much simpler strategy is to utilize all or a portion of the unified estate tax credit today (currently $2 million per person until December 2008) is to create significant leverage and fund the credit with "discounted dollars." For literally a few pennies today, future dollars can be guaranteed for delivery tomorrow through the acquisition of a life insurance policy that can fund the trust with cash instead of requiring the cumbersome liquidation or transfer of assets. It's the simple way.

The leverage created by transferring dollars today to purchase a life insurance policy inside the credit shelter trust can be helpful in many ways:

- It helps the surviving spouse because more of the decedent's estate can be transferred at the first death.
- Because the surviving spouse is a limited beneficiary of the CST the funds can be made available in the event they have a legitimate financial need, all the while keeping the "A trust" assets out the survivor's estate.

- It helps the children because the benefits are paid in cash up front, not in property. Furthermore, if property were liquidated in the "A trust," a payment of fees, commissions, and transaction costs to convert them to cash would most likely occur. The acquisition of life insurance with the credit today is more efficient and economical.

Implementation Is Easy

Furthermore, the implementation of this strategy is easy. One spouse, usually the husband, purchases a $2 million policy on his life; he pays the premiums from personal funds and names his CST as the beneficiary. During his life he controls the policy and does what he wishes with it. Upon his death, the policy proceeds are paid to his CST. The trustee makes distributions according to the terms of the trust. The $2 million death benefit is in his estate for estate tax purposes, however, are scheduled to be offset by the $2 million estate tax exclusion. Thus, no estate taxes are due. This strategy allows him to use his estate tax credit and retain both privacy and total control over the policy during his lifetime.

A Popular Strategy for Second Marriages

This approach is especially popular for those in second or third marriages. You may want to leave the bulk of your estate to your current spouse, but also want your children from a previous marriage to receive their inheritance immediately. By funding the property equivalent of the estate tax credit with life insurance, the mother or father can leave his children a substantial instant inheritance at a significant discount and transfer the rest of the estate to a qualified terminable interest property trust (QTIP) for the current spouse.

Caution: Use of IRA Funds in Your CST Can Be Dangerous

Sometimes people have few personal assets that they can place inside their "A" trust to the maximum estate tax exclusion. In these cases, an IRA or another tax-qualified account is often used to create the credit. The account owner simply names the children as the beneficiaries. Tax-qualified accounts, however, aren't an efficient use of the estate tax exclusion; primarily because the beneficiaries are required to pay income taxes in the year they receive a lump sum distribution. This causes the actual net spendable value to shrink. For example, if the beneficiaries are in the 25 percent tax bracket, every dollar they inherit is worth only 75 cents. The loss can be recovered through the acquisition of a life insurance policy funded with a portion of the tax credit and/or the $12,000 annual gift allowances.

Most CSTs are written so that the surviving spouse is a discretionary beneficiary. This means that the trustee has the ability to make distributions to the spouse during the balance of the spouse's lifetime. This protects the spouse's financial security without causing the CST assets to be taxed in the spouse's estate. It also means that there will most likely not be any distributions to the children until the surviving spouse dies.

If that is the case, it may make sense to fund the CST with a joint and survivor (JS) life insurance policy that pays benefits at the last spouse's death. (Refer to Chapter 21.) This can be an excellent wealth transfer strategy if the nongrantor spouse is financially secure and is unlikely to need money from the CST. It also can be attractive because a JS policy usually produces more death benefit per dollar of premium paid than a policy insuring a single life. Thus, there is an opportunity to increase the leverage of the first spouse's credit into more income and estate tax dollars for the heirs.

Life insurance and the CST can be tremendous partners. They can provide greater liquidity, leverage, and control if properly used before the death of the first spouse.

CHAPTER

21

The Discounted Dollar Plan

Taking Revenge on the IRS

In Chapter 18, we explored the different types and uses of irrevocable trusts. In this chapter, we will explore in detail the irrevocable life insurance trust (ILIT) and how this basic estate-planning tool makes planning for the payment of estate taxes and other settlement costs, such as income taxes, an easy task. The three primary uses of the irrevocable life insurance trust are:

1. To create
2. To replace
3. To expand

Creating Your Estate

The ILIT can be used to create an estate if you don't have one. Funds from the ILIT can also provide an inheritance, with strings attached, for individuals that want to "spend their children's inheritance now," invest in speculative investments, or simply live a "good life," all the while guaranteeing an inheritance for their family.

The availability of cash for paying estate taxes is tantamount to proper estate planning.

The main reasons funded ILITs have become a basic estate planning tool, second only to the revocable living trust, is because, if set up properly, the proceeds are excluded from the estate, while providing instant liquidity to pay estate taxes, settlement costs, or replace assets that have been gifted to a charity.

Poor Planning

Imagine this: Robert S. Kerr, U.S. senator from Oklahoma, was a wealthy politician. As a member of the establishment, he supported tax legislation that empowered Congress to confiscate up to 55 percent of a person's assets in estate taxes.

In 1978, Senator Kerr died unexpectedly. At the time, his estate was worth about $20 million. Unfortunately, Senator Kerr passed away without the most basis estate planning tool: a last will and testament. Of course, his heirs had to deal with many difficult problems at that time. But nothing as monstrous as the federal estate tax bill they received. The IRS wanted $9 million—and they wanted it in cash in nine months!

I guess you could say that Senator Kerr got his just due, considering he helped formulate the federal estate tax rules. The senator's heirs faced a dilemma: how to find the necessary cash to pay the taxman in such a short time.

Luckily, Senator Kerr's heirs were able to raise $3 million in cash without much difficulty. But the rest of his estate was in real estate that was not liquid. The family refused to sell the senator's properties at sacrificial prices, so they took out a $6 million loan. Not only did the loan have to be repaid with after-tax dollars, but the family had to pay a substantial amount of interest too.

Estate Liquidity

Estate assets can be grouped into three separate classifications to determine the degree of vulnerability or direct need for liquidity (cash) at death.

1. *Liquid assets.* These assets include cash or near-cash equivalent assets. Marketable securities, such as stocks and bonds, money market funds, and actual cash accounts are classic examples.
2. *Semiliquid assets.* These are assets that are marketable or convertible to cash but may take a reasonable amount of time to sell or convert. Examples include your personal residence, beach house, ski chalet, or other real property that may take up to one year to sell. Some semiliquid assets may be held near and dear by some family members.
3. *Nonliquid assets.* These are assets that cannot be sold or converted to cash or that may take an unreasonable or indefinite amount of time to sell. An example of a nonliquid asset is farmland that may lack a current market. Other examples include closely held businesses, outstanding notes, mortgages, and unmarketable securities that have value but no current market for their sale or disposition.

We have found a number of people under the impression that at death the IRS will collect taxes from a cross-section of all three asset groups. What these people fail to realize is that *you cannot barter with the IRS*. Consequently, the most valuable or precious property may be the first asset converted into cash to pay the IRS tax bill. A condominium used for family vacations may have to be liquidated well before the farm in Idaho. The estate tax bill is *payable only in cash* and is *due within nine months* of date of death. The IRS collects estate taxes beginning with the liquid (cash) assets of an estate and then requires the estate (or those administering the estate) to convert semiliquid assets and finally nonliquid assets to cash for the balance of the tax liability. Your estate administrators are responsible and required to convert enough assets in cash to pay the tax.

The IRS does not care what problems your estate or those administering it have in converting your assets into cash or what problems are created when all available cash is used to pay the tax liability and heirs are left primarily with nonliquid assets. It does not lament the loss of the earning power of those funds held for the future. The IRS requires that assets be converted to cash now to pay the tax debt and has no sympathy for your estate or heirs.

Figure 21.1 illustrates the true nature of the IRS and the order in which it collects taxes. This order of collecting taxes from an estate—or as we say, *IRS confiscation*—can cause extreme problems if not properly planned for.

■ Example

Consider the estate of Mr. and Mrs. Charles Johnson. The Johnsons own an office building with a net value of $3.5 million. The building is currently leased and provides a nice monthly income. Other assets consist of their personal residence valued at $750,000, a pension rollover IRA of $1.5 million, and cash and liquid securities of $500,000, for a total net estate value of $6,250,000. After properly planning their estate, their current estate plan makes use of both estate tax exclusions of $2,000,000 each. Assuming the death of the survivor occurs in 2007, the federal estate tax will be approximately $1 million. The estate's liquid cash and securities of $500,000 will be confiscated first, thus creating a tremendous problem by stripping the estate of all liquid assets; all the cash is consumed by taxes and cannot be recovered. If the residence or office building cannot be sold by the time the tax is due, the estate may be forced to borrow funds, sell the properties at liquidation prices, or worse, liquidate a portion of the IRA and pay income taxes as well as estate taxes. What if assets have to be liquidated in a down market at 50 percent of their normal value? The government has an insatiable appetite for cash with no convenient sense of timing to satisfy each individual taxpayer.

The government has an insatiable appetite for cash with no convenient sense of timing to satisfy each individual taxpayer.

FIGURE 21.1 Order in Which the IRS Collects Taxes

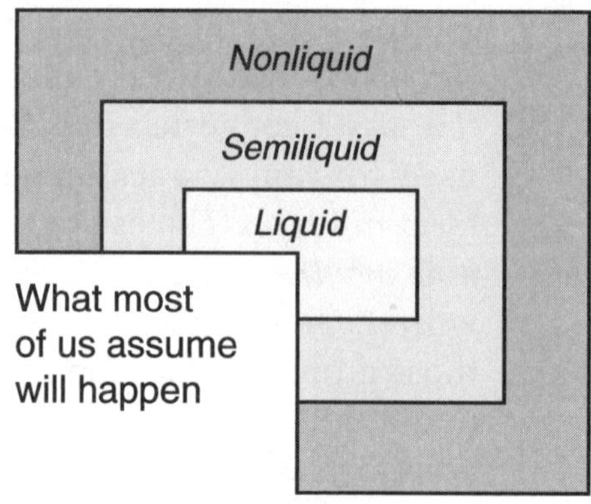

Assets

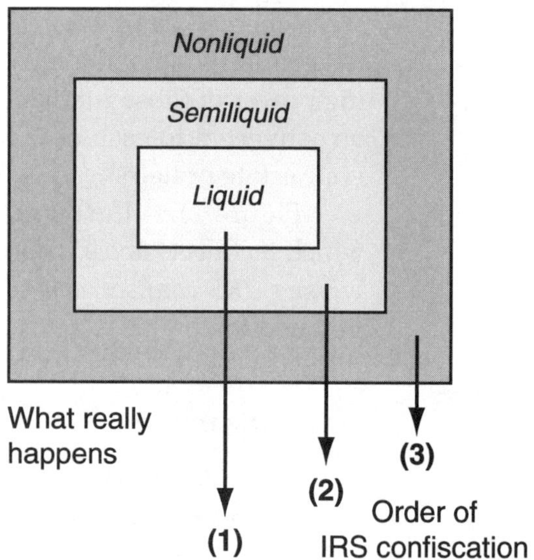

1. The IRS collects estate tax directly from the liquid assets of an estate.
2. Once all liquid assets are used and a tax balance remains, it requires semiliquid assets to be liquidated.
3. The IRS then looks for nonliquid assets.

Settling Your Estate Tax Bill

When it comes to settling your estate tax bill, creating an estate, or replacing assets gifted to a charity, your heirs have only three options. They can liquidate your assets, borrow the money, or use the *discounted dollar plan*. Let's take a close look at each.

Option 1: Liquidate Your Assets

As previously stated, a common method to settle estate liabilities, such as taxes, and replace gifted assets is for the heirs to liquidate the decedent's assets. Because every dollar paid to the IRS by this method is paid in dollars that cost at least 100 cents or more, liquidating assets is commonly known as the "100 percent cash plan." What's worse, if the assets need to be liquidated in a down market—say at 50 cents on the dollar—the 100 percent cash plan could end up being the 200 percent cash plan.

The first asset the IRS will want is your cash. And once your cash is gone from your estate, it and all future earnings are gone forever. Next, the IRS will want your most liquid assets. Generally, those are your most valued possessions. Ask yourself, "Which of my assets are the most valuable to me and my family?" Unfortunately, those prized possessions will be the second to go.

Market risks can create a problem. After all, who knows what your stocks and bonds will be worth the day your heirs are required to be redeemed to pay the taxman? Here's a frightening thought: What if your tax bill had been due on October 20, 1987, the day after the sock market crashed?

When liquidating real estate to pay estate taxes, time is usually the major obstacle. Generally speaking, real estate doesn't move fast enough. And if a buyer knows your property is up for sale under a distressed, or forced, sale, he or she will definitely not pay top dollar. And what happens if your property has depreciated? In today's fragile economy, this is quickly becoming the rule, not the exception.

We know of endless problems brought on by the lack of liquidity in taxable estates. The most acute examples usually are those estates that contain business interests. The small family-owned business or closely held corporation is usually the most adversely affected. If cash is deleted from the corporation to pay the estate tax of a primary shareholder, it can strip the corporation or business of operating capital and jeopardize the future operation of the business. Retained earnings paid to shareholders' estates in exchange for stock may be treated as dividend income and trigger adverse income tax liability.

Today, estate "fire sales" are all too common. I'm certain it wasn't the intention of the deceased to force their heirs to liquidate their assets to pay estate taxes and settlement costs. Forced liquidation is nothing more than *the confiscation of your wealth!*

Option 2: Borrow Money

Another common method to settle your estate taxes is for your heirs to borrow money. Because your family will have to repay the principal (that is, your estate tax bill) plus interest, borrowing money to settle estate taxes and settlement costs is commonly called the "100 percent plus plan." Consequently, this is the most expensive method to pay your estate tax bill and other costs.

Even though securing a loan is the most costly method, it is used all too often. That's because most Americans fail to plan the proper transfer of their wealth in advance. Without an accurate plan, heirs are left with little or no choice but to borrow money. They need cash fast to pay the taxman. It happened to Senator Kerr's heirs and countless others, too. And it could easily happen to yours.

Option 3: The Discounted Dollar Plan

The third method to settle your estate tax bill and other costs is to prepay them at a substantial discount. This innovative method is known as the **discounted dollar plan**, and is the easiest and most affordable way to avoid estate shrinkage.

The discounted dollar plan allows you to prepay your eventual estate tax bill and other costs on installments at 2 to 30 cents on the dollar. That represents a true, bona fide discount. It's as if the IRS came to you with the following proposition:

> *For a limited time, we're going to offer you a way to pay your eventual estate tax bill at a substantial discount. The discount ranges anywhere from 70 percent to 98 percent, depending on your age. If you set aside a small fraction of your estate or interest earnings today, we (the IRS) will guarantee to pay all of your estate and income taxes the day you pass away. Pay us the discounted dollar amount now, and we'll pay 100 percent of your taxes later!*

Unfortunately, the IRS doesn't make this type of offer. But in effect, the same result can be accomplished for a relatively small monetary commitment.

How Does the Discounted Dollar Plan Work?

The discounted dollar plan calls for appropriating a small percentage of your estate value or growth to purchase a relatively inexpensive life insurance policy, single life, or a joint and last survivor policy for married couples. The premium needed to secure the discounted dollar plan depends on your age, health, and amount of funds your heirs will need to cover your project estate settlement bill. Perhaps an example using our previous couple—the Johnsons—will clarify the concept.

When Mr. and Mrs. Charles Johnson, of San Diego, came to us for help in planning their estate, they were both 60-year-old, nonsmoking retirees with an estate valued at $6,250,000. Like 70 percent of other affluent Americans, they hadn't previous planned their estate, and were void of a revocable living trust and the A/B credit shelter provisions. In other words, only one $2 million estate tax exclusion could be used. The net effect would be a federal estate tax bill of $1,955,000, California currently doesn't levy a separate inheritance tax however, there is a potential immediate income tax on the $1.5 million IRA of $525,000. The loss could be as high as $2,480,000 or 40 percent.

After establishing the A/B credit shelter trust and using the new IRA "stretch" provisions, we calculated the net tax liability to be $1 million. Furthermore, earmarking $8,750 per year of the estate growth, the Johnsons were able to purchase a joint and survivor (JLS) life insurance policy to cover virtually all their estate tax liability (see Figure 21.2).

The plan was drafted inside an ILIT to help ensure that when the time comes, none of their assets will have to be liquidated to pay the taxman.

When the Johnsons decided to establish their estate liquidity discounted dollar plan, their estate was growing at an average annual rate of 10 percent, or $625,000 a year. So to create the cash to fund the discounted dollar plan, the Johnsons simply appropriated a fraction of their investment income (1.4%) to pay the insurance premium. This means that they will not experience a reduction in principal to acquire the discounted dollar plan. Bottom line: The Johnsons future estate tax liability will be satisfied using only a portion of their interest earnings to pay the premium and they'll have plenty of income left on which to live. Furthermore, the policy they obtained has a prevision that states, should Congress totally abolish all estate and capital gain taxes, they could cancel the policy and receive a total refund of all premiums paid.

Figure 21.3 illustrates the typical components of the discounted dollar plan. By placing the insurance in an irrevocable life insurance trust (ILIT), family dynasty trust, or spousal support ILIT, the funds created by the insurance policy will not be included in the insured's estate and, as such, will not increase the estate tax liability.

For one reason or another, you may hesitate at the mention of life insurance. Perhaps so-called experts in other fields have advised you against it. Perhaps you're not fully aware of the tremendous leverage and tax advantage insurance provides. Perhaps an overzealous agent or an uninformed stockbroker turned you off. Or maybe you just hate to think of your own mortality.

> The bottom line is that the proper type of life insurance, when used correctly, represents a guaranteed investment with an excellent return.

Whatever the reason, put it aside for now. The bottom line is that the proper type of life insurance, when used correctly, represents a guaranteed investment with an excellent return. In some cases, the return is as

FIGURE 21.2 Life Insurance Premiums

Joint & Survivor Life Insurance
Male Age 60
Super Preferred Nonsmoker
Female Age 60
Super Preferred Nonsmoker
$1,000,000 Insurance Benefit

Annual Premium	Premium Payment Method
$7,364	Minimum Pay to Age 99
$8,750	Continuous Pay to Age 99 Guaranteed No Lapse Coverage to Age 120
$19,123	10-Year Pay Guaranteed No Lapse Coverage to Age 120

high as 40 to 1! Of course, your actual return will vary based on your age, health, type of coverage, and the insurer(s) you select. For a 65-year-old couple, a deposit of $25,000 over seven years can easily produce $1.5 million in tax-free funds, which represents an 88 percent discount, or a 9-to-1 return on investment.

Understanding the Discounted Dollar Plan

To understand the discounted dollar plan, it is important to review the tax structure of life insurance death proceeds. Life insurance proceeds *avoid income tax*. If you are the beneficiary of a life insurance policy, you will collect the proceeds *income tax free*. If the deceased owned the policy, the life insurance proceeds are included in his or her gross estate for federal estate tax purposes, just as any asset one owned at death.

The problem with personally owning large amounts of life insurance is that not only are the death proceeds fully includable in your gross estate, but these proceeds can push what would have been a nontaxable estate into a heavily taxed estate. If the value of your estate (the sum of assets other than life insurance policies) is under the estate tax exclusion amount ($2 million) and you also own an amount of life insurance that when added to the balance of your estate pushes the total over your exclusion, you will lose a portion of your estate to estate taxation.

■ Example

Bruce Franz owns a $1 million life insurance policy. He has made his son the beneficiary. Bruce owns additional property valued at $2 million. He dies in a car accident, and his son receives the $1 million life insurance death proceeds income tax-free. Bruce's estate is valued at $3 million for federal estate tax. The estate must pay tax on the value of the insurance proceeds ($1 million). The federal estate tax due within nine months is approximately $400,000. The state inheritance tax would depend on his state of residence.

FIGURE 21.3 Typical Components of the Discounted Dollar Plan

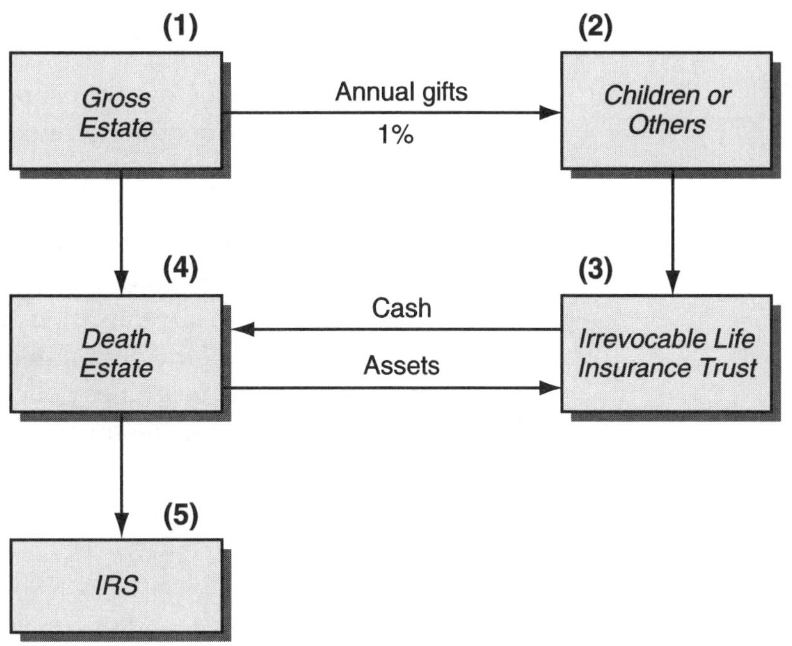

If Bruce Franz hadn't had ownership interest in the $1 million insurance policy, his son wouldn't have had to pay any estate taxes. His estate valuation for taxes would have totaled $2 million. His $2 million estate tax exclusion would be used to avoid any tax liability. Bruce could make his son the owner of the policy as well as the beneficiary and thus avoid any inclusion of the death proceeds in his estate.

One of the largest uses of irrevocable trusts is to facilitate ownership of life insurance outside the gross estate. The creator of an irrevocable trust can use the trust to apply for and own life insurance policies that prevent insurance proceeds from being included in the gross estate.

As an alternative to the irrevocable trust, many people favor naming children as owners and beneficiaries of life insurance policies. The parents are the insured; children or others are the owners and beneficiaries. However, this may cause the following unforeseen problems in the future:

- The life insurance cash values may be subject to your children's or other owners' creditors.
- The life insurance cash values can become subject to spousal election in divorce proceedings.
- Children need to unanimously agree on all aspects of the policy.

- Children or other owners may abuse cash values for their own benefit or avoid paying the premiums even in the event that parents make cash gifts to children with the expectation of premium payment.
- Owners have the right to change the beneficiary designations, and consequently people not included in your plan may ultimately become beneficiaries.

Using an ILIT, dynasty trust, or spousal support ILIT to own life insurance can eliminate all of these problems and ensure that life insurance proceeds escape estate taxation at the death of the insured.

In the structure of the discounted dollar plan, the ILIT is both applicant and owner of the insurance policy from the outset and thus prevents the insured from having any ownership in the policy.

WARNING

Life insurance proceeds are received income tax free but are not estate tax free if the insured has any incident of ownership. Rights of ownership include the right to change beneficiaries, borrow cash values, or exercise any of the standard nonforfeiture provisions included in the contract. It is vital to your estate plan that ownership of life insurance policies earmarked for estate settlement costs, wealth creation, or wealth replacement be structured correctly. Incorrect ownership will not only cause a severe loss of the net insurance proceeds caused by estate taxation but can also significantly increase the estate tax bracket on the balance of your estate.

The IRS has strict rules and guidelines concerning the transfer of existing policies to an irrevocable trust or other potential owners. If you own insurance policies and you change the ownership (transfer the policies) to other individuals or to an ILIT, you must live for three years before the life insurance proceeds will be excluded from your gross estate. Simply stated, transferring ownership of life insurance that you currently own into a new ILIT (to avoid having the death proceeds included in your gross estate) will not exclude it from your gross estate if you die within three years of the date of the transfer. This problem can be avoided with the purchase of new insurance policies if the new policies are applied for and owned correctly at the time of application. Section 1035 of the Internal Revenue Code allows for the tax-free exchange of old, low-yielding, ineffective, and improperly owned life insurance policies.

FIGURE 21.4 Ownership and Taxation of Life Insurance Contracts

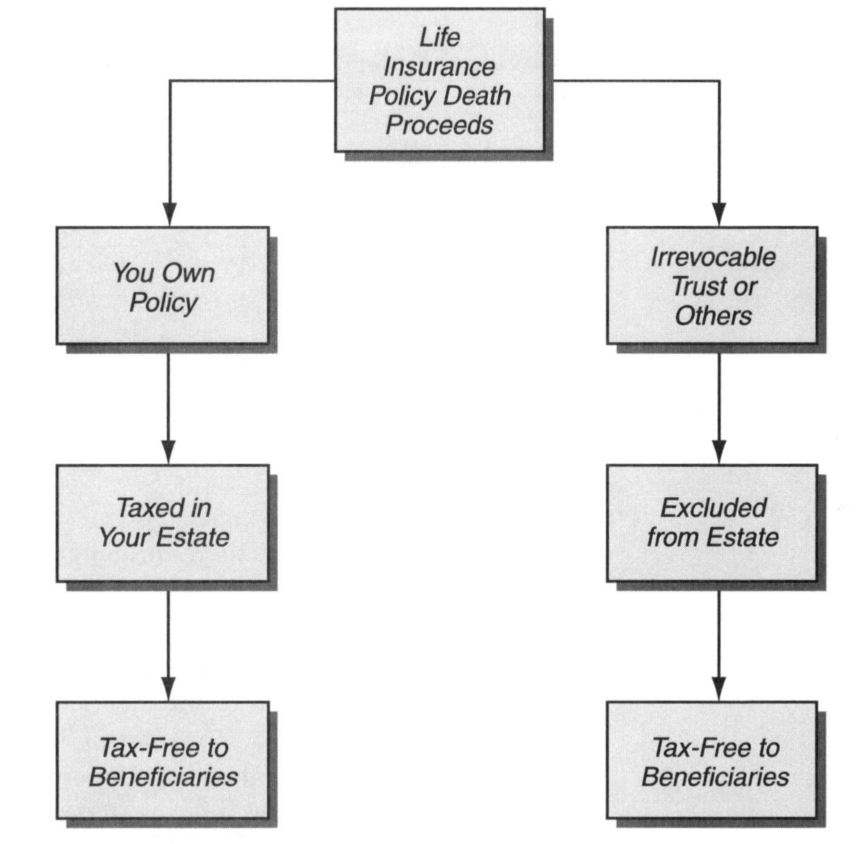

We have found that a large majority of insurance agents who do not work in the estate planning field are unaware of this potential tax trap. Consequently, we have many clients who thought their insurance policies were not included in their gross estates but, on review, discovered the opposite. In fact, we have had clients adamantly state that their insurance agent claimed that their life insurance proceeds would be completely tax free.

Figure 21.4 summarizes ownership and taxation of life insurance contracts.

The discounted dollar plan can be directed to focus on either estate liquidity needs, wealth creation or complete replacement of gifted assets. In either situation, the focus of the plan centers on the using a small percentage of your estate value to purchase life insurance. The number of years that premium requirements are necessary varies with your age, health status, cash flow, and the amount of insurance needed to ensure that your estate tax liability is paid or to create sufficient liquidity to avoid all of the problems associated with estates primarily comprised of nonliquid or semiliquid assets. Figures 21.5 and 21.6 summarize the discounted dollar plan at various ages.

The discounted dollar plan can be directed to focus on either estate liquidity needs, wealth creation, or complete replacement of gifted assets.

FIGURE 21.5 The Discounted Dollar Plan for Single Persons for Various Estate Sizes & Age–Male

Size of Estate*	Approximate Federal & State Tax Liability	Discounted Dollar Plan (Minimum Continuous Annual Premium**) 55	65	75	85
$ 2,000,000					
$ 3,000,000	$ 460,000	5,158	8,573	15,413	36,675
$ 4,000,000	$ 920,000	10,195	17,025	30,706	73,232
$ 5,000,000	$ 1,380,000	15,232	25,477	46,000	109,789
$ 8,000,000	$ 2,760,000	32,330	54,876	98,873	214,692
$10,000,000	$ 3,680,000	44,021	74,750	134,717	292,574

*Based on Current Estate Tax Exclusion (2007–2008).
**Assuming Best Risk Category.
Premiums represent a cross section of carriers.

Many clients use their annual gift tax exclusion with no diminishing effect on their lifetime $2 million exclusion. This works extremely well in family situations where you may currently be making small gifts up to the annual gift tax exclusion amount ($12,000) or would like to begin making small gifts to children or others and also fund your estate tax liability or solve a liquidity need. Considering the fact that the IRS could confiscate up to 70 percent of your estate, depending on total size and types of assets in your estate, dedicating a small percentage of the principal, or growth, annually for a number of years is minimal by comparison.

FIGURE 21.6 The Discounted Dollar Plan for Married Couples for Various Estate Sizes and Ages

Size of Estate*	Approximate Federal Estate Tax Liability	Joint and Survivor Discounted Dollar Plan (Minimum Continuous Annual Premium) 55	65	75	85
$ 2,000,000	$ —				
$ 4,000,000	$ —				
$ 5,000,000	$ 460,000	3,270	5,326	9,079	21,916
$ 6,000,000	$ 920,000	6,292	10,404	17,908	43,583
$ 8,000,000	$ 1,840,000	12,337	20,560	35,567	86,918
$10,000,000	$ 2,760,000	18,382	30,716	53,225	130,253

*Based on Current Estate Tax Exclusion (2007–2008).
***Assuming Best Risk Category.
**Based on Establishment of Proposed Credit Shelter Trust.
Premiums represent a cross section of carriers.

The Five Steps of the Discounted Dollar Plan

The five basic steps involved in the discounted dollar plan are as follows:

1. Gifts are made from the gross estate to children or others whom you want to benefit from the distribution of the trust at your death. These gifts usually are small (not over $12,000 to each person or $24,000 if both spouses participate in or split the gift) and qualify for the annual gift tax exclusion. If you have ten beneficiaries, (three children, three in-laws, and four grandchildren) you and your spouse could gift up to $240,000 per year totally gift and estate tax free, without impacting your lifetime $2 million personal estate tax exclusions or your $1 million lifetime generation skip allowance.
2. The children or others receiving the gifts waive their rights to the gifts, which qualify for annual gift tax exclusion.
3. The trustee then pays the premium for the life insurance owned by the ILIT.
4. Upon the death of the insured the life insurance policy generates cash payable to the ILIT. The ILIT then has the funds available to forward to the IRS and pay other estate settlement expenses.
5. After the tax liability is satisfied, the estate can distribute the balance of assets to heirs or other beneficiaries. The ILIT can terminate and distribute the balance of insurance proceeds (cash) to trust beneficiaries.

There are several variations of this arrangement depending on what you need to accomplish and the particular objectives of your estate plan.

In Chapter 16, we explored the family trust (trust B) and the marital trust (trust A) as means of using both estate tax exclusions, and the unlimited marital deduction in spousal estates. The use of property to purchase life insurance with an ILIT in conjunction with these trusts can complete your entire estate planning objectives without the complications of other more difficult-to-understand-and-implement estate planning strategies.

A review of what this combination accomplishes is illustrated in Figure 21.7.

The three phases incorporated in Figure 21.7 are as follows:

1. *Before the first death.* Lifetime planning includes the use of a revocable living trust for each spouse. Assets that comprise the gross estate may be retitled so that each spouse owns the equivalent of the federal estate tax exclusion. Lifetime gifts can be made to children or others that qualify for the annual gift tax exclusion. These gifts can then be used to purchase life insurance owned by the ILIT.
2. *At the first death (assumes husband).* The combination of the family trust, or B trust, provides for the use of the husband's estate tax exclusion. The balance of the husband's estate passes to the

FIGURE 21.7 Combination of Revocable Living Trust, Marital Trust, Family Trust, QTIP Trust, and ILIT

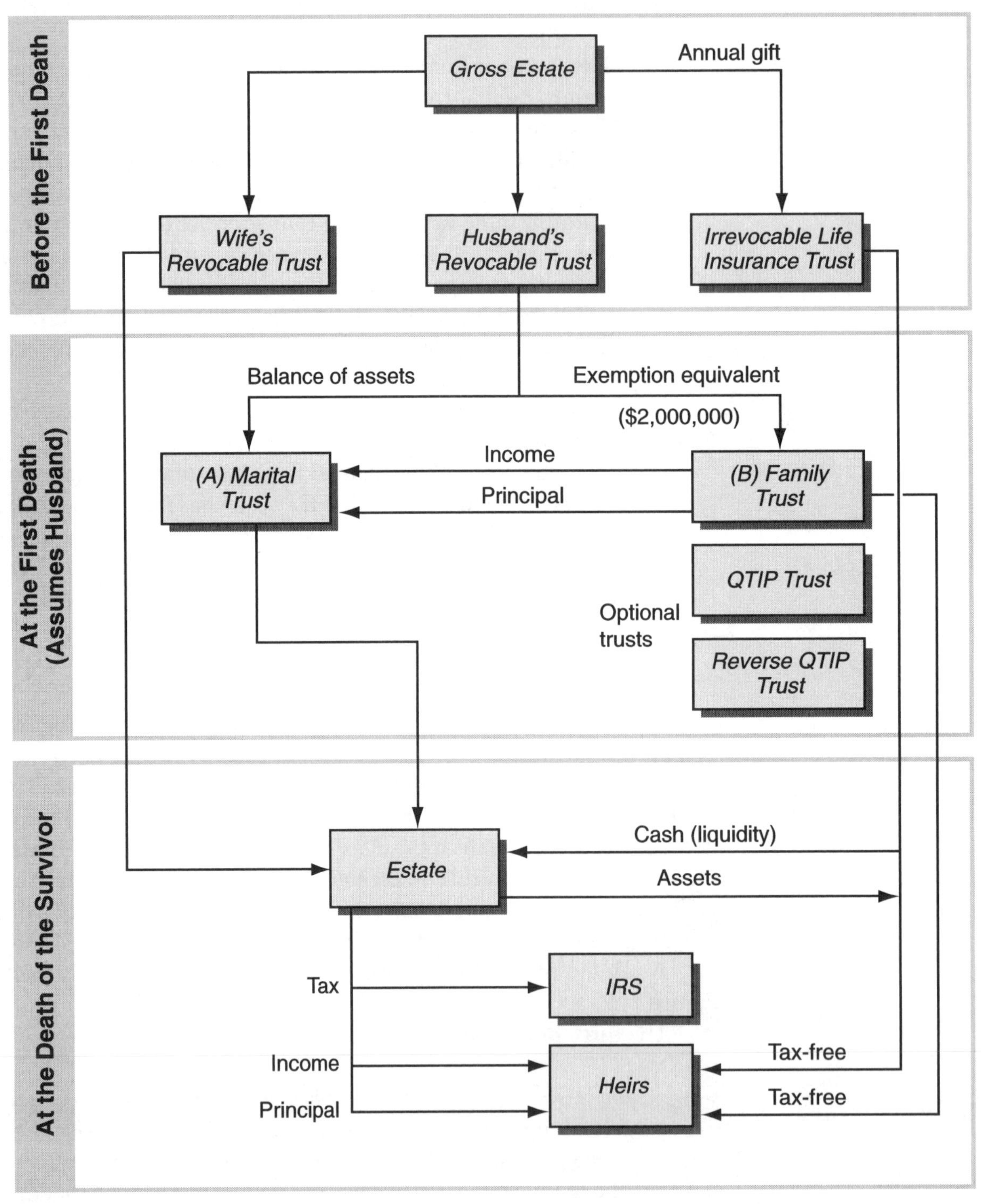

marital trust, or trust A. The QTIP and reverse QTIP trusts may be used to accomplish planning for the surviving spouse, children from previous marriages, and others as outlined in Chapter 17.

3. *At the death of the survivor.* The surviving spouse's estate elects to use the lifetime estate tax exclusion. The family trust terminates, and not only will the predeceased husband's exclusion credit pass tax free to heirs but all accumulation over and above this amount will pass both income tax free and estate tax free to heirs. The ILIT terminates and may be used to provide liquidity to the estate in exchange for nonliquid assets.

Expanding or Leveraging Your Estate

Leveraging is the major reason why life insurance has become a premier tool and continues to be one of the most effective tools as we lose other planning strategies from changes in legislation.

Leveraging in estate planning refers to shifting to the next generation or other beneficiaries an amount substantially greater than the cost of insurance. It is a true cost discount by which you can pay a few dollars now to create a significantly larger sum later.

Leveraging is the major reason why life insurance has become the premier strategic estate planning tool. Even at advanced ages, the cost of life insurance usually is substantially less than the face value that would be payable if the insured dies. Even if one spouse is uninsurable, coverage can be secured by using the better health status of the other spouse.

The insurance policy value can leverage or *expand* to many times the amount of the annual premium or gift made to others to pay the premium. Thus, huge transfers can be transacted without the application of transfer taxes.

Using Small Gifts to Fund an ILIT

The use of small gifts (to the extent of your $12,000 annual gift tax exclusion) to fund an ILIT will preserve your lifetime estate tax exclusion until your death. One of the most advantageous uses of this arrangement is that you give up very little control of your estate and estate assets during your lifetime other than the small annual gifts that you make.

In addition, the insurance trust is extremely easy to administer. Although other assets may be gifted to this trust, it usually contains only life insurance policies. Generally, there are very few management duties that a trustee has to perform. The trustee's main responsibility is to make the premium payments from gifts and collect the death proceeds and distribute these proceeds under the terms of the trust.

Using Large Gifts to Fund an ILIT

If your estate is large enough and you use proper planning to ensure adequate financial support for the remainder of your lifetime, you may want to consider using all or a portion of your lifetime estate tax exclusion (currently $2 million) and that of your spouse *now* while you are alive!

In late 1992, serious consideration was given to lowering the amount of the unified credit to $200,000.

In late 1992, serious consideration was given to lowering the amount of the unified credit. Along with their long-term health care bill for the elderly, Representatives Dick Gephardt and Henry Waxman proposed a reduction in the unified credit to reflect a personal lifetime exemption of only $200,000 in assets (today it is $2 million). Fearing this change, many people made gifts of their unified credit in an effort to *grandfather* (the government can never recall the transferred assets) the then $600,000 estate exclusion credit before proposed reductions could become law. The bill was tabled because of the pending presidential election. However, if you are in a position to gift to the extent of the current lifetime estate tax exclusion ($2 million) or in the case of spousal estates the sum of two credits ($4 million) during your lifetime, we recommend that you consider doing so before any negative changes in the exclusion are implemented by future legislation.

Using Your Unified Credit(s) Now

You should consider two key elements when making gifts to the extent of the $2 million exemption or larger amounts:

1. You should gift appreciating assets if possible.
2. You should leverage your gifts.

Gifting appreciating assets removes the assets from your gross estate and allows them to grow outside of your estate without additional taxation. This is called an *estate freeze.*

The larger your gift, the larger the leverage factor in the ILIT.

■ Example

A 65-year-old couple has an estate valued at $19 million. If both spouses gift their lifetime exclusions now, they can reduce their estate by $4 million. Not only will they have reduced the size of their estate, but also all potential future growth of the $4 million in gifted assets will be excluded from future taxation. The trust can then purchase life insurance up to $10 million with a single premium of $1.2 million to replace death tax liability. In addition, this couple can still continue to use their annual gift tax exclusion by making the $12,000 annual gifts. Remember, however, no estate tax savings idea should be implemented if it is going to drastically change your lifestyle.

Joint and Survivor Insurance: The Most Cost-Effective Way to Leverage Your Estate

Since the introduction of the unlimited marital deduction under ERTA 1981, which basically transferred the responsibility to pay estate taxes from the surviving spouse to the heirs, a number of insurance companies have introduced a relatively new type of life insurance that's ideal for paying estate taxes and replace gifted assets. It's called **joint and survivor** or **second-to-die insurance**.

The things that make JS insurance so powerful are its special tax advantages, its tremendous leverage, and its low cost. It represents a cost-effective way to preserve your estate for your children and grandchildren.

In essence, JS insurance is designed for married couples. It insures the lives of both spouses under one policy and thus costs less. The proceeds from the policy are used to pay the tax bill when the last spouse passes away. As such, it allows you to plan your estate so your heirs won't have to liquidate assets or borrow money to pay the tax liability.

If a JS plan is set up properly, the proceeds are paid exactly when they're needed—at the death of the survivor. Equally important, these proceeds can be paid to beneficiaries completely income tax free, estate tax free, probate free, and creditor free.

Before ERTA 1981, the most popular method of providing the necessary funds to pay estate taxes was to purchase life insurance on each spouse. The wife would own the husband's policy and vice versa. Proceeds from each policy were used to pay the tax liability when the time came.

While moderately effective, this method was very costly for two reasons. First, each life had to be insured separately. And second, the vehicles used at that time were expensive whole life policies.

Let's compare the cost of purchasing two separate $500,000 policies on each of two spouses to the cost of purchasing a single $1 million joint and survivor plan. (See Figure 21.8.) We assume each spouse is 65 years old and wishes to have the insurance premium (based on current assumptions) cease in ten years.

As Figure 21.8 illustrates, the last survivor plan is far less expensive. In our example, it's $151,561 less expensive!

After ERTA 1981 and the introduction of the unlimited marital deduction, many couples simply insured the youngest spouse. Obviously, they did this because taxes were not due until the surviving spouse died and insuring only the youngest spouse is much less costly than insuring both individually. In most cases, however, a joint and survivor policy is still the most cost effective method to secure estate liquidity for married couples.

FIGURE 21.8 JS Plans Can Save You Money

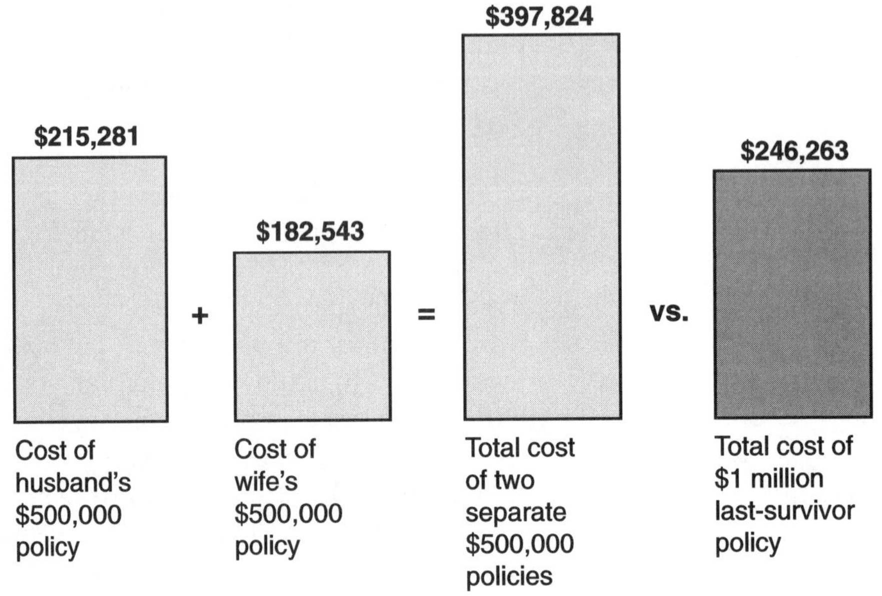

Summary

For many families, the payment of estate taxes, both federal and state, is an ominous obstacle that devours a major portion of their inheritance. The whole affair can be a nightmare; but with proper planning, it doesn't have to be a disaster. We can beat the politicians at their own game.

In summary, for a small fraction of your gross estate value or your interest earnings, the discounted dollar plan will:

- Allow your heirs to inherit your estate virtually intact
- Reduce your effective 46 percent estate tax bracket to almost nothing
- Pay your heirs proceeds totally income, capital gains, and estate tax free
- Pay your heirs proceeds free of probate and free from creditors' claims
- Allow your beneficiaries to pay your estate taxes at 2 to 30 cents on the dollar—a bona fide discount

FIGURE 21.9 Graphic Summary of the Main Benefit of the Discounted Dollar Plan

Which Check Would You Rather Use to Pay Your Estate Tax?

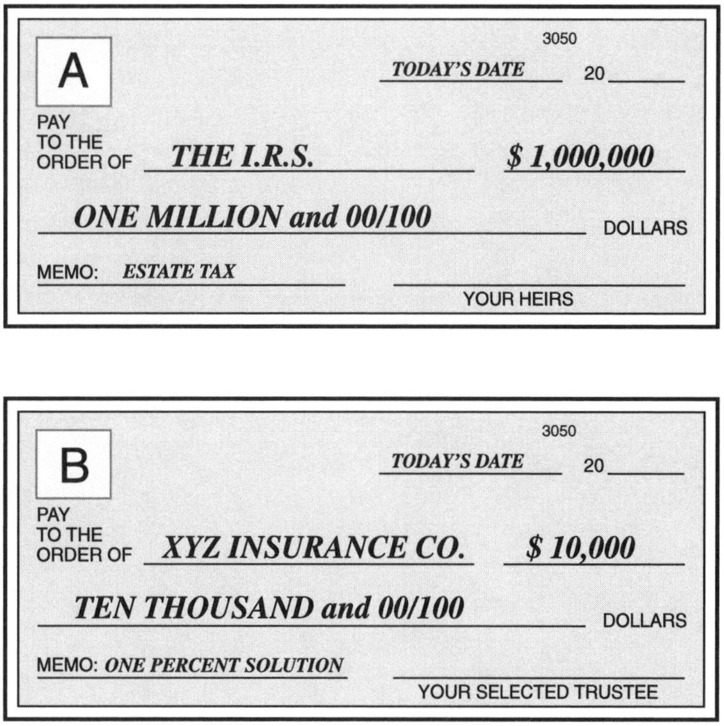

A
3050
TODAY'S DATE 20____
PAY TO THE ORDER OF THE I.R.S. $ 1,000,000
ONE MILLION and 00/100 DOLLARS
MEMO: ESTATE TAX
YOUR HEIRS

B
3050
TODAY'S DATE 20____
PAY TO THE ORDER OF XYZ INSURANCE CO. $ 10,000
TEN THOUSAND and 00/100 DOLLARS
MEMO: ONE PERCENT SOLUTION
YOUR SELECTED TRUSTEE

The Choice Is Obvious!

Figure 21.9 provides a graphic summary of the discounted dollar plan. There is simply no other money management vehicle available anywhere that offers such phenomenal benefits, strong rates of return, and superb leverage. The discounted dollar plan is the only means to effectively preserve your assets intact for your heirs, protecting the lifetime of hard work and dreams your estate represents.

CHAPTER

22

The Spousal Support Irrevocable Life Insurance Trust

A New Estate Planning Strategy with Exit Doors

The Flexible Spousal Support ILIT

A properly drafted irrevocable life insurance trust is the cornerstone of a good estate plan. While married couples create ILITs to replace income in the event of an untimely death, pay estate taxes, and equalize inheritances among children, they are often criticized as inflexible. A common complaint is that both husband and wife lose the ability to access the cash value of the life insurance policy during their lifetime. Because of this major misconception, however, many people fail to take advantage of the powerful financial leverage life insurance offers in proper estate planning. Life insurance is the only financial instrument that allows the purchase of dollars tomorrow for pennies today, and with the advent of the extremely flexible spousal support ILIT also known as the Smart Trust, continuous control of the cash build up is now a reality.

A single life insurance policy is often purchased to protect the family of the primary income earner against premature death. Such policies are usually owned by the insured or the insured's spouse. However, outright ownership of a life insurance policy by either party creates an includible asset in the estate, subject to estate taxes. In situations where the size of the total estate creates estate tax issues, the spousal support ILIT is the perfect tool.

The Single Life Spousal ILIT Strategy

A Spousal Support ILIT is simply an irrevocable life insurance trust that is drafted with enough flexibility to meet the needs of the grantor's family by allowing the trustee to make distributions to the insured's spouse and children while the insured is still alive. Such a trust gives the insured's spouse access to the policy's cash value during the insured's lifetime, while keeping the property out of both spouses' estate. It is a great hedge against potential changes in tax law and provides potential tax-favored access to policy cash value in the event of changes in family finances. A Single-Life Spousal ILIT is best explained by looking at the following example:

Gordon Crosby (age 45), a father of five, creates a single-life spousal ILIT that obtains a variable universal life policy, with an insurance benefit of $1 million on his life. Gordon will make annual exclusion gifts to the trust of $60,000 for 20 years or age 65, and the trust will use those gifts to make premium deposits. If Gordon lives in a community property state, care must be taken to ensure that he uses his separate property to fund the ILIT. Gordon's wife, Caroline, and their children are permissible beneficiaries of the trust and the trustee has the discretionary power to make distributions to them for health, education, maintenance and support.

In many states, Caroline could be the trustee if Gordon so desires. But before naming the non-grantor spouse as sole trustee of a single-life spousal ILIT, legal counsel should review applicable state law. By making Caroline a beneficiary and possibly the trustee, she has maximum flexibility to make use of policy cash values during Gordon's lifetime. The trust retains plenty of flexibility to adjust to changes in tax law and family financial situations.

If the policy is maintained until Gordon's death, as anticipated, the trust will receive the death benefit free from both income and estate taxes. At Gordon's retirement at age 65, the death benefit, assuming a 10% annual gross return will be in excess of $4 million and at his life expectancy of age 78, the insurance benefit would soar to more than $8 million.

What if by some miracle the estate tax is repealed before Gordon's death? Has the creation of the Spousal ILIT been detrimental to the financial security of Gordon and his family? Absolutely not. Listed below are some of the highlights.

- **Income Replacement in the Event of Gordon's Premature Death.** Estate planning would be easy if we knew when we were going to leave this earth. Gordon, like most of us, assumes that he will live a long and happy life. After all, he is wealthy and has access to the best health care in the world. But, is Gordon so certain of his longevity that he wants to bet the financial security of his family on it? If he dies early and his annual salary stopped, could his wife and children maintain their standard of living? Are Gordon and his wife and children willing to bet their financial security on him living to a ripe old age?
- **Supplemental Retirement Income.** Based on a gross annual return of 10% in the variable universal life contract, the life insurance contract owned by the ILIT will have a net cash surrender value of over $800,000 in year 10 and is projected to grow to $4.2 million by year 25 or age 65. If Caroline needs cash along the way, or the couple

would like to increase their retirement income, distributions can be taken from the policy without taxation in an amount equal to the premiums deposited. After that, cash value can be accessed by taking zero cost loans from the policy.

- **Tax-Free Death Benefit Available to Spouse.** Upon Gordon's death, the ILIT will receive the death benefit free from both income and estate taxes. If Caroline survives Gordon, the ILIT will not terminate until her death. Caroline and the children will remain permissible beneficiaries until her subsequent death when the ILIT will terminate and the remaining principal will pass to the children. At Caroline's death, assets remaining in the trust will not be included in her estate.

Survivorship Strategy

With few differences, a Spousal Support ILIT can be utilized with a joint and survivor policy. Unlike the single life strategy, neither spouse can serve as trustee of a survivorship spousal ILIT. When using this technique careful consideration should be given to which spouse will be the grantor of the trust and which spouse will be the permissible beneficiary. Ordinarily, it appears most advantageous to name the spouse with the longest life expectancy as beneficiary.

When creating a survivorship spousal ILIT, two common strategies are implemented to address the possibility that the grantor spouse will be the first to die, leaving no one alive who is able to pay the premiums without tax consequences.

First, consider changing the will or living trust of the grantor spouse to leave his or her remaining applicable estate tax exclusion (currently $2 million). If there is considerable remaining credit at the death of the grantor spouse, future premium payments can be paid from this amount. And by leaving this amount to the survivorship spousal ILIT, the need for a credit shelter trust is avoided. After all, the surviving spouse and children are the beneficiaries of the ILIT so there is no need to create another trust to hold the remaining estate tax exclusion.

Second, consider owning a small term life insurance policy on the life of the grantor spouse inside of the spousal support ILIT. If the husband is the grantor spouse and the wife is a permissible beneficiary, consider purchasing the survivorship life insurance on a "short pay basis", such as 15 or 20 years. Then have the trustee use the term policy with the same duration on the life of the husband to be used to pay premium payments in the event of the husband's premature death.

The survivorship spousal ILIT is an effective hedge against estate and gift tax repeal. One of the spouses can retain access to the cash value during his or her life and death benefit protection is available for the security of the family.

To further explore the incredible leverage life insurance can create in estate planning, refer to Chapter 21. By making ILITs flexible, access to the policy's cash value can be available for the family's lifetime needs without causing the death benefit to be subject to estate taxes at the death of either spouse. Spousal support ILITs can be relatively simple, but yet are often overlooked when planning one's estate.

CHAPTER

23 Premium Finance

Where to Find the Premium

Using Funds from a Lending Institution to Pay Life Insurance Premiums

One of the greatest obstacles in proper estate planning is finding the necessary cash flow to pay the required premiums to fund the life insurance required to pay the estate taxes at a discount. For whatever reason, people are sometimes more willing to allow their heirs to pay the taxes with liquidated assets at a huge loss than prefund the taxes at a true discount. This is especially true of large estates, $10 million and up.

Among the concerns is the extraction of assets from the portfolio to create the cash to pay the premium. Once money is spent, it is gone. Once assets are sold, they are gone. Wouldn't it be ideal if a lending institution would make the premium payments via a loan and the insured would only be required to pay the interest on the loan? Wouldn't it be ideal if the interest payments were made from the eventual net death benefit?

Such a concept is a reality and known as premium finance. In effect with this concept, the policy owner borrows the premium from a third party and typically pays interest only on the borrowed amount. Nonrecourse premium finance uses the policy itself as collateral for the loan against the premiums.

A premium finance loan enables individuals to obtain life insurance without tying up or expending large amounts of cash. The arrangement also allows flexibility at the end of the loan for the owner to either keep the policy and pay off the loan, settle the policy or (in the case of nonrecourse loans) walk away from the policy at the end of the loan term and have no further obligation.

Premium Financing Is Most Appropriate for the Wealthy

Premium financing is most appropriate for wealthy individuals or families who need significant amounts of life insurance protection for estate conservation, business succession and/or wealth accumulation strategies, but who do not want to liquidate personal assets to fund the insurance premiums.

In a typical premium financing scenario, the insured only pays the interest due on the premium loan each year and at a later date will pay off the loan from either a retained capital account, policy cash values, or death benefit.

Use of LIBOR (London Interbank Offered Rate)

Premium financing is subject to interest rate risk. The LIBOR (London Interbank Offered Rate) is used in most institutional funded plans and there is no guarantee that the LIBOR rate will continue to be reasonable. Because the loan rates are adjusted annually, it is possible that the rates could become considerable higher in only a few years.

Generally, the lender will require interest payments annually at the beginning of each year, although consideration can be given on a case-by-case basis to interest payments made in arrears. Lenders will generally accept the insurance policy as collateral for the loan although there may be a need for additional collateral or personal guarantees as the circumstances dictate. Loans may be paid back during lifetime or at the death of the insured.

Premium financing is a viable and innovative way of providing a source for insurance premiums. It is particularly effective in a low-interest-rate environment.

CHAPTER

24

College 529 Savings Plans

Educate Your Posterity and Reduce Your Estate

EGTRRA 2001 Provides Tax-Deferred Growth and Tax-Free Withdrawals

Today there are a few strategies left that we can implement to legally shift assets from one generation to another. We've already discussed several, such as the family limited partnership, utilization of the credit shelter trust, and the up-front use of the estate tax exclusion credit. In 1996, Congress approved Section 529 of the Internal Revenue Code, designed to help parents and grandparents establish aggressive college savings plans for their children and grandchildren (a 529 plan can actually be established for anyone). Initially the reception was lukewarm, primarily because savers had to use state-specific plans and even though the funds compounded tax deferred, withdrawals were taxed to the student.

That all changed in 2001, when, as a tagalong to the Economic Growth and Tax Relief Reconciliation Act, Congress provided that not only was growth inside 529 plans tax deferred, but all withdrawals for tuition, fees, books, supplies, on-and off-campus room and board, and even expenses for special needs students were tax-free. This spurred significant growth, so by the end of 2005, 529 college savings assets had grown to over $68 billion.

Under current law $12,000 ($24,000 per couple) can be gifted from one estate to another, gift tax-free. Under EGTRRA, up to five years' of the current exemption can be specifically gifted into a 529 plan without triggering the federal gift tax. That's currently $60,000 per person or $120,000 per couple. Additional tax-free gifts can be made in the sixth year. These gifts will not count against your lifetime federal estate tax exclusion.

Manage Each Account

The 529 college savings investment trusts are now very broad, with John Hancock Life Insurance Company leading the way through its Education Trust of Alaska. Not only can 529 plans help provide funds for a college education, with the new trusts, donors can now make decisions on how to manage their account. Furthermore, they can decide on how the money is spent when withdrawals are made, and to whom the check is made payable. If college plans change, the donor can change the beneficiary and even though contributions are totally removed from the estate, the donor can maintain control of the assets as long as he or she is the account holder. This gives great control while making extremely useful gifts to current and potential students.

Required Minimum Distributions from IRA Funds

Many 529 donors are using their required minimum distributions (RMD) from IRA accounts to benefit their grandchildren and great-grandchildren. Often we hear from retirees age $70^1/_2$ and beyond that they really don't need their RMD for living expenses. By gifting all or a portion of this income you are simply feeding education to your posterity for endless generations. (It is important to note that nonqualified withdrawals from IRA accounts are allowed, but they are taxable and subject to a 10 percent federal tax penalty if accessed prior to age $59^{1/2}$).

The generous tax-free withdrawal provisions of EGTRRA were set to expire on December 31, 2010. However, with the passage of the Pension Protection Act of 2006, the favorable tax privileges have been indefinitely extended.

In view of the fact that college expenses are on the rise, the 529 college savings plan is not only an excellent way to further build a legacy and a generation of educated heirs, it is another excellent way to shift assets from one estate to another while maintaining control.

FIGURE 24.1 College 529 Plans

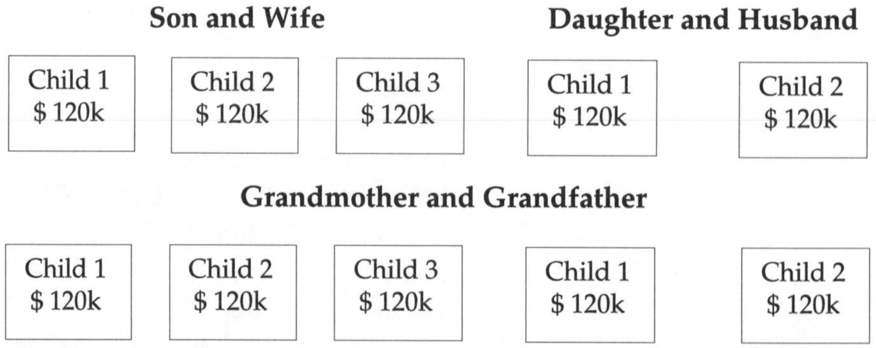

Son and Wife | **Daughter and Husband**

Child 1	Child 2	Child 3	Child 1	Child 2
$ 120k	$ 120k	$ 120k	$ 120k	$ 120k

Grandmother and Grandfather

Child 1	Child 2	Child 3	Child 1	Child 2
$ 120k	$ 120k	$ 120k	$ 120k	$ 120k

$ 360 k from Son and Wife
$ 240 k from Daughter and Husband
$ 600 k to each of the Grandchildren from the Grandparents

CHAPTER 25

Charitable Giving and the Wealth Replacement Trust

The Only Remaining Tax Shelters

The government is in no position to take on the additional burden of funding charitable institutions and the vast services they perform.

Charitable giving has evolved into one of the premier strategies in estate and financial planning. Today, 90 percent of all charitable gifts come from the private sector. Most likely you are already making contributions to your favorite charity.

The tax laws governing charitable deductions have been in existence for a long time. The only changes to the law have been the use of current mortality tables and adjustable discount rates in determining the charitable deduction. With an increasing national deficit, it is unlikely that the government will ever disallow the current tax-favored status of charitable giving. Very simply, the government is in no position to take on the additional burden of funding charitable institutions and the vast services they perform.

When to Consider Charitable Giving as an Estate Planning Tool

If you have any of the following characteristics, you might consider charitable giving even though you might not have charitable intent:

- You own highly appreciated, low-basis, and low-yielding property.
- You have a desire to reduce your estate tax liability.
- You wish to keep an appreciated asset in the family.
- You want to avoid capital gains tax on the sale of highly appreciated assets.
- You need to shift income or asset value to another family member.
- You want tax-favored income.
- You desire a current income tax deduction.
- You need a cost-effective way to pay estate taxes.

The desire to achieve even one of these objectives will in most cases also provide benefits in one or more of the other areas.

The Use of the Wealth Replacement Trust in Charitable Gifting

When assets are gifted to a charity, whether outright or in trust, the charity becomes the ultimate owner of these assets. At death, heirs or other beneficiaries cannot inherit these assets, which is why there is often reluctance in gifting significant assets, especially when the potential donor lacks the knowledge to fully appreciate the power of the union between estate planning and charitable planning.

The **wealth replacement trust (WRT)** is an irrevocable life insurance trust (ILIT) that holds an amount of life insurance to replace for heirs, assets that are gifted to charity. The reasons for making gifts to charity may have nothing to do with your concern for the charity. The enormous tax advantages (income tax, capital gains tax, and federal estate tax advantages) gained by the donor are often the primary reason people consider charitable gifting.

Charitable Gifting Techniques

This is one of the few areas today where everyone wins!

The purpose of the following examples and figures is to provide you with a description of each technique; show the cash flows that can be generated; and illustrate how you can reduce your federal estate tax liability, avoid capital gains tax, receive an income tax deduction, and increase your income by means of charitable gifting. This is one of the few areas today where everyone wins!

The Charitable Remainder Unitrust (CRUT)

The **charitable remainder unitrust (CRUT)** is designed to pay an annual income to one or more noncharitable beneficiaries for a set period of time or for their lifetimes. At the end of the designated period, the assets in the trust are transferred to one or more charitable organizations specified by the donor.

The amount of income paid to the noncharitable beneficiaries each year is determined by multiplying the value of the trust assets, calculated annually, by a percentage rate that is determined when the trust is created. The minimum percentage must be at least 5 percent, with the maximum at 10 percent, and may not be changed. Therefore, the amount of each annual payment to the beneficiaries may vary based on annual fluctuations in the value of the trust and the investment performance of the trustee.

When an individual creates a CRUT, he or she receives a current income tax deduction that is equal to the present value of the future interest ultimately passing to the charity. The tax deduction is subject to certain limitations.

The amount of the charitable deduction is controlled by the following factors:

- The type of charity
- The type of asset or property donated
- The payout rate elected at the creation of the unitrust
- The term of years in which income is to be paid to the beneficiaries and the *annual contribution base* (adjusted gross income) and additional charitable donations

As previously explored, to preserve the *value* of the asset donated to a charity for the heirs of the donor, an insurance policy is purchased to replace all or part of the value of the asset. The premium for the policy can be paid from the donor's newfound income and from the tax savings the unitrust generates. The policy is applied for and purchased by an irrevocable trust to avoid inclusion in the donor's estate. Therefore, the entire value of the life insurance proceeds pass tax-free to heirs. Because the ILIT replaces the donated assets, it is considered to be a wealth replacement trust. Figure 25.1 illustrates the use of a CRUT in combination with a wealth replacement trust.

Another form of charitable remainder trust, the **charitable remainder annuity trust (CRAT),** will be discussed later in this chapter.

One of the primary benefits in considering the use of the charitable remainder trust is the benefit of avoiding capital gains tax. Appreciated assets that are transferred to a charitable trust and sold by the trust avoid capital gains tax. Since the passage of the Taxpayers Relief Act of 1997, the capital gains tax rate for long-term capital gains assets decreased to a high of (federal) 15 percent. Even though the net capital gains tax is significantly lower than in previous years, the avoidance of this now lesser tax is still significant. Note: Many states impose their own capital gains tax, which should also be considered.

■ Example

Sam Peterson is 64 and plans to retire next year. Mary, his wife, is also 64 and is currently involved in charitable work. Mary has not been employed in a professional capacity outside the home. Sam has been employed by, and is now a senior executive with, a large corporation for the past 25 years. Sam's current salary is $135,000 a year, but his pension with the company will only provide him $50,000 per year before taxes. Sam knows he and his wife will need more than his pension on which to live.

With a total estate in excess of $3 million, Sam and Mary's children will not have to pay estate taxes if they establish a credit shelter trust. Sam and Mary plan to leave a portion of their estate to their church and the remainder

FIGURE 25.1 Combination of a Charitable Remainder Unitrust and a Wealth Replacement Trust

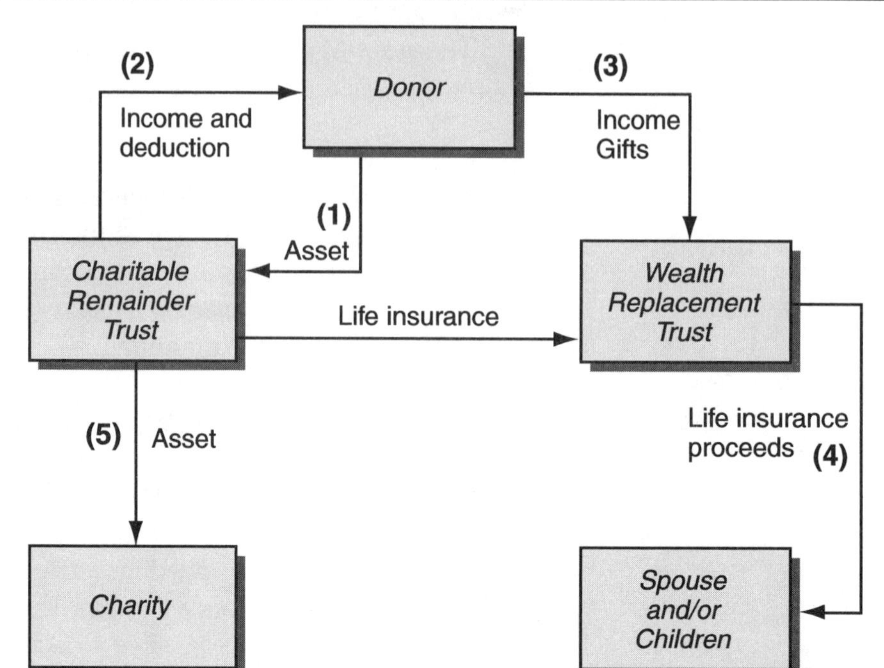

1. The donor transfers the asset(s) to the charitable remainder unitrust and avoids capital gains tax on the sale of the asset(s).
2. The donor receives an income tax deduction and income from the trust.
3. The donor gifts part of the income to the wealth replacement trust for the purchase of life insurance.
4. When the donor dies, the life insurance replaces the amount that was gifted to the CRUT.
5. At death of the last beneficiary, the ultimate CRUT value is transferred to the charity or charities.

to their three children. They are looking for ways to increase their current monthly income while still accomplishing their estate planning goals.

Sam owns a piece of non–income-producing real estate that has a current market value of $1 million. He purchased the land 25 years ago for $100,000; and no debt is associated with the land.

Sam would like to sell the land and reinvest the cash. He knows there would be a substantial capital gains tax to be paid, both federal and state of 20 percent of the gain—the estimated tax is $180,000—which would only leave $820,000 to reinvest for additional retirement income. In addition, the amount he could leave to his children and church would be reduced by the $180,000.

Sam and Mary's goals are to

- avoid the capital gains tax on the sale of the property,
- provide additional retirement income, and
- maximize the amount of the estate passing to their heirs and the church.

A CRUT will achieve all the goals Sam and Mary have established.

How the Goals Are Accomplished

Avoid the capital gains tax. Sam and Mary establish a CRUT with the help of an estate planning specialist (quarterback) and an estate planning attorney. They then gift the property to the trust. The CRUT sells the land for $1 million. Because the property was sold by the CRUT, no capital gains tax is paid; creating an immediate savings of $180,000 in capital gains tax avoidance.

Provide additional retirement income. The trust Sam and Mary establish is designed to pay them an annual income for as long as either of them is alive. The trust has $1 million to be invested. They elect that the trust should pay them 8 percent annually. Sam and Mary now have an additional income of $80,000 per year, before taxes, to supplement their retirement income. As the $1 million investment increases through the years, their income will increase as well. For example, if the account increases to $1.5 million, their 8 percent annual income will jump to $120,000. Whether Sam predeceases Mary or Mary predeceases Sam, this stream of income will continue on to the survivor for his or her lifetime.

Maximize the amount of the estate passing to beneficiaries. The CRUT will terminate when the survivor dies, at which time the remaining value of the trust will pass directly to their church without tax consequences. Sam and Mary have also used a portion of the annual income and tax savings created by the gift to purchase a $1 million joint and last survivor policy, which is owned by an irrevocable trust with their children as the beneficiaries. The children therefore will receive $1 million totally tax-free to replace the asset given to the charity.

Additional Benefits

By gifting the property, Sam and Mary have removed $1 million from their taxable estate and avoided estate taxes on that amount should the estate tax exclusion be reduced. In addition, they receive a significant current income tax deduction for the charitable gift portion of the trust. If they are unable to fully deduct all of the income tax deduction for their contribution base, they can carry the excess forward for up to five years.

FIGURE 25.2 Benefits of the CRUT for Donors Sam and Mary Peterson versus Outright Sale of Property

We have used the following assumptions:
Value of the property donated: $1,000,000
Amount Sam paid for the property: $100,000
Trust rate of return: 8%
Trust payout rate: 8%
Payments to be made: annually
Income tax bracket: 28%
Capital gains tax bracket: 20%
Federal estate tax bracket: 50%
Sam's age on the date of the gift: 64
Mary's age on the date of the gift: 64

	Outright Sale	**CRUT**	**Difference**
Asset value	$1,000,000	$1,000,000	$ 0
(–) Capital gains tax	180,000	0	180,000
(+) Tax savings	0	65,520	65,520
(=) Net to invest	820,000	1,065,520	245,520
Average investment income	47,232	61,374	14,142
(×) Number of years	20	20	20
(=) Total net income	944,640	1,227,480	282,840
(–) WRI* premium	0	175,000	175,000
(=) Net spendable income	944,640	1,052,480	107,840
Asset value in the estate	820,000	0	820,000
(–) Estate tax	410,000	0	410,000
(+) Appreciation	0	0	0
(+) WRI* benefits	0	1,000,000	1,000,000
(=) Net to heirs	410,000	1,000,000	410,000
(+) Future gift to charity	0	1,000,000	1,000,000
(=) Total benefits	$1,354,640	$3,052,480	$1,287,840

*WRI = wealth replacement insurance.

Figure 25.2 summarizes Sam and Mary's CRUT, illustrates the benefits the CRUT creates, and compares the benefits of the CRUT with the alternative of selling the asset and reinvesting the proceeds. An additional use of the CRUT is to fund for retirement using the tax-favored aspects of the CRUT with the ability to make a large gift to your favorite charity.

Reducing Estate Taxes by Using a CRUT

Another strategic use of the CRUT is for the reduction of estate taxes.

■ Example

Bill Maxwell is 67, and his wife, Linda, is 66. Bill is retired and has an adjusted gross income of $750,000 per year. Their lifestyle is such that they spend almost all of their income. Their estate is valued at $10 million.

Bill and Linda plan to leave their estate to their three children. They also plan to leave a piece of land to the university where Bill and Linda met. The land is worth $1 million and has a cost basis of $200,000, but it is not developed and does not produce an income.

Bill and Linda know that 27 percent of their estate will be eroded by estate taxes. They have put off any planning, but now they are at the age where they realize their own mortality and are wanting to discuss their planning options.

Their goals are to

- *maintain their current level of spendable income,*
- *reduce the size of their taxable estate,*
- *initiate a cost-effective way to pay estate settlement costs, and*
- *make a substantial gift to Bill's alma mater.*

These goals will be met by their making a deferred gift of the land to the university using a CRUT rather than waiting until their death.

How the Goals Are Accomplished

Maintain current level of spendable income. Bill and Linda create a CRUT and gift the piece of raw land to the trust. The trust sells the land and pays no capital gains tax. Because the land produced no income and thus no tax had to be paid, there has been no effect on their net spendable income.

Reduce the size of their taxable estate. By gifting the land to the trust, the value of their estate has been reduced by $1 million plus any future appreciation the land may have had, resulting in a corresponding reduction in estate taxes.

Initiate a cost-effective way to pay estate settlement costs. Having created the CRUT, Bill and Linda have provided a new source of additional cash flow to fund their estate liquidity needs.

The cash flow, which is made up of the tax savings and all the income to Bill and Linda from the trust, is gifted to an irrevocable trust. The trustee uses the gift to purchase a life insurance policy. In most cases, the irrevocable trust would be the beneficiary of the life insurance and would use the proceeds to pay the estate taxes.

Make a substantial gift to Bill's alma mater. The trust assets will pass to the university when both Bill and Linda have died. Should the trustee's investment performance exceed a 9 percent yield, the gift to the university could be well in excess of $1 million.

The objectives in designing the trust are to maximize the cash flow generated and purchase as much joint and survivor life insurance coverage as possible. We assume a 9 percent before-tax yield and examine the effects on the cash flow by varying the number of years the trust runs. Our example in Figure 25.3 includes joint lives, one life and 17 years certain, and a ten-year term. Years certain is the guaranteed number of years the trust would pay out to the creator or other beneficiaries.

Example of Maximizing a Charitable Gift

John and his wife, Mary, are both 45 years old. They have a joint income of $58,000 per year. Several years ago, one of their children was critically ill. Thanks to the assistance of the local children's hospital, their child has fully recovered and leads a normal life.

John and Mary want to repay the hospital for its help with their child. They decide to begin making cash contributions to the hospital on an annual basis. Their gift currently is $1,800 per year. They would like to do more for the hospital, but their funds are limited.

John wants to make an ultimate gift of $100,000 to the hospital using an insurance policy on his life. He asks the hospital to use his annual gift to pay premiums for the life insurance policy. The hospital is owner and beneficiary of the policy, but John still receives his current deduction for the gift. The policy is designed so that based on current interest assumptions, it will require only ten premium payments.

The after-tax cost of the plan to John will be $12,960 over a ten-year period, and the ultimate gift to the charity will be $100,000.

WARNING

Some states will not allow the type of gift John made because of the insurable interest question. Please check with the charity or an estate planning attorney before making this type of transaction.

FIGURE 25.3 Comparison of Alternative Trust Periods for Sample CRUT

	Rem. Unitrust	**Rem. Unitrust**	**Rem. Unitrust**
Assumptions	Technique #1	Technique #2	Technique #3
Time period projected			
Income payout rate			
Income paid	annually	annually	annually
Investment period measured by	2 lives	1 life/17 yrs.	10 yrs.
Contributions			
Fair market value of property	$1,000,000	$1,000,000	$1,000,000
Income tax deduction	247,290	211,350	431,372
Capital gains tax on sale	0	0	0
Cash Flow			
Income during life	1,337,755	1,133,970	741,976
(–) Out-of-pocket premiums	92,530	92,530	92,530
(–) Premiums paid by reinvesting	1,272,955	1,068,492	676,498
(+) Net spendable income	(27,730)	(27,502)	(27,502)
Estate for Heirs*			
Gross value of estate	0	0	0
(+) Life insurance death benefit	4,740,561	4,266,212	3,750,932
(–) Estate taxes	0	0	0
(=) Net estate for heirs	4,740,561	4,266,212	3,750,932
Benefit Summary			
Net income + net estate			
(=) Total family benefit	4,712,831	4,239,160	3,723,880
(+) Endowment to charity	1,000,000	1,035,352	1,035,352
(=) Total benefit	$5,712,831	$5,274,512	$4,759,232

*Estate for heirs assumes estate tax exclusion not taken.

Additional Charitable Giving Tools

The previous sections have dealt specifically with charitable giving techniques in which life insurance is used as an integral part of the plan to replace the value of the gifted asset and was referred to as the *wealth replacement trust.* In this section, charitable giving techniques are discussed that can, but do not necessarily, involve the use of life insurance with the wealth replacement trust. *It is important to be familiar with these other concepts as they too are a viable part of charitable giving and estate planning strategies.*

Grantor Charitable Lead Unitrust

A *grantor charitable lead unitrust* is designed to pay an annual income equal to a fixed percentage of the net fair market value of the trust assets, valued annually, to a qualified charity for a period of years or the lifetime of one or more individuals. At the end of the designated payout period, the assets that had been generating annual income to the charity revert to a noncharitable beneficiary or beneficiaries.

To determine the amount of income to be paid to the charity, the annual fair market value of the trust assets is multiplied by a fixed percentage. For example, a gift of stock valued on the annual valuation date at $100,000 multiplied by a 5 percent payout rate equals $5,000 paid that year to the qualified charity:

$$\$100{,}000 \times .05 = \$5{,}000$$

This form of a charitable lead trust can provide the donor with a large charitable contribution deduction in the year the trust is funded for ascertaining the fair market value of the assets on the date of the transfer into the trust minus the present value of the remainder interest. However, there is a cost for getting such a large deduction in a given year and designating the noncharitable remainder beneficiaries: the income that is payable to the charity must be included as taxable income (for income tax purposes) by the donor each year. For individuals with large incomes, a grantor charitable lead unitrust provides substantial income tax savings in a current year. The deduction can be used to offset up to 30 percent of the donor's contribution base with a five-year carryover available for any deduction amount that could not be used in the year of the contribution.

For individuals with large incomes, a grantor charitable lead unitrust provides substantial income tax savings in a current year.

Example of the grantor charitable lead trust. Stephen Lewis has worked for almost 30 years for a computer company. He is a cofounder and major shareholder of the company. Four years ago, the company developed a system for the personal computer market that had Wall Street believing it could be a major player in the computer field. Since becoming a public corporation two years ago, Stephen's stock has grown from a value of just over $2 million to a recent valuation of $25 million, which represents 40 percent of the outstanding shares, or 400,000 shares. The stock pays $4.38 per share in dividends. Stephen and Elaine have three grown children and would like to make gifts of some or all of the stock to them and/or their grandchildren, but they want to minimize the gift tax consequences. Stephen's salary from the corporation this year will be about $430,000. After this year (in addition to the income from the stock), Stephen will have a retirement income of $100,000 annually paid from his company's pension plan.

John and his wife are considering retirement at this time. They are looking at ways to plan for their retirement and at the same time minimize their

FIGURE 25.4 What the Grantor Charitable Lead Trust Can Accomplish

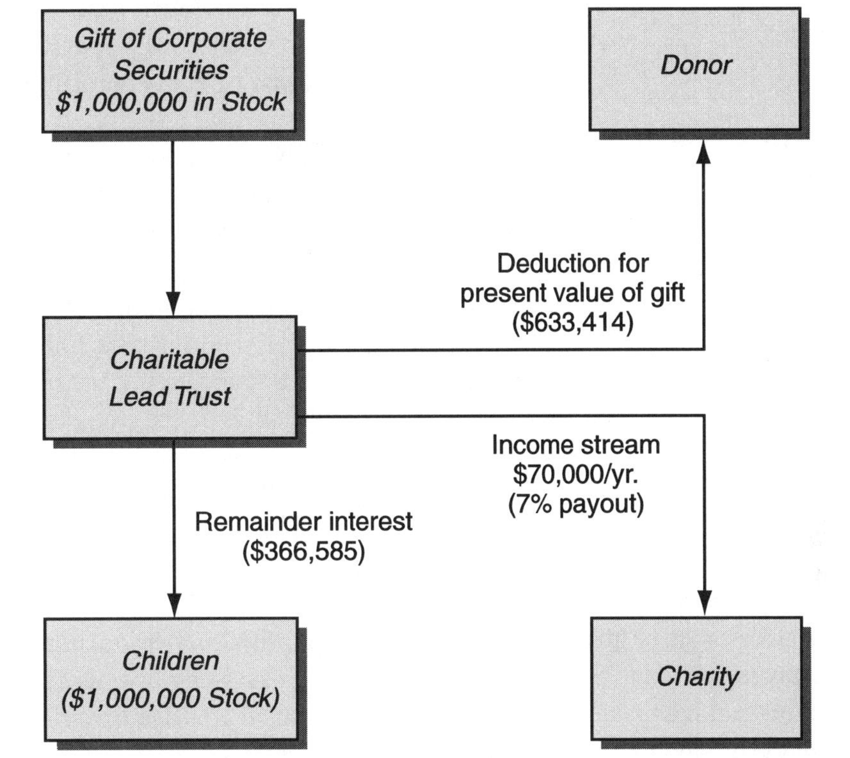

estate and income tax liabilities. One method is to establish a grantor charitable lead trust in which they would gift $1 million worth of stock to the trust.

By transferring $1 million in stock and providing a 7 percent (equivalent to the current dividend rate) income payout to a qualified charity for Stephen's lifetime (estimated by using a mortality table), they will receive a present-value charitable contribution deduction for the value of the income to be received by the charity ($633,414). The remainder of the trust then passes to their children, with a remainder interest value of $366,585.

Stephen's income this year is made up of his $430,000 salary plus stock income of $1,752,000 (400,000 shares $4.38/share), for a total of $2,182,000. By using the charitable gift arrangement, he receives a substantial deduction against his current adjusted gross income. He can use this to offset up to 30 percent of his contribution base and carry over anything in excess of this amount over the next five years. He can further increase his deduction if he decides to contribute even more shares of stock, but the amount of the deduction is still limited to 30 percent of his contribution base in the year of the gift. The "cost" of the large current deduction is that Stephen will be taxed under the grantor trust provisions of the Internal Revenue Code on the trust income as it is earned (as if he had received it).

Figure 25.4 illustrates what John has accomplished by means of this charitable gift arrangement.

Charitable Lead Annuity Trust

A nongrantor **charitable lead annuity trust** is designed to pay an annual income to a charity for a specified period of time, for the life of one or more individuals, or for a combination of the life of a person plus a specified time period. At the end of the agreement, the trust assets are transferred to individuals other than the donor. The trust can be created during a donor's lifetime or by his or her will.

The amount of income paid to the charity each year must be ascertained on the date the property is transferred. It usually is determined by multiplying the fair market value of the property transferred by the annuity rate, or may be a stated sum that is fixed at the time the trust is created. The same amount will be paid to the charity each year regardless of the fluctuations in the trust value or the investment performance of the trustee.

A nongrantor charitable lead trust does not provide the donor with an income tax charitable deduction. However, income generated by assets within the trust is not taxable as income to the donor, and the donor obtains a gift tax deduction for the present value of future income payable to the charity.

One purpose for creating a nongrantor charitable lead trust is to decrease, for estate or gift tax purposes, the value of the assets that will pass from the trust to the donor's heirs.

One purpose for creating a nongrantor charitable lead trust is to decrease, for estate or gift tax purposes, the value of the assets that will pass from the trust to the donor's heirs. If the remainder is irrevocably gifted to the donor's heirs, the actuarial value of the remainder on the date of the gift is includable in the donor's estate.

Example of the charitable lead annuity trust. Sam Watts has decided that his church's recent plea for income donations is something on which he should act. He currently owns $1 million of shares in his company's business that were purchased 20 years ago for $150,000. He ultimately wants the shares to pass to his three children but he has no current need for the income generated by them. To help make the church's budgeting process easier, Sam would like to promise a fixed annual donation.

A charitable lead annuity trust might be the best solution for him. By transferring the stock with an appreciated value of $1 million to the trust and using an annuity rate of 7 percent, the trust can provide the church with an annual payment of $70,000.

At the end of the trust agreement, the stock will pass to Sam's three children at a decreased value for gift tax purposes of $536,950. (This represents a tax deduction of $463,050, which is the present value of the income interest paid to the charity during the trust years.) If the remainder is irrevocably gifted to the donor's heirs, the actuarial value of the remainder on the date of the gift is includable in the donor's estate.

Sam is able to provide a fixed income to his church during his lifetime and at death pass the value of his stock to his children at a discount. This plan is illustrated in Figure 25.5.

FIGURE 25.5 Example of Charitable Lead Annuity Trust

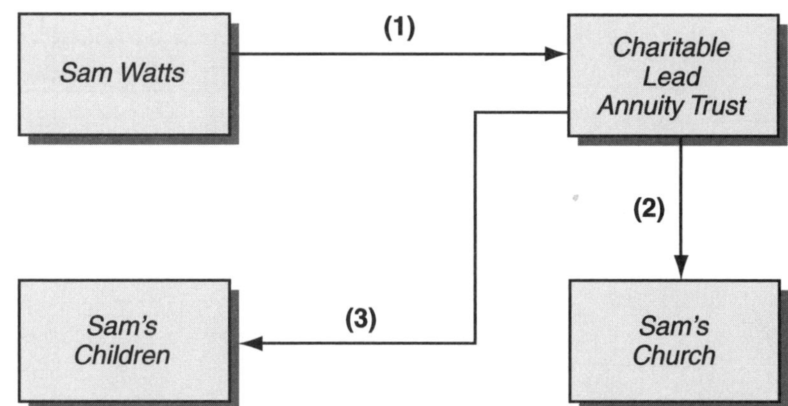

1. Sam transfers $1 million in stock to a charitable lead trust.
2. The trust pays an annual fixed income of $70,000 to Sam's church for his lifetime.
3. At the end of the agreement, assets pass to Sam's children at a discounted value for estate and gift tax purposes ($536,950). If the remainder is irrevocably gifted to the donor's heirs, the actuarial value of the remainder is includable in the donor's estate.

Charitable Remainder Annuity Trust (CRAT)

A *charitable remainder annuity trust* is designed to pay an annual income to one or more noncharitable beneficiaries for a specific amount of time that is no more than 20 years or for the length of the beneficiaries' lives. At the end of the agreement, the assets are transferred to the charity for its use.

The amount of annual income paid to the beneficiaries is determined by multiplying the fair market value of the asset transferred by the annuity rate. This amount is fixed at the time the trust is created but can be no less than 5 percent of the initial net fair market value of the property. The same amount of income will be paid to the beneficiaries each year regardless of fluctuations in the trust value or investment performance of the trustee.

The donor receives an income tax charitable deduction equal to the present value of the future gift that will go to the charity.

Example of the charitable remainder annuity trust. Irma Stricklin, the owner of a chain of dry cleaning stores, is wrestling with the dilemma of what to do with her sizable estate. She has never married. The thought of having a large portion of her estate go to the government for estate taxes makes her cringe. Irma is looking into ways to reduce the taxable

FIGURE 25.6 Example of Charitable Remainder Annuity Trust (CRAT)

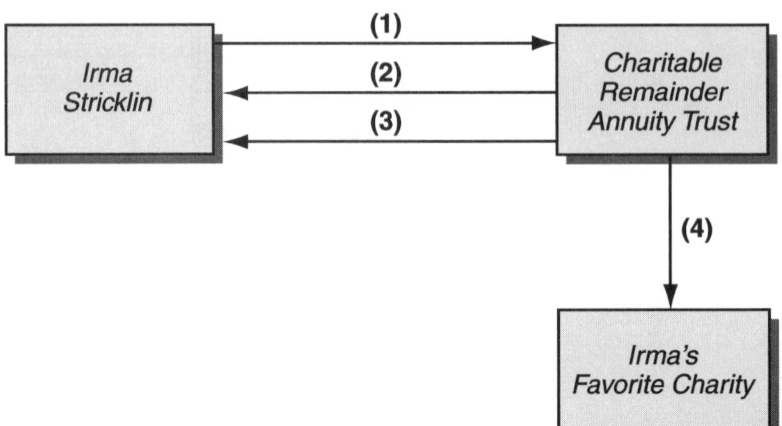

1. Irma gifts the land to a charitable remainder annuity trust for her favorite charity.
2. Irma receives an income tax deduction of $536,950.
3. Irma receives $70,000 annually for life.
4. At Irma's death, assets in trust pass to her favorite charity for its use.

size of her estate. She has recently read about the concept of charitable giving and wants to know if there is any way she can give to charity and still retain some of the benefit from her property for herself.

Irma has several pieces of property in her estate that she bought 25 years ago when she was thinking of expanding her dry cleaning empire. One particular piece of property is in a prime development location. She purchased it for only $100,000, and it now has a market value of $1 million.

Irma desires as much certainty in her future as possible. Thus, she considers a CRAT arrangement for her property.

By placing her property in a trust for her favorite charity and having the trust sell the property, Irma can avoid the capital gains tax on the property that she would have paid had she sold it herself. The trust's annuity arrangement will provide her with a fixed annual payment of $70,000 for her lifetime (based on a 7 percent annuity rate).

Irma will also receive an income tax deduction of $536,950 that she can carry forward for 5 years for the present value of her future gift that will go to charity, as illustrated in Figure 25.6.

Pooled Income Fund

With a *pooled income fund,* the assets of one or more donors are transferred to a trust fund maintained by the charity. The fund is designed to pay an annual income to the donors, including their living beneficiaries, for life. At the end of the agreement (the death of the last donor), the assets from the fund are turned over to the charity for its use.

FIGURE 25.7 Example of a Pooled Income Fund

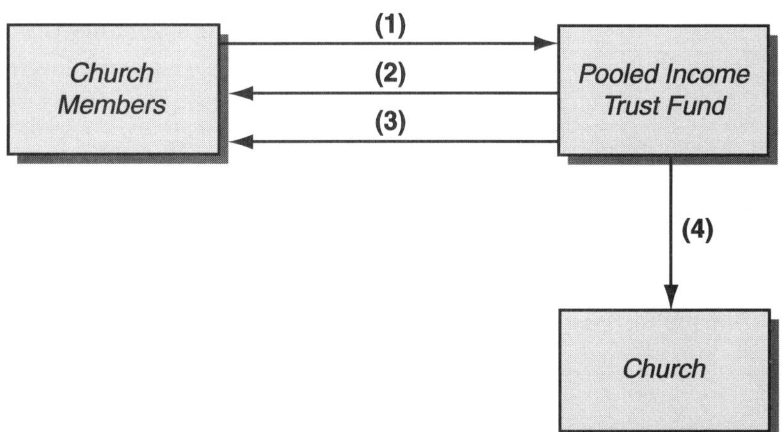

1. Church members gift assets to the pooled income trust fund.
2. Each member receives an income tax deduction for the present value of his or her future gift to the church.
3. Members receive an annual income for life that is based on the unit value of their gift.
4. The remaining value of the trust is passed to the church for its use at the final member's death.

The fund's annual investment performance and the proportion of the individual donor's contribution determine the amount of income paid to the donors each year.

When an individual makes a contribution to a pooled income fund, an income tax charitable deduction is allowed. It is equal to the present value at the date of transfer of the future gift that will go to the charity.

Example of the pooled income fund. Some members of the local Congregational church want to create a way for providing their church with future funding. These people are the charter members of the church, and they're concerned about what will happen after they're gone. They themselves are not in financial positions that would allow them to give large gifts. However, they feel that if there is a way for them to combine their resources, their total contribution could be quite substantial.

A pooled income fund is the best way to meet their objectives. Under this arrangement, each member donates cash or appreciated property to a pooled income trust fund in return for an income tax deduction. They also receive an income for life from the trust based on the value of their gift in proportion to the total trust. After the trust agreement ends at the death of the last donor, the funds are released to the church for its use. Figure 25.7 illustrates the pooled income fund.

The guidelines for establishing various charitable remainder trusts are complex, but the benefits are outstanding. The summary contained in Figure 25.8 outlines the various points of operation in establishing these trusts. The assistance of a professional is necessary when considering the use of this unique strategy.

FIGURE 25.8 Summary of Income Tax Deduction Rules for Charitable Gifts by Individuals

Annual Limit	Description
50% of contribution base	Includes contributions to public charities, certain private foundations, and governmental units (50% charities). Deductions for contributions to 50% charities are always taken first in the order of calculation.
30% of contribution base	Includes contributions to certain other private foundations and charitable organizations (30% charities). Contributions to 30% charities are always considered after those to 50% charities in the order of calculation. Can use this limit if you haven't used up 50% limit for the tax year. For example, donor deducts 15% for contribution to a 50% charity. Donor can deduct the full 30% for a subsequent contribution to a 30% charity.
Additional limits for capital gains property (Limits apply when you contribute more than your 20% to your annual contribution base.)	If you contribute certain appreciated capital gains property, your deduction will be subject to 30% and 20% limitations as follows: for contributions to 50% charities, your deduction is limited to 30% of your contribution base; for certain 30% charities, the limit is 20% of your contribution base. Special rules limit when these deductions can be made. There also are rules that provide for carryovers.
"For the use of" contributions	Deductions for contributions "for the use of"(rather than "to") 50% charities are limited as follows: the lesser of 30% of the annual contribution base or 50% of the contribution base minus the deductible contribution to 50% charities.
Contribution base	Generally, adjusted gross income for the year in which the contribution is made.
Order of calculations for deduction (You can deduct for contributions until your annual limit is reached.)	First, deduct your 50% charity limit; if your annual limit isn't reached, deduct your 30% capital gains property limit. Next, deduct your 30% charity limit. Finally, deduct your 20% capital gains property limit from your remaining annual limit, if any. For example, assume that you have an adjusted gross income of $60,000. You contribute $5,000 in cash and stock that is worth $20,000 to a 50% charity. You bought the stock two years ago for $5,000. In addition, you give $8,000 in cash to a 30% charity. Your annual 50% contribution limit is $30,000 (50% of $60,000). You deduct your $5,000 cash gift to the 50% charity. Next, you deduct $18,000 of your stock contribution,which is your 30% limit for a contribution of appreciated capital gains property, to a 50% charity (30% of $60,000). The remaining $2,000 for the stock contribution is carried over and can be applied next year to your 30% limit. Finally, you deduct $5,000 of the $8,000 cash gift to the 30% charity and carry over the remainder

FIGURE 25.8 Summary of Income Tax Deduction Rules for Charitable Gifts by Individuals (*Continued*)

Annual Limit	Description
	for use as a 30% limit deduction next year. The reason your 30% charity contribution is limited to $5,000 is that the amount of your remaining 50% contribution limit must be calculated as if you had deducted all of the $20,000 stock contribution instead of only $18,000 ($30,000 less $5,000 cash less $20,000 of stock equals $5,000 unused 50% contribution limit available for your 30% charity contribution).
Carryovers	You can carry over excess contributions for each of the five years after the year of your actual contribution. Carryovers are deducted, with the earliest year first, as follows: after actual gifts made to 50% charities are deducted, then 50% charity carryovers are deducted; if the 50% annual limit isn't used up, actual 30% charity gifts are deducted, then 30% charity carryovers are deducted.

Amount Deductible	Kind of Property
Full value	Cash or check; long-term stocks and most other long-term capital assets.
Donor's basis	Short-term stocks or other short-term assets; inventory and ordinary income property (includes life insurance policies). Long-term capital assets of tangible property if use by the donee is not related to charitable purpose of charity. Long-term assets to certain 30% charities.

CHAPTER

26

Private Foundations

The Ultimate Zero Estate Tax Plan

Very few of us realize that we can create and use private foundations either during our lifetime or at our death to gain significant income tax advantages and, more significantly, eliminate death taxes altogether.

Most of us are not strangers to the world of philanthropy. We have been asked to lend our name, time, and financial support to a number of charitable causes. Educational institutions, churches, hospitals, museums, and other organizations have benefited from our generosity. Some of us serve on boards of directors or advisory councils of charities. However, very few of us realize that we can create and use private foundations either during our lifetime or at our death to gain significant income tax advantages and, more significantly, eliminate death taxes altogether.

Tax incentives for establishing private foundations are enormous. Individuals or donors who make gifts to foundations during their lifetime can claim income tax deductions for their contributions. Cash contributions to a private foundation may be deducted at up to 30 percent of the donor's adjusted gross income. A donor may also contribute appreciated property, or capital assets on which capital gains tax would be paid if sold, to a private foundation. Appreciated property may be deducted at up to 20 percent of the donor's adjusted gross income when contributed to certain types of private foundations.

Sizable income tax deductions alone are a very tempting incentive for gifts or transfers to foundations during a donor's lifetime. *However, it is in the estate planning area that establishing a private foundation presents the greatest tax advantages.* At death, contributions or transfers to private foundations by outright bequest, will, trust, beneficiary designation, or other means are *fully deductible at 100 percent* for estate tax purposes. Depending on the size of your estate and the proportionate amount (legacy) left to a private foundation, transfers will substantially reduce the federal estate tax (50 percent in the highest estate tax bracket) or eliminate federal estate tax all together. For most estate holders, the ability to leave 100 percent of the estate's assets to a foundation or other qualified charities will eliminate or nearly eliminate all death tax!

The Zero Estate Tax Plan: A Potential Planning Opportunity

Consider leaving the current estate tax exclusion amount (currently $2 million per person, $4 million jointly for husband and wife) to heirs and the balance to a foundation to accomplish a zero estate tax plan. If you need to leave heirs additional amounts, consider further planning to include tax-free life insurance benefits as outlined in Chapter 21, "The Discounted Dollar Plan."

Those familiar with various tax structures point out that an individual may deduct direct cash contributions to publicly supported charities of up to 50 percent of adjusted gross income. While the tax benefits available to those who exercise their charitable intent exclusively through private foundations are sometimes smaller (30 percent), many donors realize major tax planning benefits by a combination of giving both to a private foundation and to public charities during both lifetime and deathtime planning.

The Unique Benefits of Private Foundations

A number of benefits, both social and personal, makes contributing to private foundations either during an individual's lifetime or at death a very special and appropriate investment into the future. Unlike a direct gift, which usually benefits one recipient on one occasion, a private foundation continues the donor's generosity for as long as it exists. Foundations can continue giving to more recipients over a longer period of time than can other types of charities.

Private foundations play a vital role in financing social, scientific, and cultural progress. They finance new ideas as society changes over time. It is the private foundation that can respond to new needs as they occur. One-time direct gifts do not provide this flexibility.

Several important personal benefits accrue to donors who establish private foundations. Many use private foundations as nonending tributes to loved ones, continuing memorials that are not set monuments but living, changing entities. Many donors also find that setting up a foundation is an effective means for organizing their charitable efforts and for regulating the amount given by other family members. A foundation is a system for giving that intervenes between the donor and potential recipients.

Who Should Consider Establishing a Foundation?

Not everyone should consider establishing a private foundation. However, for those individuals and families who want to have an impact not only in their own time and place but on the future, foundations can certainly contribute. When people operate a private foundation, they join the ranks of those who have not only voiced their concern for humanity but have translated this concern into action.

Individuals that establish foundations are predominantly

- wealthy individuals,
- individuals whose heirs are already well off,
- individuals with strict philanthropic motivation,
- individuals whose estates are subject to death tax and who would like to reduce their tax liability, and/or
- individuals who would like to favor charities instead of indemnifying the government through confiscatory estate taxation (death tax).

Size Considerations

Unless a certain amount of principal is available to generate funds for grant-making from the foundation, it may not be worthwhile to incur the costs of forming and operating a private foundation. There is no legal minimum on the amount that justifies establishing a foundation; however, there are some practical economies of scale and other general guidelines.

One economy of scale (measure) dictates that an annual minimum of $10,000 should be available for grant-making. The $10,000 amount may be generated by endowment, by annual contributions to the foundation, or by a combination of the two. Another guideline is that when an endowment is the sole source of grant-making funds, a minimum endowment of $250,000 may be an appropriate measure. However, to a large degree the amount necessary to justify a foundation depends solely on the donor's interests, objectives, and motivation in creating the foundation. Many small foundations (those well under $250,000) have been established to provide modest academic scholarships.

Three types of private foundations are widely recognized exceptions to the rules governing size. One is the "standby" foundation, which is set up to receive lifetime annual contributions and stands to receive a major bequest at a donor's death or on termination of a trust. Until then, the donor gains experience with management and grant-making procedures. The second exception is a "flow-through" foundation, which converts appreciated and/or real property into cash and immediately distributes the proceeds to publicly supported charities. The third exception is the "support organization," or "named fund," which is closely tied to a publicly supported organization or institution.

Surveys of existing private foundations show a range of assets from approximately $2 billion with annual grants of almost $150 million to small foundations with total assets of $200,000 or less and obviously small grants.

Surveys of existing private foundations show a range of assets from approximately $2 billion with annual grants of almost $150 million to small foundations with total assets of $200,000 or less and obviously small grants.

Types of Assets

The types of assets available to an individual or family that is considering establishing a private foundation play a part in determining what kind of foundation should be set up and whether a private foundation is an appropriate charitable outlet.

Stock in a Privately Held Corporation

Historically, such stock has accounted for almost one-half of all contributions to private foundations. When a foundation, together with its related persons, holds more than a 20 percent equity interest in a private corporation, special rules apply. The foundation must divest itself of its excess holdings within five years. In addition, payout requirements may cause liquidation of stock holdings when the dividend yield is less than 5 percent of the stock's market value. Generally, within these limits donors may make annual deductible contributions of stock up to 20 percent of their adjusted gross income.

Appreciated Property

Rules governing contributions of tangible or intangible appreciated property to private foundations are complex. When appreciated property is given to a grant-making foundation, a maximum deduction of 20 percent of adjusted gross income is allowed and there are no carryover privileges. Technical requirements are invoked when appreciated property is given to a flow-through, operating, or support foundation, and professional advice should be sought. (An operating foundation is defined below.)

Real Property

Donations of real property to a foundation are usually deductible up to 20 percent of the donor's adjusted gross annual income. Deductions of up to 30 percent may be allowed when the property is suited to a specialized use, such as ecological study or public recreation, and the donor elects to establish an operating foundation for the express purpose of using the land in a special fashion.

Whatever assets are donated, an independent appraisal is required to establish deductibility. The fair market value of the property must be determined by an independent appraisal for determining the allowable income tax deduction for an individual's contribution base.

Types of Foundations

Many fundraising organizations include the word *foundation* in their names. Many bear no relationship to private foundations, which exist to make grants for charitable, educational, or religious purposes, or, in some cases, to carry out such activities themselves. The major types of private foundations are discussed below.

Private operating foundations. As the name suggests, these are not primarily grant-making entities. They operate facilities or institutions devoted to a specific charitable activity spelled out in their charters. Some conduct research while others provide a direct service by operating museums, facilities for the handicapped, historical sites, and the like.

Corporate foundations. These are private grant-making foundations with close ties to the corporation that provides their funding. They are often flow-through foundations that use funds received last year to make grants this year. Philanthropic priorities are usually set by the chief executive officer of the corporation or by a committee appointed by the foundation's board of directors. Other corporate officers may serve as directors or trustees for the foundation.

Support foundations. Sometimes called named funds, these are foundations within a larger public charity or institution and are attractive alternatives for donors whose philanthropic activity of choice is already being served by a large public charity, institution, or community foundation. Support foundations, or named funds, are less administratively complex than independent, grant-making foundations because the public charity they benefit can assume many ongoing management responsibilities. Such foundations allow donors or donor families to maintain a continuing relationship with their chosen charitable enterprises. Although much grant-making discretion is lost, the donors can often exercise considerable control of the funds within a publicly supported organization or institution.

Community foundations. These are public charities supported not by any one donor or donor family but by the pooled contributions of a large number of individuals. The community foundation is a viable philanthropic outlet for donors who wish to serve the good of a particular community, and or would like the advantages of a private foundation, but without the costs. Community foundations usually confine their grant making to a specific locale, and decisions are made by trustees who represent a broad spectrum of the community's residents. The Cleveland Foundation and the Metropolitan Atlanta Community Foundation are examples of community foundations. Donors whose anticipated principal is less than the rule of thumb $500,000 may find that a gift to a community foundation, with instructions for its use, will serve their philanthropic goals quite well. The National Heritage Foundation (*www.nhf.org*) is an excellent national community foundation designed specifically to allow entry into the world of charitable estate planning, with all its tax, control, and income benefits for much less in personal expense than other methods.

Private nonoperating foundations are usually incorporated under state law as nonprofit corporations or organized as charitable trusts. The Internal Revenue Service recognizes them as tax-exempt organizations.

Private nonoperating foundations are usually incorporated under state law as nonprofit corporations or organized as charitable trusts. The Internal Revenue Service recognizes them as tax-exempt organizations.

A board of directors or trustees usually makes grant-making decisions, and this board may be either autonomous or largely controlled by the donor or donor family. While grant-making is the sole activity of some foundations, other foundations participate actively in conferences, publications, and research related to their field of interest. All private foundations must set forth exempt purposes in their charters.

Payout Requirements

A private foundation must distribute for its charitable purpose an amount equal to its "adjusted net income" or its "minimum investment return," whichever is greater. Adjusted net income is defined as all income of the foundation except for gifts and long-term capital gains. The minimum investment return is defined by law as 5 percent of the fair market value of all the foundation's assets as determined by periodic appraisal. Failure to spend at the required level will result in tax liability.

Establishing a Private Foundation

Seeking Advice

Individuals or families that are considering the establishment of a private foundation should seek technical assistance from an estate planning professional who is experienced in handling nonprofit tax matters. Potential foundation grantors can acquire names of professionals in their area by consulting *The Foundation Directory*, which has become a standard reference work, for the names of foundations in all geographic areas. *The Foundation Directory* is available at most public libraries. You may also refer to the National Heritage Foundation (*www.nhf.org*) for further information.

Tax-Exempt Status and Organization

All private foundations must qualify as tax-exempt organizations. Within 15 months after formation, the foundation must file an application for tax exemption (Form 1023) with the designated district director of the Internal Revenue Service. The IRS will then determine whether the foundation meets the requirements for tax-exempt status. In addition, the new foundation will probably have to file with a state regulatory body and, when applicable, apply for exemption from state sales or property tax.

Private foundations are organized as corporations, unincorporated associations, or trusts. Characteristics of these organizational types are discussed below.

Corporation. Most incorporated private foundations are set up as nonprofit corporations and have no stock. Articles of incorporation are filed with the appropriate secretary of state and with the register or recorder of deeds in the county where the foundation's main office is located. Such a corporation, in general, operates like a for-profit corporation. The foundation's board of directors elects officers, carries out the foundation's activities, and records its deliberations.

Unincorporated association or trust. A private foundation organized as a charitable trust is governed by a trust instrument that sets up the initial appointment of trustees, sets forth their powers, and provides for the orderly selection of future trustees.

Formalizing an exempt purpose. The exempt purpose set forth in a foundation's charter or trust instrument defines the arena in which its grant making will take place. In defining a purpose, the donor or donor family may wish to seek the opinions and advice of others. The founders, managers, and directors of other private foundations can be especially helpful. There is a bewildering array of human and social needs, and each private foundation has the opportunity to select which of these it wishes to address.

Choosing Foundation Managers

It is essential that private foundations, like commercial enterprises, have established management structures. Whether organized as a corporation, an unincorporated association, or a trust, a foundation must have mechanisms for making and implementing decisions. It is recommended that individuals with diverse backgrounds be included in the management process.

The types of foundation managers are described below.

Directors or trustees. The majority of private foundations have boards of directors or trustees. Members of the boards are usually chosen by the donor or donor family and are often members of the donor family. Ideally, the boards should take an active role in setting the foundation's purposes and distributing its income. Sometimes, however, foundation boards meet infrequently and are poorly informed about the organization's charitable endeavors. It's best to select as directors or trustees individuals with a high level of interest in, and commitment to, foundation activities.

Officers. Foundation boards usually elect officers to assume the ongoing administrative duties associated with foundation operation. As a rule, these officers are usually selected from among the members of the board or the donor family.

Operations

Grant-Making Policies and Procedures

To a large extent, the exempt purpose of a private foundation determines how grants will be made. A foundation that exists solely to channel funds to a specific public charity or institution will not need to advertise the availability of grants or review applications. But a foundation whose purpose is to address problems of inner-city poverty, for example, must be prepared to receive and evaluate a wide variety of applications.

A clear set of policies and procedures for implementing the foundation's purpose should be determined by the donor in conjunction with directors or trustees or, when applicable, with paid staff or representatives of the community. Any geographical or other major restrictions on grant making should be determined. When contacted by potential recipients, a foundation should respond promptly with a fact sheet and a straightforward explanation of procedures for receiving and processing grant applications.

Reporting and Recordkeeping

Federal Requirements

All private foundations must file a federal tax return, Form 990-PF. In addition to information about the foundation's assets, income, and expenses, this form requires that the foundation list its substantial contributors, foundation managers, and highly compensated employees as well as all payments made to these persons.

In addition, any private foundation that has assets exceeding $5,000 at any point during its taxable year must file an annual report, Form 990-AR. The IRS makes copies of these annual reports available for public inspection. The foundation must also make a copy of its annual report available at its office, and must publish notice of its availability in a newspaper of general circulation.

State Requirements

Copies of the federal tax return (Form 990-PF) and annual report (Form 990-AR) must be filed with the attorney general's office of the state in which a private foundation is located. Some states may impose additional reporting requirements on private foundations, and advice concerning these should be sought from an attorney or certified public accountant.

Family Matters

Family continuity can be strongly encouraged and achieved through the use of private family foundations. Consider using children and grandchildren as trustees and grant makers.

In addition to the many tax-saving elements of private foundations, we have discovered a significant one that is often overlooked. Family continuity can be strongly encouraged and achieved through the use of private family foundations. Consider using children and grandchildren as trustees and grant makers. Invariably this forces all those who are included to work closely together, and it can go a long way in teaching these individuals about financial matters through a hands-on approach. Family members are usually drawn closer together through interaction involved in joint or committee decision making and they can receive a director's fee from the charity.

At first glance the establishment of a Private or Family Foundation can appear overwhelming, and the annual reporting a task only suitable for an accountant. If however, you work through a community or national foundation such as the National Heritage Foundation (www.nhf.org) not only are the fees, by comparison, extremely low, but the annual work load is shifted to the community or national foundation. The net results are incredible. Because of the costs and complexity, in past years private family foundations were only available to the ultra wealthy, with names like Rockefeller, Kennedy and Gates. Today, with the introduction of the community and national foundations you can set up a Charitable Remainder Trust with the Family Foundation as the ultimate charitable beneficiary for less than $1,000.

CHAPTER

27

The Charitable Gift Annuity

Now You Can Give and Receive

Creating a Lifetime Income

Charitable gift annuities (CGA) are among the oldest and most respected methods of charitable giving, with the first CGA having been issued by the American Bible Society in 1843. Charitable gift annuities currently play a prominent role in the planned giving programs of hundreds, if not thousands, of charitable organizations across the nation, from The National Geographic Society and The United Way to every major university and religion.

Each year, thousands of Americans make generous charitable gifts to CGAs. In so doing, they are able to support charities of their choice while enjoying the significant financial advantages a CGA provides. With proper planning, many common financial objectives can be met and exceeded through a CGA, such as increasing income, reducing taxes, securing value to heirs, and creating a lasting social legacy.

A CGA is one of the easiest forms of planned giving. In exchange for an immediate gift to a legitimate 501 (C) (3) charity, the donor is promised a specified lifetime income. The exact amount of that gift is agreed upon inception. Typically, the life income goes to the donor or is shared as a 100 percent joint and survivor annuity to the donor and spouse. There is an agreement of understanding between the donor and the charity. Obviously, if you choose to receive your CGA income directly from a charity, the institution's stability and reputation is critical.

The maximum rates of return that are typically paid by a CGA are established by the American Council on Gift Annuities, taking into consideration current interest, mortality assumptions, and current actuarial tables.

Substantial Tax Benefits

There are three primary ways in which a CGA can assist in tax management. First, when transitioning the ownership of a highly appreciated capital asset (marketable securities, real estate, business interests, etc.) to a charity in exchange for lifetime annuity income, the donor does not realize a lump sum capital gain distribution. The capital gain is reduced significantly and then amortized over the donor's life expectancy. This means that a portion of the donor's CGA income will be taxed at the lower capital gains rate.

Second, a substantial, immediate income tax deduction is given, which can be used to offset current income taxes up to a certain amount based on the adjusted gross income. Any surplus deduction can be carried over up to a five additional years. The amount of the tax deduction is based upon the projected value of the ultimate gift to charity.

Third, transitioning an asset to a CGA removes the asset from the donor's taxable estate, which can greatly reduce potential estate taxes. In some cases, depending on the type of asset, transitioning an asset can also avoid income with respect to a decedent (IRD) taxation at the time the estate is settled.

Guaranteed Benefit—Income

When entering into a CGA contract, most donors want to make certain the charity has a safe method of protecting funds that will be used to make their lifetime income payments. Charities are required to meet specific financial requirements on a state-by-state basis. In addition to these safeguards, a few charities will use a portion of the gift to purchase a single premium immediate annuity (SPIA) for the life of the donor(s) from a highly rated life insurance company, "reinsuring" and guaranteeing that the monthly annuity payments will be paid.

Perhaps an example would be helpful. Let's assume you are 58 and your wife is 53, and you sell a duplex for a net profit and capital gain after loan and expenses of $1 million. Your original cost basis was $300,000, so your capital gains tax on April 15 of the year after the sale would be $140,000, assuming a total tax of 20 percent. You want a guaranteed income for life from the proceeds. You love going to the symphony, and you would like third row seats for two without paying for the season pass. You also could use a sizable tax deduction.

By establishing a Charitable Gift annuity, either directly with the symphony or through Legacy Global Foundation, *www.legacyglobal.org*, you will be guaranteed a 5% lifetime annual income for you and your spouse of $50,000 per year, of which $20,482 would be received free of income tax. You would also receive an income tax deduction of $313,840. And for the $1 million contribution to the symphony either directly or through the

Legacy Global Foundation, you would get your two third row seats, center to the symphony for life.

Guaranteed Benefit—Charitable Legacy

When charities "reinsure" their payment obligation to its CGA donors through insurance companies, meeting their reserve requirement, they can use the remainder of the gift today for its charitable mission. A few charities allocate a portion of the remainder gift to a donor advised fund (DAF) that is funded at the death of the donor(s). This permits the donor to have some say, in an advisory capacity, as to how the charitable funds are used, and provides an excellent method of establishing a perennial legacy. Some charities will maximize this remainder allocation to a donor advised fund by using a portion of these funds to obtain a life insurance policy to increase the DAF value at the death of the donor(s), significantly increasing the original gift to the charity.

In conclusion, a CGA can provide both a donor and a charity several important financial planning advantages. Donors can increase their income while obtaining significant tax reductions. Charities can tap into sources of funds that would not become available until the death of the donors. The charitable gift annuity is a classic "win-win" opportunity for both donors and charities.

FIGURE 27.1 The Charitable Gift Annuity

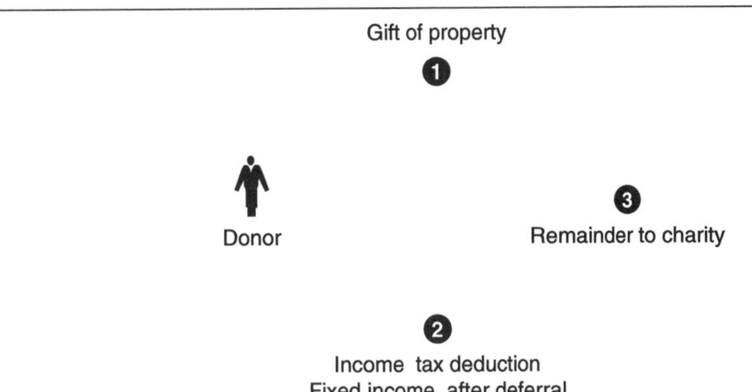

How It Works

❶ You transfer cash, securities, or other property to charity.

❷ You receive an income tax deducation and may save capital gains tax. The charity pays a fixed amount each year to you or to anyone you name for life. Typically, a portion of these payments is tax-free.

❸ When the gift annuity ends, its remaining principal passes to the charity.

FIGURE 27.2 Charitable Gift Annuity with a Family Foundation

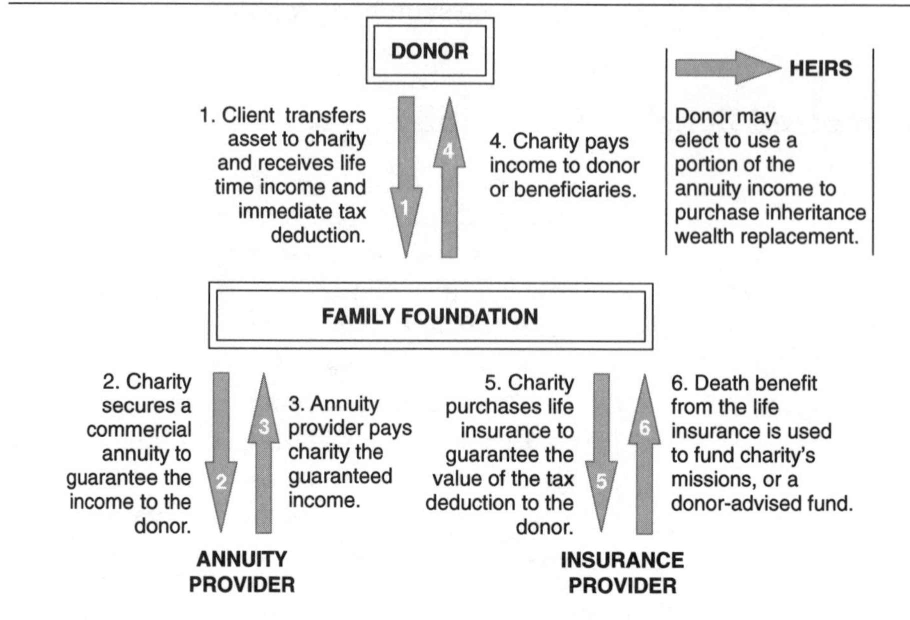

CHAPTER

28

Qualified Personal Resident Trust

Keeping Your House in the Family

For most Americans, the largest single asset is their home with its equity created by payments, time, appreciation, and inflation. In just a few years, a home can increase two, three, even ten times in value. While the home is the source for most of a family's enduring memories, it can also become an albatross as the growing equity increases the overall net estate and the eventual estate tax when the surviving owner dies.

Under the QPRT concept, you transfer your residence into a trust through which you retain all rights to the use of the residence for a specified number of years.

Even if the home was sold, the equity would still exist until, of course, it is spent. So the dilemma is what to do with the equity? How can you live in the comfort you are accustomed to and avoid the eventual estate taxes that will be levied against your most valuable asset?

QPRT to the Rescue

To the rescue comes the **qualified personal resident trust** (QPRT), or what lawyers and accountants now call the "Q-pert." Under the QPRT concept, you transfer your residence into a trust through which you retain all rights to the use of the residence for a specified number of years. At the end of the term, the property can be transferred directly to the remaining beneficiaries. While living in the home during the trust period, you are responsible for all related costs just as you would be if you continued to own it outright. At the end of the term, your free use of the residence is up, leaving you with the following five options:

1. You can choose to no longer live in the residence and have the trustee administer it as part of the trust, either holding it for the remaining beneficiaries, leasing it, or selling it.

2. You can provide for the residence to be held in a new trust for the benefit of the remaining beneficiaries (that is, your children or spouse). If your spouse is a remaining beneficiary, he or she can allow you to live in the residence rent free during his or her lifetime. On your spouse's death, the residence can go to your children and you could rent the residence from them or give up its use.
3. You can arrange to buy the home from the trust for its current fair market value. Because the QPRT is a grantor trust, there is no gain on a sale. If the residence is held to your death, your estate will receive a step-up in basis.
4. You can buy the residence from the remaining beneficiaries at the end of the QPRT term. While such a purchase would cost the trust or the remaining beneficiaries to incur capital gains measured against the benefits of the leverage gift from the beginning, the purchase may still be advantageous.
5. Most common, you can enter into an arms-length lease arrangement with the new owner, which would be the QPRT or the remaining beneficiaries, and pay fair rent. If the residence stays in trust at the end of the QPRT term and the trust remains a grantor trust, you could arguably rent the residence with no income tax consequence. As the grantor, you would be paying rent to yourself. The rent payment would also remove additional assets from your estate.

One basic point is that the whole idea of the QPRT is to reduce the exposure of what's probably your most valuable asset—your home. Also eligible, however, can be your vacation home, boat, or mobile home, all of which would also be acceptable property as long as they provide sleeping space, a toilet, and cooking facilities.

Choosing the Term for the Trust

The QPRT was created in 1990 and not only allows you to transfer your home out of your estate, but also allows the transfer of all future appreciation out of your estate as long as you outlive the term of the trust. You, the grantor, must determine the length of the trust at the time it is set up. Your retained interest is then calculated based on this term, your (the grantor's) age, and the value of the residence. The value of the gift is then calculated by subtracting the value of the retained interest from the market value on the date of the transfer. Because the gift will be considered a future interest gift, your $12,000 annual gift tax exclusion will not apply. However, if you haven't used your $2 million estate tax exclusion, the exclusion may be applied to reduce the gift tax due on transfer of the residence into the trust, which may result in little or no tax payment.

■ Example

Two grantors, ages 60 and 62, transfer a residence with a fair market value of $500,000. Following are the taxable gifts for the various trust terms:

Term	*Taxable Gift*
5 years	*$346,664*
10 years	*240,203*
15 years	*116,642*

A 60-year-old with a $400,000 equity interest in his home and a ten-year QPRT will be able to slash $227,924 from the $400,000 value of the home for the ten years of use, leaving just $172,076 subject to gift tax. At the end of the ten-year term, his children take title tax-free to an asset at a fraction of its true market value. What started at a market value of $400,000 could be worth $100,000 to $150,000 more as the result of inflation and growth during the intervening decade. It's a win-win situation for the man and his children. Only Uncle Sam walks away with less.

You can see that the length of the term chosen for the trust has a great impact on the amount of the gift. The grantor must balance two aspects: (1) the desire for a smaller gift tax and (2) the term of years that the grantor must live. If you are the grantor and you die during the period of the trust, the full market value of the residence will be included in your estate and an adjustment will be made at your death to individual taxable gifts, thus putting you in the same position as if you had never transferred the asset into the trust.

Exclude the Value of Your Home from Estate Taxation—Forever

There is, however, a simple solution to the apparent flaw in the QPRT mentioned above: Simply establish a term life insurance policy for the period of the trust and for the additional estate tax that would be due as a result.

If, for example, your estate was valued at $4.5 million, your home had equity of $500,000, and you and your spouse, ages 62 and 60 respectively, established a ten-year QPRT, your approximate estate tax would be $250,000 if you both should die during the time period of the QPRT. The solution: secure a ten-year level term life insurance policy for the healthiest and youngest spouse, in this case the 60-year-old wife.

■ Example

Assumptions: *Male 62/Female 60*

Home equity – $500,000
50% Estate tax bracket
QPRT trust period — 10 years
Approximate tax — $250,000

Solution: *Ten-year level term policy on 60-year-old female spouse*
Annual premium — $1,065
Owner — An irrevocable trust

Result: *The Insurance company pays the $250,000 estate tax for pennies on the dollar.*

Getting Qualified Help

You can see that a QPRT is not the type of estate planning strategy that you should attempt by yourself. You most definitely need legal assistance in drafting a qualified personal resident trust. One final note: The trust should be drafted as a grantor trust even though it creates taxable income to you, the grantor; but it also allows you to continually deduct the mortgage interest and property tax payments. You will also qualify for benefits under Internal Revenue Code Section 1031 if the property is sold and another one is purchased for equal or greater value.

You can see that the qualified personal residence trust is an excellent tool that can be used to reduce your estate, thus reducing your family's estate tax liability.

WARNING

You can see that a QPRT is not the type of estate planning strategy that you should attempt by yourself. You most definitely need legal assistance in drafting a qualified personal resident trust.

CHAPTER

29

The Reverse Mortgage

Extract Your Home Equity and Reduce Your Estate While Never Leaving Home

1989: The FHA Developed the First Reverse Mortgage

Millions of senior Americans find themselves in a dilemma: They have significant equity in their home with little cash to spend on life's basic needs, let alone on luxuries. As a result, they live extremely frugal lives, and when the surviving spouse dies the home is inherited by the heirs. Shortly after the funeral, the children sell the home and divide the equity. In some parts of the country, homes that were purchased 30 or 40 years ago for $50,000 are now worth over $1 million. Before, the only alternative was to secure a home equity loan that had to be repaid.

In 1989, the Federal Housing Administration (FHA) developed the reverse mortgage program to allow homeowners (all parties must be 62 or older) the opportunity to access the equity in their home while being able to continue to live in their home until the surviving spouse is no longer able to do so. Once the surviving spouse vacates the home (for 12 consecutive months), the heirs can repay the reverse mortgage with other funds in order to keep the property. If this isn't done, the lender will require the sale of the property to secure repayment.

When the reverse mortgage is repaid, the lender (bank or mortgage company) receives the total amount of principal advanced to the borrowers including any financed expenses for payments made on the borrowers' behalf, as well as the accumulated interest. If the proceeds from the sale of the property are greater than what is needed to repay the reverse mortgage, all excess funds flow to the heirs. If, however, the sale of the property does not bring in enough funds to repay the reverse mortgage in full, the heirs are not required to pay the shortfall.

As long as the home is used as a primary residence, property taxes are paid, and it is kept in good repair, the loan does not have to be repaid.

Most reverse mortgages have costs similar to traditional mortgages, including interest charges, origination fees, closing costs, inspections, and insurance.

Four Types of Reverse Mortgages

There are four basic types of reverse mortgages:

1. The single purpose reverse mortgage
2. The home equity conversion mortgage (HECM)
3. The Home Keeper reverse mortgage
4. The proprietary reverse mortgage

The single purpose reverse mortgage. As the name implies, this type of reverse mortgage is designed to provide funds for a specific use, such as repairing a home, making modifications to accommodate a disability, or paying property taxes or a special assessment. In most cases, these loans are earmarked for low or moderate-income homeowners.

The home equity conversion mortgage. Federally insured through the Federal Housing Administration, the HECM guarantees that as long as the homeowners remain in the home, they will receive the loan advances initially promised them, even if their home declines in value or the institution making the loan goes bankrupt. Furthermore, homeowners are not required to have income or good credit to qualify for any version of the reverse mortgage.

The Home Keeper program. This is a proprietary reverse mortgage developed by the Federal National Mortgage Association (Fannie Mae), a privately owned company. The Home Keeper reverse mortgage limit for 2006 is $417,000, and as a result, this program offers a higher principal limit that the HECM. Like the HECM, the Home Keeper funds can be received as a lump sum, a monthly income, or a line of credit.

The proprietary reverse mortgage. These private mortgage instruments are offered and owned by the financial institutions that develop them (banks, mortgage companies, etc.). Generally speaking, the eligibility requirements, payment options, and repayment obligations for proprietary reverse mortgages are similar to the HECM. However, because they are private loans, there is virtually no limit to amount that can be borrowed. As a result, they are used for individuals with huge equity and minimal cash flow.

The Four Reverse Mortgage Determination Factors

For an HECM, the maximum amount a homeowner may receive is based on four factors:

1. *Age.* While all borrowers must be age 62 or older, the amount a homeowner may receive is determined in part by the age of the youngest borrower. Older borrowers will receive larger loans.
2. *Home value.* The more the home is worth, the greater the maximum principal limit.
3. *FHA loan limits.* Set annually by the FHA, these limits reflect the average home value for the properties in specific geographic areas.
4. *HECM interest rates.* Higher rates mean lower principal limits.

Four Methods to Access Your Home Equity

Lenders are required to offer an interest rate that is adjusted annually and the rate can't increase more than 2 percentage points in a year or more than 5 percentage points over the life of the loan.

With an HECM, the borrower may elect any one or a combination of the following four options:

1. A lump sum payment
2. An increasing line of credit
3. Monthly cash advances for a predetermined number of years
4. Monthly cash advances for as long as the homeowner occupies the residence

Homeowners using an HECM must receive counseling from an agency that is approved by HUD. This counseling is designed to make certain that the borrowers have a clear understanding of the program and all details and ramifications.

One of the side benefits of the reverse mortgages in general is that when death occurs to the surviving spouse, the heirs are disinherited with the exception of any new net increase in property value. A life insurance policy can be purchased on the life of the borrowers to replace the lost inheritance, and if the policy is purchased correctly the proceeds will be received totally income and estate tax free (see Chapter 21 on how to properly purchase replacement insurance).

Summary

Simply put, a reverse mortgage is a loan a lender gives to an individual or couple based on the equity in their home. This is passive money that can now be released to be used for a multitude of planning strategies. With a reverse mortgage, one can:

- Tap into the equity in their home
- Receive tax-free cash in either a lump sum, a monthly income, a line of credit, or a combination of the three
- Have no monthly mortgage payment
- Have no risk of every losing the home
- Live where they want for as long as they want
- Not be subject to income or credit qualification

For further information, contact Freedom Financial, 1-800-301-6171, or visit *www.financialfreedom.com* or *www.aarp.org/money/revmort/*.

CHAPTER

30

Life Settlement

Selling Old Ineffective Life Policies for Cash

The Distinction Between Viatical and Life Settlements

In the mid-1980s, a few bold businessmen created a financial instrument designed to purchase life insurance policies from HIV-positive clients. The idea was simple: Based on statistics, the client would not have long to live, and so the businessmen would pool their money, make an up-front cash settlement, take over the policy payments, and wait for the illness to run its short course. The concept was called a viatical settlement. While these types of arrangements had a few successful years, legislators felt that evil doings could become a common occurrence because a client needed to be terminal to be accepted. Thus, "viaticals" have been highly scrutinized by state lawmakers. From this early beginning, a new "cottage industry" has evolved now known as life settlement, and has grown into a $10 billion business.

The main distinction between a viatical and a life settlement program is that a life settlement provider will consider any person who will sell their life insurance policy at a discount as long as they meet the following guidelines:

1. The insured should be over age 65
2. There should have been a negative change in health since the policy was issued
3. The policy must be in force for over two years
4. The insured should have a life expectancy less than 12 years
5. The policy should have a minimum death benefit of $100,000

Reasons for Choosing a Life Settlement Program

Reasons for selling a life insurance policy through a life settlement include:

- The insured no longer needs or wants the insurance policy.
- The policy is going to lapse due to lack of funds to pay the premium. In other words, it is no longer affordable.
- The insured needs the money in advance to cover current expenses such as medical bills or other debt.
- The insured estate has decreased or estate laws have changed, and the insured no longer requires the insurance to pay the estate taxes.
- The current policy is failing due to unrealized assumptions. In other words, the policy will cease to exist under the current payment structure unless more cash is infused.
- The retirement or termination of a key employee or business partner that is insured with a key-man or buy-sell agreement life insurance policy.
- The intended beneficiary has died before the insured.

Types of Life Policies to Consider

The buyer makes the minimum premium payments necessary to keep the policy in force and holds the policy until termination (death of the insured).

The types of policies to consider that can be sold via a life settlement include: whole life, universal life, variable life, and even term life insurance, if it still has the right to upgrade (convert) from term to permanent.

It is also important to note that there shouldn't be a tax liability if the settlement amount is less than the cost basis of the policy.

While life settlements have not yet become mainstream and focus on morbid events, they are becoming more prevalent as our society ages and older policies (usually those over ten years old) become imperiled due to unfulfilled projections, low interest earnings, and poor mortality experience. Furthermore, most life insurance agents have access to life settlement programs, and there are those that feel agents and financial planners have a responsibility to disclose the ramifications, options, and possibilities of life settlement. Many Americans have had changes in their lives that could make a life settlement advisable, so if you meet the criteria, it may be to your advantage to have a specialist review your options.

Figure 30.1 Life Settlement Actual Examples

Male: 68 (Bypass History)	**Male: 56 (Prostate Cancer History**
Policy Type: Convertible Term Life Face Amount: $200,000 Cash Value: $0 Reason for sale: No longer needed coverage	Policy Type: Convertible Term Life Face Amount: $1,500,000 Cash Value: $0 Reason for sale: To enhance retirement income
Life Settlement: $40,500	**Life Settlement: $360,000**
Female: 76 (Healthy)	**Joint and Survivor—Female, 74—(Husband deceased)**
Policy Type: Universal Life Face Amount: $1,500,000 Cash Value: $400,000 Reason for sale: To use settlement funds to acquire a new fully guaranted death benefit policy	Policy Type: Universal Life Face Amount: $10,000,000 Cash Value: $1,800,000 Reason for sale: Husband had passed, and his wife no longer wanted to fund the premium. Wanted to maximize value.
Life Settlement: $605,000	**Life Settlement: $2,500,000**

CHAPTER

31

Protecting Your Assets

Watching Your Backside

You don't need to be told how litigious our society has become. People sue at the drop of a hat. The number of lawsuits isn't nearly as important as the growing size of the awards for negligence, personal injury, and malpractice, which can only be described as absurd and exorbitant. The huge awards are becoming established benchmarks and insurers are withdrawing from liability markets or raising premiums to unaffordable levels.

The reality is that if you have accumulated a modest to large personal net worth, the odds are high that you will be sued at some time in the future.

The lack of effective tort (wrongful act) reform and the justice system in general are now producing a substantial level of litigation against professionals, trustees, company directors, corporate executives, and business owners. The reality is that if you have accumulated a modest to large personal net worth, the odds are high that you will be sued at some time in the future. Therefore, you must be aware of the need to protect your wealth, commonly referred to as asset protection, against contingent creditor action.

The U.S. Legal System and the "Deep Pocket" Attitude

The richer you are, the more likely you will be sued. Why? It doesn't do lawyers or their plaintiff clients any good to sue someone who doesn't have the money or insurance coverage to pay off a successful lawsuit. That is why lawyers look for someone with "deep pockets" when evaluating a case. The deeper your pockets, the more attractive you are as a lawsuit defendant.

The devastating increase in litigation has contributed to the exorbitantly high cost of professional malpractice insurance for physicians, accountants, architects, engineers, lawyers, and entrepreneurs. Premiums are often so costly that professionals are forced to forgo malpractice insurance.

The legal community has created contingency fees ranging between 33 and 40 percent of an eventual settlement. With such high fees, a strong economic incentive leads contingency fee law firms to file as many lawsuits as possible in the hopes that the majority will settle out of court.

Many critics see the heart of this problem is the U.S. legal system, which has created approximately 314 attorneys per 100,000 individuals. The state of California alone has approximately 120,000 attorneys licensed to practice law. England has 112 attorneys per 100,000 people, and Japan has only 12 attorneys per 100,000 people. The United States has by far the largest number of attorneys, which in turn results in its being the most litigious country in the world. Furthermore, a lawsuit is filed in this country every 1.75 seconds, according to the American Bar Association.

A lawsuit is filed in this country every 1.75 seconds, according to the American Bar Association.

And don't forget about juries. Jurors, not lawyers, are the ones who determine award levels. And jurors are notorious for nonsensical verdicts. No matter which side of the O.J. Simpson trial you were on, you no doubt can understand how unpredictable the U.S. jury system is.

An industry newsletter, *Lawyers Alert*, made some dire predictions about the U.S. legal system: "Juries will hand down bigger damage awards for emotional distress and tort suits; more verdicts will come under attack because of the claims of bias and jury selection; lawsuits over toxic waste cleanup will pour in from real estate agents, developers, building contractors, and insurance companies trying to shift blame from themselves; and multimillion-dollar jury awards for personal injuries will become more frequent."

It Could Happen to You

Don't think that it can't happen to you. Many potential problems may become a legal liability for you as a result of an opportunistic plaintiff or lawyer. Here is a short list of some potential problems:

- Problems related to your home or commercial property, including loose gravel, wet sidewalks, clean glass windows, uneven pavement, doors that people walk through, swimming pools, and open gates
- Accidents caused by your children
- Accidents or incidents caused by someone in your employ or by a subcontractor, including auto accidents involving autos while on company business, or potential harassment
- Auto accidents
- Equipment malfunctions
- Recreational outing accidents
- Professional malpractice
- Slips and falls
- Exposure as a director or officer of a corporation

Asset Protection Planning

The following are just a few examples that illustrate why *asset protection planning* has become a crucial part of estate planning.

■ Example

A female customer of a Florida furniture company was awarded $2.5 million, which the furniture company had to pay after its deliveryman stabbed her. The court ruled that the company had failed to do elaborate screening when they hired the deliveryman and held the company liable for negligence.

■ Example

A family in Escondido, California, owned an auto repair business. Ten years before California imposed a $7.9 million order on the family, the family had a disposal company remove hazardous materials from the property it owned. California declared the yard site unsafe, the removal company subsequently filed bankruptcy, and as a result, California imposed a fine of $7.9 million on the family and its legal next of kin. Even though the family had made strenuous efforts to work within the state's environmental guidelines, California still imposed this large penalty.

■ Example

The case of Mrs. W. shows how litigation fever can affect anyone. Mrs. W. loaned her 18-year-old grandnephew $18,000 to buy a 1981 Chrysler. After a long party that, according to court records, included smoking marijuana and drinking, the grandnephew and his friends started driving the car, subsequently lost control of it, and drove off a railroad bridge. As a result, one of the passengers lost his leg in the accident and was paralyzed from the chest down. The paralyzed passenger subsequently sued Mrs. W., and a jury found the 91-year-old woman liable to the paralyzed patient. The court ordered her to pay the paralyzed passenger $950,000.

Preventing Litigation with Asset Protection Planning

Businesspeople and professionals in the United States have for years used two concepts to maintain and create wealth: (1) financial planning and (2) estate planning. These two types of planning are primarily concerned with building and maintaining one's estate. A third type of planning has been developed to minimize the risk of exposure to economic loss from the litigious nature of our society and is called *asset protection planning,* which utilizes various techniques to protect assets from potential creditors. The key to asset protection planning is the *preventive* planning that occurs *before* creditors file claims.

The key to asset protection planning is the *preventive* planning that occurs *before* creditors file claims.

Those especially vulnerable to litigation are physicians, surgeons, dentists, financial planners, investment advisors, attorneys, accountants, natural resource developers, manufacturers, developers, architects, contractors, insurance agents, board directors, business owners, and real estate owners. These people can minimize their risk of exposure through various techniques to protect their assets from potential creditors. The key is preventive asset protection planning rather than trying to protect assets *after* a creditor has filed a lawsuit or acquired a judgment or lawsuit against you.

The explanation for so much litigation in today's society is found in economic factors and not necessarily in the pursuit of justice. The primary goal of asset protection is to render unattractive the assets that were once attractive to potential plaintiffs through the use of various asset protection techniques.

Asset protection is a process whereby individuals divest themselves of legal ownership of particular assets that are vulnerable to judgment creditors while at the same time maintaining or regaining control of those assets for their own use and enjoyment.

Asset protection is a process whereby individuals divest themselves of legal ownership of particular assets that are vulnerable to judgment creditors while at the same time maintaining or regaining control of those assets for their own use and enjoyment. The process of asset protection planning and the establishment of various asset protection planning techniques and strategies must be made in advance of any claims by creditors. Asset planning protection cannot be done at the 11th hour or after a creditor has obtained a judgment or filed a claim against you.

The first caveat of asset protection planning is that there is *no absolute technique or techniques to fully protect your assets* from potential creditors. Nothing is guaranteed to work 100 percent of the time. In light of this, the objective of asset protection is to create a legal fortress around your assets to an extent that makes it impractical for creditors to penetrate it.

Requirements for Creating an Asset Protection Plan

It is very important that you meet the following requirements in order to establish an asset protection plan:

- You must be solvent at the date assets are transferred.
- Your motivation and intent cannot be to avoid creditors.
- There can be no intent to make a fraudulent transfer.
- You must make a full disclosure to the IRS.

The legal system has recently witnessed the erosion of traditional legal techniques to limited and individual liability. Certain states have expanded the rights of creditors so much that lawyers have searched out new and more effective ways to protect their clients' assets from creditors and judgment creditors. We will focus on two techniques that we have found to be extremely effective not only for asset protection but for estate planning purposes: the family limited partnership and the limited liability company.

The Family Limited Partnership (FLP)

The **family limited partnership** is a unique entity that provides ultimate control and management of partnership assets while at the same time providing asset protection benefits. In a family limited partnership, there are one or more general partners who are vested with the management control of partnership affairs and assets. Limited partners, of which there can be one or more, do not have any control or management in partnership affairs or the management of assets. The limited partner's role is passive and therefore has limited liability for the obligations of the partnership. Often a husband and wife are the general partners and their children and/or grandchildren are the limited partners.

A family limited partnership is a technique for protection against potential creditors. A creditor may successfully sue and obtain a judgment against you, but because you are a general partner of a family limited partnership, the creditor must go to court again and obtain a *charging order* against your partnership interest, allowing the creditor an interest in the income of the partnership only rather than in the principal.

The general partner(s) have the discretion of how to invest the assets of the partnership and how much, if any, of the income is to be distributed to the partners. The partnership agreement is drafted in such a way as to give the general partner(s) the discretion to distribute income to the partners, which provides you two defenses against judgment creditors. First, you can invest the partnership assets in such a manner that they do not generate current income, such as nondividend paying growth stocks. And second, any income that is generated does not have to be distributed.

Keep in mind that partners have an obligation to pay income tax on partnership income regardless of whether it is distributed. This is analogous to reinvested mutual fund capital gains and income distributions. Even if you reinvest those distributions, you must still pay income taxes as if you received them. The same is true of family limited partnerships, which to judgment creditors is a substantial barrier. Creditors will be obligated to pay income taxes on the partnership income even if they don't get it. This obligation is a definite drawback when a plaintiff's attorney is determining whether to file suit against you.

Supervision is written into the family limited partnership in that the general partner or partners have the power to make or not make partnership distributions. Thus, in the event that there is a charging order against a partner's share in the partnership, the general partners can effectively turn off the income stream to that partner and allow the income to accumulate and be reinvested within the partnership. If the debtor partner does not actually receive income, the judgment creditor with the charging order will not receive income either.

If the family limited partnership itself becomes subject to a lawsuit, all the assets within the partnership will become subject to the claims of the plaintiff. Negative circumstances can potentially occur if an asset within the partnership can cause liability. For example, a tort claim will most likely happen as the result of a faulty apartment complex that has not been maintained for years. Under this circumstance, it is best to segregate out from the estate any particular asset or assets that may cause liability in and of themselves, and place them in a separate family limited partnership. This technique is often used if you own separate commercial buildings or apartment buildings. Each apartment would be transferred to a separate family limited partnership. If there is a slip-and-fall case on one of the apartment building premises, the separate family limited partnership that holds the particular apartment building within the estate would be subject to the plaintiff's claims, and the other apartment buildings within the estate would be free from liability.

The Limited Liability Company (LLC)

The limited liability company is the fastest growing form of enterprise in the United States. At the present time, 44 states have statutes specifically approving LLCs. The following provides a summary of the characteristics of this organizational form and includes such topics as the taxation of an LLC, the advantages of the LLC over other business forms, unsettled issues that could lead to adverse consequences, and the estate planning implications of LLCs.

What Is an LLC?

A **limited liability company** is a hybrid that combines a corporation and a partnership and attempts to select the most favorable characteristics of each. The objective of an LLC is to pass through income, deductions, and credits without passing through liability. The LLC is thus an unincorporated organization that protects its equity owners (called members) from personal liability for the entity's debts and obligations. The LLC must be created either for transacting business or for holding investments, and it is created by filing articles of organization with the appropriate state agency.

Some of the standard (but not universal) traits of these creatures of state statute include:

- An LLC must consist of at least two members, but there is no limit on the number of members an LLC may have.
- Managers, essentially the same as a corporation's board of directors, oversee the LLC members.

- Distributions are made and profits and losses are allocated proportionately according to the respective contributions of the members.
- All members and managers are protected from personal liability for the LLC's debts and other obligations. In other words, the limit of liability in an LLC is the extent of a member's investment.
- Members may freely assign or transfer the economic rights associated with their interests.
- Rights other than economic rights, such as voting, may only be assigned with the consent of other members.
- The entity dissolves on the first to occur of: unanimous consent of all members, a date specified in the articles of the organization, voluntary withdrawal of a member, death of a member, expulsion of a member, bankruptcy of a member, or decree of court.
- The LLC may conduct almost any type of business unless prohibited by law.
- Individual members, unlike partners in a partnership, cannot act on behalf of the LLC without express authority.
- An LLC operating agreement states the terms upon which the organization will do business and may be modified only by unanimous vote of the members.
- Members can resign after giving six months' notice at which time the firm must distribute cash, assets, or both with fair market value equal to the member's interest.
- Distributions are prohibited to the extent that would render the LLC insolvent.

How Is an LLC Formed?

Assume you and other associates, investors, or family members decide to start a business together, and all would like protection against personal liability. You would all like to take early losses of the business and apply them against taxable income that each of you anticipates from other sources. Neither a partnership nor a corporation would satisfy both of these goals. All parties would contribute cash, property, and their services, and in return receive a membership in the LLC. The members would file articles of organization with the state authorizing the business and draw up an operating agreement listing the specifics of your association. The profits and losses of the business, as well as any cash and property distributions, would be apportioned according to the relative value of the members' contributions unless all of you provide some different allocation in the operational agreement.

You can, under most circumstances, convert a partnership or a corporation into an LLC.

Benefits of an LLC

Protection against creditors. This protection is the single most important characteristic of the LLC and is a key distinguishing factor vis-à-vis a partnership, which provides limited liability for its limited partners but not its general partners. It is also the characteristic that makes it similar to a corporation. The LLC is the only business entity that allows every member, including managers, to enjoy limited liability while the entity is treated as a partnership for federal income tax purposes. This insulation is particularly important if the underlying business or asset may involve environmental claims, product liability claims, or similar exposures.

Management without personal liability. Unlike a limited partnership, because an LLC allows any member to be involved in management without exposure to personal liability, the LLC is very appealing to senior family members.

Conversion of passive income or losses. It may be possible for an active participating member of an LLC to convert what might otherwise be treated as passive losses for tax purposes. Likewise, passive income can be converted into active income. This potential is not possible for limited partners in a family limited partnership who are restricted to passive income and passive loss treatment.

Avoidance of ancillary administration. Because an interest in an LLC is personal property (even if the LLC holds only real estate), it provides a way to convert real property to personal property and thus avoid probate in the state in which the real property lies. Avoidance of ancillary probate can save significant aggravation and expense.

Economies of scale. An LLC can serve as a consolidating vehicle for a great deal of your wealth. Rather than giving one child one asset and giving another child another asset, thereby incurring multiple administration costs, one centralized management (either you or the person/party appointed by you to manage the LLC) will handle all the assets uniformly. In this manner, the children will share equitably in both growth and income from *all* the transferred assets.

Family business and estate planning tool. Because the LLC may be structured to be taxed under partnership laws, it has many of the same features of a partnership used in business and estate planning. First is the avoidance of the double tax at the corporate level. Because income is taxed directly to the members, use of an LLC can shift income to family members who cannot, or do not want to, work in the business. Second, interests in a family LLC can be shifted to other family members with little physical or financial cost, a shift that makes wealth sharing among family members relatively easy. Third, because many states have highly flexible LLC laws, a great deal of additional income and estate planning can be achieved.

Potential multiple gift/estate tax valuation discounts. These discounts are very similar to the discounting of assets in family limited partnerships. As soon as cash, stocks, real estate, a business, or any other asset is placed within the wrapper of an LLC, its utility to the buyer diminishes. The consequent reduction in marketability leads to a valuation discount that is realistic and reasonable. Furthermore, the LLC can be fragmented into pieces, and control can be vested in the interests held by the senior generation. Together, the lack of marketability coupled with the lack of control may result in a discount in excess of 35 percent.

Tax Transfer Implications

Estate taxes. There is no major difference in the estate tax treatment of an LLC from the treatment of a family limited partnership. If it can be shown that the value of a membership interest has less marketability than the liquidation value of the underlying investments of the LLC, a valuation discount should be allowed for estate (and gift) tax purposes. It may also be argued that a legal right to cash out of the LLC is worth little if it is relatively liquid.

Gift taxes. If you make a gift of an interest in an LLC to a family member, that transfer should qualify for the annual gift exclusion under the same conditions as would a gift of stock or partnership interests. If the gift is outright, there should be no question about qualification for the $12,000 exclusion. Likewise, if you put money or other assets into the LLC and do not reflect the contribution in the form of an increase in your relative membership interest, then you are making an indirect gift to other members.

Why Is an LLC Preferable to a Partnership?

The following are advantages of an LLC over a partnership:

- All members avoid liability exposure except to the extent of their investment. Even a limited partnership must have one general partner.
- LLC members can convert passive losses/gains into active losses/gains, which is not permissible in family limited partnerships.
- All members can actively participate without losing limited liability status. Conversely, a limited partner who participates in management loses limited liability status.

Why Is an LLC Preferable to an S Corporation?

A number of significant distinctions between an LLC and an S corporation are as follows:

- Most of the typical restrictive corporate tax laws apply to S corporations in spite of the pass-through election.
- There are strict eligibility rules for S corporations that do not apply to LLCs. An LLC, for example, can have more than 35 members, and many more types of persons or entities can be owners of LLCs than of S corporations. Therefore, LLCs are preferable to S corporations because the owners do not all have to be individuals or U.S. citizens, and may be nonresident aliens.
- LLC interests can be passed to trusts for estate planning purposes without meeting the requirements of a qualified subchapter S trust (QSCT).
- Special allocations of income and losses are possible that would violate the one-class stock requirement for S corporations.
- Assets of the LLC avoid the tax on built-in gains applicable to S corporations under U.S. Code Section 1374.
- Appreciated property can be contributed tax free to an LLC without meeting the 80 percent ownership requirement.
- The LLC or its members may be vehicles to avoid the transfer-for-value rules. No such exception exists for transfers of life insurance policies to S corporation shareholders other than the insured.

Discounts During the Lifetime Using Family Limited Partnerships

The family limited partnership or limited liability company structured as a partnership may provide an outstanding opportunity for you to reduce your estate tax liability. These estate planning tools are being used to a large extent in estates congruent to yours where appreciated and appreciating assets are involved and there is a desire by the estate holders to transfer assets to family members before death to avoid estate taxes.

The plan is relatively simple. You create and then contribute assets to the FLP or LLC and retain both a general partner and limited partnership interest. There is no income tax liability on the completed transfer. You then make gifts of limited partnership interests to your children and grandchildren while retaining the general partnership interest.

As the general partner, you have exclusive management and investment control over the partnership assets and have broad discretionary powers to determine the amount and timing of any distributions to the family limited partners. During the term of the partnership, no partner is entitled to demand a distribution or a return on his or her share.

The transferred partnership interest should not be included in the transferor's (your) estate at death, even though as general partner you retained substantial control. In addition, the family limited partnership provides a convenient vehicle with which to effectuate leveraged lifetime gifts, including *annual gift tax exclusion gifts* and *unified credit gifts* ($600,000 each).

The real advantage is that the value of the transferred limited partnership interests can usually be significantly discounted for gift tax purposes. Gifts of limited partnership interests may be valued significantly less than the proportionate value of the underlying partnership assets because of their lack of marketability and a minority owner discount.

Under Internal Revenue Code Section 2512, gift tax is determined by reference to the fair market value as the price at which such property would change hands between a willing buyer and seller. In arriving at the fair market value of interests in closely held businesses, the IRS considers many factors, including the degree of control associated with the asset. A minority discount reflects the inability of a shareholder or limited partner to compel liquidation and therefore to realize a pro-rata portion of the entity's underlying net asset value.

The lack of marketability reflects concern that there is not a ready market available for an owner to sell his or her interest. Each of the above factors—lack of control and lack of a ready market—will reduce the price a potential buyer will pay for a limited partnership interest. The discounts vary depending on the facts and circumstances, but they may be quite substantial and often range from 20 to 70 percent.

Summary

LLCs are not the perfect solution to all estate and asset protection planning problems, but they are potentially one of the most exciting new tools of the decade. Nationwide acceptance and uniform rules will not be immediate but will occur more quickly than almost any other concept currently employed by estate planners. LLCs are important because of their almost magical ability to vest a large element of control while shifting the tax burden on huge amounts of wealth subject to that continuing control. As trust substitutes, LLCs answer many problems that have concerned trust grantors, including (1) loss of control over the assets placed into the trust, (2) access to the assets for emergencies or opportunities, and (3) an ability to make changes to key terms and provisions.

The family limited partnership, in sum, is a unique entity that provides ultimate control and management of partnership assets while, at the same time, providing asset protection benefits. In a family limited partnership, there are one or more general partners who are vested with the management control of partnership affairs and assets. Limited partners, of which there can be one or more, do not have control or management in partnership affairs or the management of assets. A limited partner's role is passive and therefore has limited liability for the obligations of the partnership.

A family limited partnership is a better technique for protection against potential creditors than any other instrument used for asset protection. Once creditors obtain a judgment against you as a general partner, they must obtain a *charging order* against your partnership interest, giving them an interest in the income of the partnership only, rather than the principal. This is very limited because the judgment creditors now must pay income taxes on both the undistributed profits and the income of the partnership in proportion to their interest as determined by the charging order even if no income is distributed by the partnership.

Thus, the judgment creditors become assignees and are liable for taxation on income that they don't receive. The partnership agreement is drafted in such a way as to give the general partner the discretion to distribute income to the limited partners. This then becomes a definite barrier to a plaintiff's attorney when deciding to file suit against you or the general partners.

In very general terms, you should consider an LLC if you own assets that can create a large liability, such as an apartment complex or business. Conversely, you should consider an FLP if you, not the asset, are subject to liability claims as a physician or architect. Both offer effective asset protection but are useful under different circumstances. Of course, you should consult competent legal counsel before taking any action.

Asset protection planning is a highly specialized area of the law. We have found few law firms in the United States that can adequately deal with these issues. Many say they do, but most cannot. If you are considering this type of planning, we strongly recommend that you find a firm that specializes in this area, even if it means traveling out of state.

CHAPTER 32

Getting Started

Taking the Next Step—Our Invitation to You

Take this simple test. For a few moments, close your eyes and think about the potential problems that would arise if you died today. Try to answer some of the following questions:

- How will my estate pass to my family or heirs?
- Have I made it perfectly clear who is to get what and when they are to get it?
- Will family members have enough income to continue with their accustomed lifestyles?
- Can the business continue without me?
- Will those to whom I want to leave my estate actually receive it?
- Who will gain guardianship of my minor children?
- Will my estate be subject to probate?
- Have I taken the necessary steps to tax advantage of both estate tax credits?
- How much will my estate have to pay in federal, state estate taxes and other costs?
- What transformations will my estate have to go through to pay the tax bill?

These are just a few of the common questions that death creates; the list goes on and on.

Where Do You Start?

To come up with an estate plan, where do you start? Having facilitated hundreds of estate plans, we recommend that you find an estate planning quarterback—a person who can summarize your current estate planning (if any is in place), identify problems, and help you set objectives and format and execute a plan.

To begin the process, you must first make a choice. Who would you like to inherit your estate—your children and other heirs or the federal government, the state government, and the legal system? If you are like most people, the answer is simple. However, ensuring that your choice becomes a reality is not so easy.

George was right on target, unfortunately, the harsh reality is that government and the legal system are set up to get your money and make it their money.

Unfortunately, the harsh reality is that government and the legal system are set up to get your money and make it their money.

Somehow, much of what the United States stands for has been twisted like a pretzel. We have lost sight of the premise that we are a free society that allows and encourages its citizens to become successful. Why does it now follow that having a high income and net worth make you a bad person, one who is considered greedy and money hungry?

In the '60s, George Harrison of The Beatles wrote a satirical song, "Taxman" about the taxes in Britain. It could have been written with the IRS in mind as well. The song was a verbal complaint of the vast number of taxes citizens of the crown were charged throughout their life. It ends with the verse:

"Now my advice for those who die,
Declare the pennies on your eyes.
Cause I'm the taxman,
Yeah, I'm the taxman
And you're working for no one but me."

In our estimation, there has been a reversal in the psychology of the public because of the hard times we've been through in the past few years. The recession of the early 1990s fostered a sense of jealousy and created, as Dr. Gary North coined it, "an age of envy." It is now politically correct to say that those who have the audacity to make a lot of money should pay for their "crimes." And the government will do this by "taxing the heck out of you."

The government and legal system do not profit unless your affairs are disorganized and vulnerable to an exorbitant tax bill.

Sadly, the federal system is not alone in the effort to reduce your net worth. Much of the legal system stands to gain from your wealth as well.

Therefore, you need to organize your financial affairs so that you pay the least amount of legal fees along with the lowest taxes possible. The government and legal system do not profit unless your affairs are disorganized and vulnerable to an exorbitant tax bill. The legal system is designed so that an attorney's motivation is often different from your own.

Between the reality of the current political climate, the likelihood of increases in federal estate taxation, and the lack of incentive for the legal system to organize your affairs accurately, holding onto your assets is more difficult than ever. What does this mean to you? It means that you need to plan now for the future.

The following situations are standard occurrences in our society.

■ Example

Sam is a 64-year-old corporate executive. His wife Janet is also 64 and not employed, having been active in charitable organizations most of her adult life. Sam plans on retiring at 65. He has been with the same large corporation for the past 24 years. Over the course of his career, Sam has paid as much as 50 percent of his annual earnings in federal and state income taxes. Sam and Janet are currently in a 35 percent tax bracket. For each dollar Sam makes, they are able to keep only 65 cents.

Sam and Janet have accumulated assets valued at $5.5 million that include Sam's qualified retirement program (approximately $1.5 million). Under current law, if both Sam and Janet die today, their federal estate tax will be $1,610,000 before any other person or heir receives a penny. The IRS will require the estate to pay this tax, in cash, within nine months after their death. Their children will also have to pay an income tax on Sam's retirement plan of up to $525,000.

Their tax loss can be measured, and with proper planning they can avoid the ravages inflicted on a poorly planned estate. *Estate taxes and huge legal bills are not necessary.* With proper planning, the estate and income taxes and legal fees for Sam and Janet can be legally reduced to zero!

■ Example

Tom and Frances started their manufacturing company in Seattle almost 20 years ago. The gross annual sales of the company are approximately $3 million. Tom's son, Greg, has been involved in the business for about 15 years. Two other children are not involved in the business and live out of state.

Today, Tom is 67 years old and wants to retire. He has thought about selling the company in order to do so, but hasn't for two important reasons. First, Greg's hard work and determination have helped build the Tom James Company to its current level of success. Greg shares his father's desire to keep the business in the family and to one day pass it on to his own children. Second, if Tom sells the business, he will face a capital gains tax on the sale of approximately $700,000.

Tom's net interest in the company is valued at about $3.5 million. If Tom dies today, the federal estate tax on the value of his estate (including his business interest) will be about $2.5 million. Tom's estate has very few liquid assets to pay this liability. It is also true that the company has very little cash to redeem Tom's stock.

Tom is concerned that the tax liability could severely impact the future operations of the business, not to mention the income outlook for Frances if she survives him. He would like to leave the business intact for Greg and Greg's family and wants to leave his other children and grandchildren an equivalent amount of inheritance.

Tom and Frances recognize the potential problems with the company and their estate but don't know where to start to solve them.

WARNING

Estate planning is no longer an option; it is a necessity.

We have covered many techniques that a family can utilize to reduce or even eliminate estate taxes and legal costs:

- You can remove hundreds of thousands of dollars from your taxable estate while retaining the ability to receive income from the assets.
- You can work with your family to reduce your taxable estate without losing control of it.
- You can discount the value of your stock in your company, using methods of which most planners are unaware.
- You can leave millions of dollars to your grandchildren, saving hundreds of thousands of dollars in estate taxes in the process.
- Your heirs can stretch the distribution of your IRA and annuities
- You can help develop and sustain the charities of choice

These are just a few of the options that will allow you to save hundreds of thousands, even millions, of dollars in estate taxes and legal fees.

You may wonder why your CPA and attorney haven't discussed these opportunities with you. We have found that if professional advisors don't specialize in estate planning, they will be vague about the techniques that we have outlined. In addition, a good portion of these professionals spend their time correcting the past, not planning for the future. When was the last time your accountant showed you how you could save in future income tax? Generally, accountants tell you only what is due and make certain that it is paid before they sign the return.

When was the last time your accountant showed you how you could save in future income tax?

This area of tax planning is very complex, and many professionals who don't specialize in estate planning don't have the time and the expertise to facilitate your estate plan correctly.

If you don't effectively plan your estate, any of the following can happen:

- Your family can lose thousands of dollars to estate taxes and spend tens of thousands of dollars on unnecessary legal fees.
- In the event of your death or disability, your family may be left without any direction from you on how to proceed.
- Your heirs may be forced to sell assets to create liquidity for estate taxes.
- The transfer of your estate can be a financial and emotional nightmare.

A well-planned estate will pass to your heirs in its entirety and in the manner you design. Therefore, you should seek assistance from a professional planner who can help you through the maze of estate planning options.

Figure 32.1 contains a very simple personal estate planning profile. This profile (or an equivalent one) is the basis for starting your estate planning. It will allow an estate planner to determine fundamental problems when there isn't an existing estate plan, amend problems with current plans that have been recently executed, or update plans that have been in place for many years.

The Next Step: Creating Your Own Estate Plan

Completing your personal estate planning profile is an important first step. Our offer to you is to help you create an effective estate plan that will allow you to achieve your goals. If you do not have an estate planner and are just beginning the process of planning, we offer you an estate planning summary of your current estate at the end of this book.

Our detailed summary serves several purposes. It will

- identify probate assets and multiple probate assets;
- assess probate costs;
- calculate federal estate tax liability at your death and then at the death of your spouse;
- identify how assets are owned and compare alternative ownership;
- identify specific problems, such as a lack of liquidity for federal estate tax liability, and outline ways to correct these problems;
- Make certain your heirs can "stretch" the distribution of their inherited IRA and annuity
- assess current gifting strategies and suggest ways to improve these strategies; and
- identify specific problems as outlined in the text of this book and format strategies to solve these problems in a clear, concise, and detailed report.

If you already have an estate plan in place but have not implemented the strategies described in this book (e.g., the discounted dollar plan) and

FIGURE 32.1 Personal Estate Planning Profile

PERSONAL ESTATE PLANNING PROFILE—CONFIDENTIAL

IF YOU ARE SINGLE, WIDOWED OR DIVORCED, SIMPLY PROVIDE YOUR PERSONAL INFORMATION AND DISREGARD ALL REFERENCES TO A SPOUSE

FULL NAME			
DATE OF BIRTH / /	SMOKER? ❑YES ❑NO	CITIZENSHIP	OCCUPATION
WITHIN THE PAST FIVE YEARS HAVE YOU CONSULTED A PHYSICIAN, MEDICAL PRACTITIONER OR BEEN CONFINED TO A HOSPITAL, CLINIC OR MEDICAL FACILITY? ❑YES ❑NO IF YES, PLEASE GIVE DETAILS:			

SPOUSE'S FULL NAME			
DATE OF BIRTH / /	SMOKER? ❑YES ❑NO	CITIZENSHIP	OCCUPATION
WITHIN THE PAST FIVE YEARS HAVE YOU CONSULTED A PHYSICIAN, MEDICAL PRACTITIONER OR BEEN CONFINED TO A HOSPITAL, CLINIC OR MEDICAL FACILITY? ❑YES ❑NO IF YES, PLEASE GIVE DETAILS:			

HOME ADDRESS	CITY, STATE, ZIP	HOME PHONE ( )	BEST TIME TO CALL
MAILING ADDRESS	CITY, STATE, ZIP	WORK PHONE ( )	BEST TIME TO CALL

ASSETS & LIABILITIES Key: Use to indicate how title is held:
H=Husband's separate W-Wife's separate CP=Community property JT=Joint property TC=Tenancy in common TE=Tenancy by the entirety

DESCRIPTION OF ASSETS	FAIR MARKET VALUE	LIABILITY	NET VALUE	NOW TITLE IS HELD
RESIDENCE				
OTHER REAL ESTATE				
STOCKS & BONDS				
BUSINESS & INTERESTS				
CASH IN BANK (CDs, MONEY MARKETS, ETC.)				
NOTES RECEIVABLE				
PERSONAL EFFECTS (AUTOS, BOATS, ETC.)				
RETIREMENT PLAN (NOT RECEIVING INCOME)				
VALUE OF ALL ANNUITIES				
OTHER ASSETS				
OTHER DEBTS				
TOTAL VALUES				

LIFE INSURANCE (PLEASE LIST ADDITIONAL POLICIES ON SEPARATE PAPER)

COMPANY	INSURED	OWNWER	BENEFICIARY	POLICY DATE	FACE AMOUNT	CASH VALUE

CHARITABLE GIFT TOTAL VALUE OF ASSETS THAT YOU WILL BEQUEATH, BASED ON CURRENT DESIGNATION, TO CHARITIES AT YOUR DEATH: YOU? $______ SPOUSE? $______

INCOME JOINT ANNUAL GROSS EARNED INCOME $__________________ JOINT ANNUAL GROSS INCOME FROM INVESTMENTS $__________________

CHILDREN (LIST ALL LIVING CHILDREN: S=SELF SP=SPOUSE J=JOINT)

NAME	AGE	SEX ❑M ❑F	PARENT ❑S ❑SP ❑J	NAME	AGE	SEX ❑M ❑F	PARENT ❑S ❑SP ❑J
NAME	AGE	SEX ❑M ❑F	PARENT ❑S ❑SP ❑J	NAME	AGE	SEX ❑M ❑F	PARENT ❑S ❑SP ❑J

GRANDCHILDREN (IF YOU ARE PLANNING TO LEAVE AN INHERITANCE TO ANY OF YOUR GRANDCHILDREN, PLEASE INDICATE BELOW: S=SELF SP=SPOUSE J=JOINT)

NAME	AGE	SEX ❑M ❑F	GRANDPARENT ❑S ❑SP ❑J	NAME	AGE	SEX ❑M ❑F	GRANDPARENT ❑S ❑SP ❑J
NAME	AGE	SEX ❑M ❑F	GRANDPARENT ❑S ❑SP ❑J	NAME	AGE	SEX ❑M ❑F	GRANDPARENT ❑S ❑SP ❑J

PLEASE INDICATE THE ESTATE PLANNING TOOLS YOU CURRENTLY HAVE IN PLACE

❑ UPDATED WILL
❑ CREDIT SHELTER OR BYPASS TRUST
❑ REVOCABLE LIVING TRUST
❑ MEDICAL POWER OF ATTORNEY
❑ DURABLE POWER OF ATTORNEY
❑ FAMILY DYNASTY TRUST
❑ FAMILY LIMITED PARTNERSHIP
❑ FAMILY OR COMMUNITY FOUNDATION
❑ CHARITABLE TRUST
❑ IRREVOCABLE LIFE INSURANCE TRUST
❑ ESTATE LIQUIDITY THROUGH LIFE INSURANCE
❑ LIMITED LIABILITY COMPANY
❑ QUALIFIED PERSONAL RESIDENCE TRUST
❑ COMMON LAW TRUST
❑ GRANTOR RETAINED INCOME OR ANNUITY TRUST
❑ OFFSHORE ASSET PROTECTION
❑ OTHER (EXPLAIN) ______________________
____

The best time to have planned your estate is yesterday; but if you failed to complete your planning yesterday, then *today* is the second-best time to start.

you would like actual numbers or illustrations on any of the outlined strategies in Part Two, see the survey form at the back of the book.

The problems that are created at death are devastating. The best time to have planned your estate is yesterday; but if you failed to complete your planning yesterday, then *today* is the second-best time to start.

Figure 32.2 illustrates why procrastination can become a problem. It doesn't have to happen to you!

FIGURE 32.2 Procrastination Will Be Dangerous to Your Wealth

Glossary

adjusted gross estate The gross estate less debts, administration expenses, and losses during administration.

adjusted taxable estate The adjusted gross estate less any marital and/or charitable deductions.

adjusted taxable gifts Gifts that exceed the lifetime federal estate tax exclusion (currently $2 million), and the annual gift tax exclusion (currently $12,000). Gifted amounts over and above the exemption and annual exclusion at death are added back to the taxable estate and are subject to estate taxes.

administration The formal process of settling an estate. Various duties include valuing the estate, filing tax returns, paying taxes, and distributing assets to heirs.

administration expenses Expenses incurred while administering an estate. These include legal fees, appraisal fees, and distribution and disposition costs.

administrator Person appointed by a court to manage the estate of a person who dies without a will.

after-born child A child born after the death of a parent.

alternate valuation date A date used by the personal representative to value a decedent's estate that is not to exceed six months after date of death. The value of the assets must be lower and result in a reduction of the gross estate and a reduction in the estate tax liability to qualify for its use.

ancillary probate Term for probate if decedent had real property in another state.

annual gift tax exclusion The right of each individual to make small annual gifts to other individuals each year to the extent of $12,000 (under current law). The number of these gifts is unlimited. These small annual gifts are in addition to the lifetime estate tax exclusion credit (currently $2 million) and do not reduce the exclusion credit.

annuities Contracts established through life insurance carriers in two formats. The deferred annuity, which provides tax deferred wealth accumulation and a future guaranteed lifetime income. The immediate or income annuity, which provides a guaranteed lifetime income. There are three basic types of deferred annuities: (1) The fixed interest annuity, where the life insurance company's board of directors determine the rate of return, (2) The variable annuity, where the performance of the variable fund (comparable to a mutual fund), determines the rate of return, and (3) The index annuity, where the performance of an outside index, like the S&P 500 determines the rate of return. Only in recent years do all three forms of annuities offer full interest guarantees.

ascertainable standards Involves the right of a surviving spouse to invade the family trust, or B trust, without causing the property to be included in his or her estate. The power is limited to such needs as health, education, maintenance, and support.

assets All types of property which can be made available for the payment of debts.

basis The original amount paid to acquire an asset or the fair market value of an asset on the date it was acquired.

beneficiary The person and/or organization that receives trust property after the death of the trust grantor; also refers to those who receive property under a contract (such as an annuity or life insurance policy) through a beneficiary designation.

bequest A *specific* bequest is a gift by will of a designated class or kind of property (e.g., a gift of the decedent's residence to a named individual). A *general* bequest is one that is accomplished from the general assets of an estate (e.g., a bequest of a sum of money without reference to any particular account or investment from which it is to be distributed).

book value Value that equals assets less liabilities in valuing businesses. It is the net worth of the business.

b trust A trust created at death under a provision in the will (testamentary) or by provision in a trust. This trust is often referred to as the *family trust* and usually holds the lifetime federal estate tax exclusion credit (in spousal estates) of the first spouse to die. It also qualifies assets placed into the trust for the use of the lifetime estate exclusion credit. Also known as a credit shelter trust.

bypass trust A trust designed not to qualify for the unlimited estate tax marital deduction. Commonly referred to as the *family trust*, or *b trust, credit shelter trust* it is designed to make use of the lifetime $2,000,000 exclusion credit.

capitalization of earnings The measure of earning capacity when valuing a business.

charitable deduction A deduction allowed for a gift to a qualified charitable organization.

charitable gift annuity Establish directly through a charity to provide guaranteed income for while receiving a significant income tax deduction for the contribution to the charity. The charitable gift annuity can also be established through donor advised fund, allowing personal control of the investments.

charitable gifting Gifts of cash or other assets made to qualified charities (under the IRS definition) for which the donor receives various tax deductions.

charitable remainder trust (CRT) The donation of property or money to a charity, whereby the donor reserves the right to use the property or to receive income from it for a specified time. When the agreed-upon period is over, the property belongs to the charitable organization. The donor in turn receives various tax deductions and tax advantages. The most common CRTs are the charitable remainder annuity trust (CRAT) and the charitable remainder unitrust (CRUT).

codicil A revision, change, or modification to an existing will.

college 529 savings plans A program established in 1996 by Congress to allow parents and grandparents the ability to gift funds to heirs specifically designated for college education. Under EGTRRA 2001 up to five years ($60,000 per person) of the current exemption ($12,000) can be gifted without triggering the federal gift tax. If the funds are withdrawn by the student for education expenses they do not incur any income or gift tax on the principal or the gain. A few life insurance carriers have 529 plans that allow the donor the ability to invest the funds as they choose.

community-owned property Property acquired during marriage in which both husband and wife have an undivided one-half interest. Not more than one-half of community property can be disposed of by a will. The eight current community property states are Arizona, California, Idaho, Louisiana, New Mexico, Nevada, Texas, and Washington. Wisconsin also has enacted laws that closely resemble those of community property states.

conservator A person who is appointed by a court to manage the estate of a protected person who, because of age, intellect, or health, is incapable of managing his or her own affairs.

corpus The principal property of a trust. Separate from trust income, it is property transferred to the trust and is also referred to as *principal.*

credit estate tax Also known as the B trust, family trust, or bypass trust, is designed to take advantage of both available federal estate tax lifetime exclusion for married couples.

credit shelter trust A state death tax imposed to take full advantage of the amount allowed as a credit against the federal estate tax.

crummy power The power held by the beneficiary of a trust to withdraw a certain amount annually from the trust.

curtesy A man's entitlement through common law to all property held or owned by his wife. (See also **dower.**)

death tax Tax imposed by the federal government that can be in excess of 46 percent and a tax that is imposed by some state governments.

decedent A deceased person.

deed A legal instrument used to transfer title to real property in the eyes of the law.

deemed transferor The parent of the transferee most closely related to the grantor. A parent related to the grantor by blood or adoption is deemed closer than one related by marriage. This relationship is important in understanding the taxation of generation-skipping transfers.

devise Legally, a gift of real estate under a will as distinguished from a gift of personal property.

direct skip The transfer of assets or gifts made directly to second-generation beneficiaries, skipping the middle generation. For example, gifts made by a grandfather to a grandchild while skipping the grandfather's children.

discounted dollar plan A program involving a small portion of the total gross estate to fund the purchase of life insurance inside an irrevocable trust. The purpose is to provide liquidity for estate tax payment or to replace the loss of estate property as a result of taxation for pennies on the dollar. A maximum use of leverage. Dollars tomorrow for pennies today.

domicile State and place of one's official residence.

donee The recipient of a gift, but may also refer to the recipient of a power of appointment and to an individual or entity capable of owning property.

donor A person who makes a gift or grants a power of appointment. Limited to individuals only.

dower A woman's entitlement to an interest in all the property of her husband that was owned during their marriage. (See also **curtesy.**)

durable power of attorney Allows the power of attorney to survive any disability the principal could suffer.

dynasty trust An irrevocable life insurance trust (ILIT) used by wealthy people to create nontaxable generation-skipping transfers to several generations.

Economic Growth and Tax Relief Reconciliation Act of 2001 Sweeping legislation that passed Congress June 7, 2001, commonly known by its abbreviation EGTRRA, pronounced "egg-terra." The Act made significant changes in many areas of the US Internal Revenue Code, most significant were those addressing federal estates taxes, gradually increasing the federal estate tax credit to $3,500,000 in 2009, and decreasing the highest bracket to 45 percent, with complete estate repeal in 2010. The most notable characteristic of EGTRRA is that its provisions are designed to *sunset* (revert back to pre-EGTRRA laws) on January 1, 2011, unless further legislations is enacted.

Economic Recovery Tax Act of 1981 (ERTA) A broad-based tax reform legislation signed into law under the Reagan administration. The legislation, as it pertains to estate planning, created the unlimited marital deduction, increased the estate and gift tax exemption, and restructured the estate and gift tax rates.

estate analysis A formal written estate plan that analyzes estate taxation, property ownership, probate costs, current planning, etc., and formulates a plan to achieve various objectives. It is a road map for achieving the objectives, format, and execution of an effective estate plan.

estate freeze Method whereby highly appreciating business and personal assets are shifted out of an estate so that future appreciation will not be included in the gross estate.

estate planners Individuals who specialize and devote 100 percent of their time to the issues and practice of planning estates and whose backgrounds can vary from law to finance.

estate tax A tax that may be imposed not only by the federal government but also by state governments on the right of a person to transfer property at death. The federal transfer tax is currently applicable to estates valued over and above the $2 million federal lifetime estate tax exclusion credit.

estate tax base An amount on which the federal estate tax is levied that is determined by subtracting the allowable expenses, deductions, and exclusions from the gross estate and adding back in any adjusted taxable gifts.

estate tax credit Formally referred to as the unified credit the estate tax credit is the amount of assets you can transfer from one generation to the next without incurring federal estate tax. Resulting with the passage of EGTRRA 2001, the credit is set to be $2 million per person through 2008, increasing to $3.5 million in 2009, repealed for 2010, and then revert back to $1 million in 2011.

estate tax states Those states that impose a death tax directly to the estate and do not share in revenues collected by the federal government.

fair market value The value at which estate property is included in the gross estate for federal estate tax purposes; the price at which property would change hands between a willing buyer and a willing seller under any compulsion to buy or sell and both having knowledge of all the relevant facts.

family allowance Money available from an estate for the testator's spouse and children while the estate is being settled.

family limited partnership (FLP) A legal entity that provides ultimate control and management of assets while at the same time providing asset protection.

family trust (See **b trust**.)

federal estate tax An excise tax levied by the federal government on the right to transfer property at death. It is imposed on and measured by the value of the estate left behind by the deceased.

fee simple Outright ownership of property with absolute rights to dispose of, or gift, it to anyone at death.

fiduciary A person in the position of great trust and responsibility, such as the executor of a will or the trustee of a trust.

five and five power A provision that allows a trust beneficiary to withdraw the greater of $5,000 or 5 percent of the principal from a trust without causing the entire trust property to be included in his or her estate for federal estate taxation.

foreign asset protection trust A revocable living trust established under the laws of a foreign country.

foreign death tax credit A credit against estate and gift taxes on an amount that is paid to foreign governments as a death tax.

formal written estate plan summary (See **estate analysis.**)

format The planning tools used in the process of estate planning. Trusts, wills, CRTs, etc., are all estate planning formats.

funded insurance trust An insurance trust provided with income-producing property, the income from which is used to pay the premiums on the policies held in the trust.

future interest The postponed right of use or enjoyment of property.

generation-skipping transfer (GST) A transfer of property, usually in trust, that is designed to provide benefits for two or more generations of beneficiaries who are younger than the generation of the grantor.

generation-skipping transfer tax (GSTT) A transfer tax generally assessed on gifts in excess of $1 million to grandchildren, great-grandchildren, or others at least two generations below the donor.

gift splitting A provision allowing a married couple to treat a gift made by one of them to a third party as having been made as one-half by each, provided it is consented to by the other on a gift tax return.

gift tax Tax on gifts generally paid by the person making the gift rather that the recipient.

gift-tax annual exclusion The provision in the tax law that exempts the first $11,000 (as adjusted for inflation) in present-interest gifts a person gives to each recipient during a year from federal gift taxes.

gift tax marital deduction A deduction allowed for a gift made by one spouse to another. Outright gifts and life estates qualify for the deduction if the donee has the right to the income from the property for life and a general power of appointment over the principal. Certain qualified terminable interest gifts also qualify. The amount of the deduction is unlimited.

grantor The person who establishes a trust who is also called the *creator, settlor, donor,* or *trustor.*

gross estate The total value of all property in which a deceased had an interest that must be included in his or her estate for federal tax purposes.

guardian A person appointed to have custody over the person or the property or both of a minor or incapacitated person.

health, education, maintenance, and support (HEMS) (See **ascertainable standards.**)

heir A person who is entitled to inherit assets of the decedent when the decedent left no will; also specified as *next of kin.*

holographic will A will written entirely in the testator's own handwriting.

incidents of ownership Rights applying to ownership interest in an insurance policy. These include the right to change a beneficiary to borrow on a policy, to change premium modes, and so on.

inheritance tax A tax imposed by a number of states that is based on the value of the property that taxpayers inherit. It is levied on the right to receive property, not on the right to transfer property.

insurance trust A trust established to own insurance policies in order to prevent them from being included in an estate.

intangible property Property that does not have physical value, such as a stock certificate or savings bond.

inter vivos trust A trust, also called a *living trust,* created during a person's lifetime. It operates during that person's lifetime as opposed to a testamentary trust, which does not operate until the grantor dies.

intestacy laws Individual state laws governing the distribution of the property of a person who dies without leaving a valid will.

intestate The situation of a person who dies without having a valid will; that person is said to have died *intestate.*

irrevocable life insurance trust (ILIT) A trust that cannot be changed or canceled once it is created.

irrevocable trust A trust created for the permanent transfer of property.

joint and survivor life insurance A relatively new type of life insurance that provides an insurance benefit at the death of the surviving spouse or partner. Generally, this method of providing estate liquidity for married couples is the most cost-effective strategy. It is also known as survivorship insurance and second-to-die insurance.

joint ownership Ownership that occurs when two or more people own the same property. The death of a joint owner immediately transfers ownership to the surviving joint owner(s).

joint tenancy Ownership shared with an unlimited number of individuals whereby each tenant owns an equal undivided share of the property.

joint tenancy with rights of survivorship (JTWRS) The holding of property by two or more individuals in a manner that, on the death of one tenant, the survivor or survivors succeed to full ownership by operation of law.

lapse The failure of a bequest in a will because the intended recipient died before the testator.

last will and testament The usual formal term referring to a will.

legacy A gift of personal property by will that is usually referred to as a *bequest;* the recipient is called the *legatee.*

leverage A true cost discount by which one can pay a few dollars now to create a significantly larger sum later.

leveraged dollars The present use of a sum of money to create a true discount in the future; using current premium dollars now to create a large amount of dollars in the future in life insurance contracts.

life estate The title to the income interest vested in a life tenant.

life insurance Insurance customarily used to discount the actual tax liability, create an estate, replace an asset, or insure liabilities.

life insurance trust A trust that has the proceeds of a person's life insurance policy as its principal.

life interest or life estate An interest that a person has in property enjoyed only during life.

life tenant The person, often referred to as the *income beneficiary,* who receives the income from a legal life estate or from a trust fund during his or her own life or that of another person.

limited power of appointment A special power granted to a donee that is limited in scope as opposed to being general.

lineal descendant One who is, by blood relationship, in the direct line of descent from an ancestor.

liquid assets Cash or assets that can be easily converted into cash without any serious loss, such as bonds, life insurance proceeds paid in a lump sum, bank accounts, and certificates of deposit.

liquidity The measure of liquid assets. In estate planning, it is detrimental to measure the amount of liquid assets available for paying death taxes and expenses.

living trust (See **revocable living trust.**)

long-term care insurance A product created by the insurance industry to help pay the exorbitant costs of long term medical expenses. The younger you are the most reasonable the premium. Based on recent legislation the premium can be tax deductible if you meet certain minimum income requirements. Several life insurance companies have designed cutting edge long term care policies that couple savings, life insurance and long term care coverage for comparable premium.

marital deduction The portion of a deceased spouse's estate that may be passed to the surviving spouse without becoming subject to the federal estate tax.

marital trust A trust consisting of the property that qualifies for the marital deduction.

multiple probate Property owned by a decedent in states other than the state of domicile that will be subject to probate; usually refers to real estate owned in several states that becomes subject to each individual state's probate system at time of death.

net taxable estate The total value of an estate after all deductions have been subtracted.

nonliquid assets Assets that are not easily converted into cash without the risk of serious loss, such as real estate, a business interest, or art objects.

nonmarital (nonmarital deduction) trust A trust consisting of property that does not qualify for the marital deduction.

nonprobate property Property passing outside the administration of the estate other than by will or intestacy laws. Examples include jointly held property passing by right of survivorship (law), life insurance proceeds payable to a named beneficiary (by contract), and property in a living trust (property not titled to an individual).

nonresident alien Usually the noncitizen (alien) spouse of a deceased U.S. citizen. Special rules apply to prevent this spouse from removing property from the United States. Use of the marital deduction is usually not allowed unless certain conditions are met.

nonskip The transfer of property to the next-in-line generation such as when a father transfers property directly to his children as opposed to his grandchildren.

nuncupative will An oral will dictated by the testator before witnesses during a final illness and later converted to writing.

objectives In estate planning, the formulation of each individual's needs and desires regarding distribution of his or her estate and the various intricacies involved in the transfer.

operation of law Assets that pass outside of a probate estate by certain ownership. Property held between spouses as joint tenants with rights of survivorship passes to the surviving tenant by operation of law.

optimal marital deduction Using the unlimited marital deduction in a trust arrangement to gain a tax liability of $0 at the death of the first spouse.

outright ownership Complete ownership of property by an individual that can pass directly to another individual at death.

payable on death (POD) An arrangement whereby a depositor elects that a sum of money or account be payable to named individuals on death; similar to a beneficiary arrangement.

per capita A way of distributing an estate so that the surviving descendents will share equally regardless of generation.

Pension Protection Act of 2006 On August 12, 2006, President George W. Bush signed into law the 1,000 page Pension Protection Act. Among the many changes and safeguards to retirement accounts the act now allows non-spousal beneficiaries of an IRAs, 401k and annuities the ability to "stretch" their inheritance over their lifetime. The decision to implement the "stretch" can be made before (by the owner) or after the death of the of the owner. Giving maximum control to distributions of retirement accounts beyond this lifetime.

personal representative A person appointed by the court to settle an estate.

per stirpes A way of distributing an estate so that the surviving descendents will receive only what their immediate ancestor would have received if he or she had been alive at the time of death.

posthumous child A child born after its parents' death.

pourover Refers to the transfer of property from one estate or trust to another estate or trust that is triggered by the occurrence of an event such as a death. For example, property disposed of by will can "pour over" into an existing trust.

power of appointment The right given to a donee to dispose of property that the donee does not fully own within the limits set forth by the donor, which can cause the value of the asset to be included in the estate of a donee who holds the power of appointment.

power of attorney A document which authorizes a person to act as another person's agent.

premium finance A method to purchase significant amounts of life insurance where the policy owner borrows the premium from a third party and typically pays interest only on the borrowed amount.

present interest As applied to a gift, the present right to use or enjoy the property. A gift must have this characteristic to qualify for the annual $12,000 gift tax exclusion.

pretermitted heir A child or other descendant omitted from a testator's will.

principal The property funding a trust, from which income is expected to be earned. Trust principal is also known as *res* or *corpus.*

probate The process of providing the validity of a will in court and executing its provisions under the guidance of the court. When a person dies, the will must be filed before the proper officers of the court, giving the court jurisdiction in the matter to enforce the document commonly referred to as "filing the will for probate." When the will has been filed, it is said to be "admitted to probate." The process of probating a will involves recognition by the court of the personal representative named in the will (or appointment of an administrator if none has been named), the filing of proper reports and papers as required by law, determination of the validity of the will if it is contested, and distribution and final settlement of the estate under the supervision of the court.

probate court A court with the power to probate Wills and settle estates.

probate property Property that passes under the terms of a will. If there is no will, it passes under the state intestacy laws.

qualified charity A charity that qualifies to receive gifts for which an income tax charitable deduction is allowable.

qualified domestic trust (QDOT) A special trust to which assets are transferred so that a spouse who is not a U.S. citizen (a nonresident alien) will be entitled to claim the benefit of the unlimited marital deduction.

qualified terminable interest property (QTIP) Property qualifying for the marital deduction at the election of the donor or the decedent's personal representative. The spouse retains a qualified income interest in the property for life, with the income payable at least annually. The corpus ultimately passes to a specified *remainderman* under a special power of appointment given to the spouse.

qualified terminable interest property trust (QTIP trust) A trust that qualifies for the unlimited marital tax deduction. No estate tax is imposed on the value of the property transferred to the surviving spouse in a QTIP trust on the first spouse's death as long as the surviving spouse receives all income at least annually. The purpose of the QTIP trust is to enable an estate to avoid tax while the grantor still designates who will receive the property remaining in the trust on the second spouse's death.

quarterback An estate planner who specializes in the practice of estate planning and who coordinates the entire effort for a client. The effort involves designing the plan, based on the objectives; suggesting a format; and executing the plan in conjunction with other professionals or providing outlets for the accounting, legal, and all additional aspects of execution.

remainder interest A future interest that comes into existence after the termination of a prior interest. For example, individual A creates a testamentary trust under a will in which the principal is to be retained with income paid to individual B until B's death, at which time the principal or remainder interest will be passed to individual C.

remainderman The person entitled to receive the principal of a trust when the intervening life estate or estates terminate.

remedy of partition The separation of shares of property held jointly by the direction of a court.

residuary estate The remaining part of a decedent's estate after debts, expenses, and distributions have been made. Wills usually contain a clause on disposing of the residue of the estate that the decedent has not otherwise bequeathed.

reverse mortgage A program established in 1989 by Congress to allow home owners the ability to extract their equity while remaining in their home.

reverse QTIP The use of a QTIP trust to preserve a decedent's $1 million generation-skipping exemption.

reversionary interest The possibility that property will return to the donor after it has been given away.

reversionary trust A trust limited to a specified term of years or for the life of the beneficiary at the end of which period the trust is terminated and the property returned to the grantor.

revocable living trust A written legal document into which grantors place all their property with instructions for its management and distribution on their disability or death.

revocable trust A trust that can be altered, amended, terminated, or revoked during the grantor's lifetime with all property being recovered by the grantor.

right of election The surviving spouse's right to a share of the augmented estate rather than accepting the amount provided by will or intestate succession statues. The percentage is based on the length of marriage.

right of survivorship Property held jointly whereby at the death of one joint owner, the other owner or owners succeed to full ownership by surviving under law.

semiliquid assets Assets that can be converted to cash within a reasonable amount of time—usually within one year.

settlor Another term for the grantor or creator of a trust.

shrinkage A reduction in the amount of property that passes at death caused by loss of capital and income resulting from payment of death costs. It may be greatly increased if assets must be sold for cash to pay such costs.

skip person In generation-skipping transfers, the person of the generation that is skipped. The child of a parent who makes gifts favoring only grandchildren is considered a skip person.

spousal support ILIT An irrevocable life insurance trust that allows the spouse lifetime access to the cash build up within life insurance policies, providing maximum flexibility when obtaining life insurance to pay estate taxes, create an estate or replace an asset that is gifted.

sprinkling or spray trust A trust under which the trustee is given discretionary powers to distribute any of the income among beneficiaries in equal or unequal shares and to accumulate any income not distributed.

state death tax credit A format of many states to calculate and collect their portion of state-imposed death taxes.

state inheritance tax A tax imposed by specific states for the transfer of property from one generation to the next.

step-up in basis A decedent's capital gains property that passes to others and escapes the capital gains tax when sold by the person who inherits the property. Persons inheriting capital gains property receive the property at date-of-death fair market value. In effect, the basis in this property is deemed to be "stepped up" and does not reflect the decedent's original cost basis for determining applicable capital gains tax on the sale of the property.

"stretch" IRA or annuity Provisions created by EGTRRA and PLR 200151038 that allow generational distributions from tax deferred retirement accumulations vehicles such as an IRA or an annuity to be "stretched" over the life expectancy of the beneficiary based on the required minimum distribution (RMD) table established by the IRS.

successor trustee or executor An individual or institution which takes the place of a trustee or executor who can no longer hold office.

super trust A package of trust instruments that includes a revocable living trust, an A/B bypass trust, and an irrevocable life insurance spousal support trust.

tangible property Property that has physical substance, such as a house or car.

taxable distributions Distributions from qualified retirement plans that are fully taxable and that can also refer to distributions from a trust when working with generation-skipping transfers.

taxable terminations In generation-skipping transfers, interests in trusts that terminate (e.g., income rights).

Tax Reform Act of 1986 (TRA 1986) An encompassing tax act that made many changes in estate and gifting rules.

tenancy by entirety Ownership of property by a husband and wife so that such property may not be disposed of during life by either spouse without the other's consent; at one spouse's death, the property goes to the survivor.

tenancy in common Ownership of property by two or more persons so that each has an undivided interest and, at the death of one, is passed by will to the deceased's heirs. It does not pass automatically to the surviving tenants in common.

terminable interest An interest in property that will terminate in the future; usually associated with the right to income from a trust that terminates at the death of the grantor.

testamentary At death.

testamentary trust A trust set up in a will that only takes effect after death.

testate The situation of a person who dies with a will.

testator, testatrix A person who dies with a will. A male is a *testator;* a female is a *testatrix.*

transferee The person receiving property transfers.

transfer on death (TOD) Designation on securities that allows the naming of a beneficiary to receive them upon death of a party.

transferor The person who makes transfers of property to others.

trust An arrangement for holding legal property and managing the property for the benefit of another.

trustee The holder of legal title to property for the management, use, or benefit of another.

unfunded insurance trust An insurance trust that is not provided with cash or securities to pay the life insurance premium, which is usually paid by someone other than the trustee.

unified credit With the passage of EGTRRA the unified credit is now referred to as the "lifetime federal estate tax exclusion credit" and is the amount every taxpayer is allowed to exclude from estate tax.

unified probate code A standardized probate process adopted by many states in an effort to simplify the probate process.

unitrust (See **charitable remainder trust.**)

unlimited marital deduction Property that qualifies as marital deduction property. Under ERTA 1981, the ability to pass unlimited amounts of property that qualifies for the marital deduction became law. At present unlimited amounts of marital deduction property may pass to a surviving spouse without estate or gift tax consequences.

wealth replacement trust (WRT) An irrevocable life insurance trust that replaces the value of gifted assets made to charities used in conjunction with charitable remainder trusts (CRTs).

wealth transfer Process and strategy for transferring property to others with minimal estate and gift tax liability.

will A written document with instructions for disposition of property at death that can be enforced only through the probate court.

witness A person who observes the signing of a will and attests to the signature.

Index

D

E

F

G

O

P

Q

R

S

THE NEXT STEP

❑ Please provide me with additional personalized information on the following:

❑ I would like illustrations and numbers specific to my personal estate on the following:

- ❑ **Estate Planning Strategies for the 21st Century**
- ❑ **Revocable Living Trusts**
- ❑ **Gifting**
- ❑ **The Discounted Dollar Plan**
- ❑ **Asset Protection**
- ❑ **Family Limited Partnerships**
- ❑ **Annuities**
- ❑ **Family Dynasty Trust**
- ❑ **Spousal Support ILIT (Super Trust)**
- ❑ **Charitable Gift Annuity**
- ❑ **Private Family Foundation**
- ❑ **Reverse Mortgage**
- ❑ **Life Settlement**
- ❑ **Estate Analysis**
- ❑ **Charitable Remainder Trusts**
- ❑ **QTIP Trust Planning**
- ❑ **Irrevocable Trusts**
- ❑ **Estate Freeze Techniques**
- ❑ **Limited Liability Company**
- ❑ **"Stretch" IRA and Annuities**
- ❑ **How I Can Correct Estate Planning Mistake 1 2 3 4 5 6 7 8 9 10 (Circle those that apply—See Chapter 3.)**
- ❑ **How to Avoid the Six Retirement Tax Time Bombs**

YOUR FULL NAME		
DATE OF BIRTH	CITIZENSHIP	OCCUPATION

SPOUSE'S FULL NAME (if applicable)		
DATE OF BIRTH	CITIZENSHIP	OCCUPATION

HOME ADDRESS	CITY, STATE, ZIP	HOME PHONE ( ) Best Time to call:
MAILING ADDRESS	CITY, STATE, ZIP	HOME PHONE ( ) Best Time to call:

❑ **I request a telephone conference with an estate planner.**

❑ **I would like an estate planner (quarterback) in my vicinity to contact me.**

❑ **I would like you to recommend an estate planning attorney in my vicinity.**

❑ **Other**

RETURN TO:

Estate Planning Specialists
3165 South Alma School Rd.
Suite 29116
Chandler, AZ 85248
888-892-1102 – 480-899-1102
Fax 480-899-6723

Or Go To

www.estateplanningmadEZ.com